H. Pemberton

A Winter Tour in Spain

H. Pemberton

A Winter Tour in Spain

ISBN/EAN: 9783337187507

Printed in Europe, USA, Canada, Australia, Japan

Cover: Foto ©Andreas Hilbeck / pixelio.de

More available books at **www.hansebooks.com**

THE COURT OF LIONS.—PALACE OF THE ALHAMBRA.

A WINTER TOUR IN SPAIN.

BY THE AUTHOR OF

"DACIA SINGLETON," "ALTOGETHER WRONG,"

ETC., ETC., ETC.

THE ESCORIAL.

LONDON:
TINSLEY BROTHERS, 18, CATHERINE ST., STRAND.
1868.

[*Right of Translation Reserved.*]

A

WINTER TOUR IN SPAIN.

BY

H. PEMBERTON.

LONDON:
TINSLEY BROTHERS, 18, CATHERINE ST., STRAND.
1868.

[*Right of Translation Reserved.*]

LONDON:
BRADBURY, EVANS, AND CO., PRINTERS, WHITEFRIARS.

TO

MY TRAVELLING COMPANIONS

THESE REMINISCENCES OF OUR

WINTER TOUR IN SPAIN

ARE AFFECTIONATELY INSCRIBED.

London, June, 1868.

PREFACE.

In publishing "A Winter Tour in Spain," our principal object is that it may prove an acceptable work to those who, having travelled in Spain, may like again to glance over scenes (imperfectly sketched, yet true so far as they go,) that must be remembered with pleasure; for it seems to us impossible that anyone can have learnt to know Spain and the Spaniards, and not also have learnt to appreciate both the country and people; though neither may be free from defects.

CONTENTS.

	PAGE
INTRODUCTORY REMARKS	1

CHAPTER I.
FROM LONDON TO BAYONNE 9

CHAPTER II.
BIARRITZ—SAN SEBASTIAN 17

CHAPTER III.
BURGOS 25

CHAPTER IV.
MADRID 36

CHAPTER V.
MADRID—*(continued)* 52

CHAPTER VI.
MADRID—*(continued)*—A BULL-FIGHT 69

CHAPTER VII.
THE ESCORIAL 87

CHAPTER VIII.

TOLEDO 98

CHAPTER IX.

CORDOVA 112

CHAPTER X.

SEVILLE 120

CHAPTER XI.

SEVILLE—(*continued*) 138

CHAPTER XII.

SEVILLE—(*continued*) 154

CHAPTER XIII.

JEREZ DE LA FRONTERA—SHERRY 171

CHAPTER XIV.

CADIZ 174

CHAPTER XV.

GIBRALTAR 184

CHAPTER XVI.

MALAGA 195

CHAPTER XVII.

GRANADA—THE ALHAMBRA 208

CHAPTER XVIII.

GRANADA—(*continued*) 224

A WINTER TOUR IN SPAIN.

INTRODUCTORY REMARKS.

THERE are but two classes of travellers to be met with in Spain; those who go there for climate, and those who go for pleasure, and even of these the number is very limited. None flock here, as they do to most other European countries, for education or economy; these are two objects as yet unattainable. Neither invalids nor tourists, however, will be disappointed, for they will each meet with what they seek. The climate in the south and along the east coast of Spain is magnificent; the scenery and objects of interest throughout the country must fulfil the expectations of all.

But climate is not everything to those who, on account of health, are driven from their own country, though it may appear to be, and is, the main object. There are many drawbacks to contend with in encountering a winter in Spain. The journey is long if by land, and longer still if by sea; railway travelling has not yet arrived at perfection in this far behind-hand, procrastinating land. The trains always start at most unconscionable hours in the morning—hours utterly impossible for an invalid, and most disagreeable to every one; or else they start at night. The Spaniards arrange these matters to suit themselves and not winter travellers; the railway guides are at present published but once a year, and that in summer; thus against the scorching heat of that season do they seek to escape exposure during the day. They are far too indolent to dream of having a change made for the winter months; they travel then so little themselves, and their winter is so short, that in more ways than this do they, from the want of a little energy, cause people to experience discomfort, and keep hundreds from visiting their beautiful country.

Medical men are much needed—English, of course—there are plenty of Spanish, too many of them; but if Nature does not cure, they cannot, and it is best to avoid them; in but very few places are English doctors to be found, and those there are, are not altogether such as could be desired. Another great want is fireplaces; in none but a very few of the largest and best hotels in the principal towns are they to be found, and then only in the best sitting-rooms. This, to an invalid, and indeed to many in health, is a very serious discomfort and privation. The evenings are often chilly, and one becomes more sensitive to the least cold from the great heat of the sun during the day; and with all the bright and glorious sunshine which favours this magnificent land, between November and April, days will sometimes dawn that remind one of the season, and then, if no fire can be had, an extra shawl or cloak is far away better than a headache-giving, stupifying *brasero*. These *braseros* are the only fires of the country; they are large pans (like big copper soup-plates) containing lighted charcoal, which are placed in the middle of the room on a wooden frame, and are extremely unhealthy, affecting both the respiratory and nasal organs, and should be carefully avoided; besides, the heat they give is very trifling.

Hotels are, as a rule, not good; they are deficient in comforts; and the food, though far better than what we were led to expect, is hardly such as is suited to an invalid. Beef and mutton are very poor; pork is excellent, and is the best meat throughout Spain; this arises from the manner in which the pigs are fed, but it is hardly the right food for a delicate person. Then the cooking: it certainly will not tempt appetite, if it does not completely destroy it. To the tourist, who is of course strong and healthy, or ought to be, all these objections and disagreeables are too trifling for him to give them a thought; he, on the whole, rather likes getting up in the middle of the night to start by a 4 or 5 a.m. train; he neither wants doctors nor fireplaces, and, with a good appetite, the unartistic dishes put before him perhaps even meet with approbation; at any rate they are not condemned.

The best towns for those who seek climate are Alicante, Seville, Málaga, and Gibraltar, if we can call the Rock, Spain. The best hotels in the country are, the Hôtel des Princes at Madrid; the Hôtel Bossio at Alicante, and the Hotel Washington Irving at Granada.

Money is indispensable to all travellers; by money, we mean a good supply, as everything, gloves excepted, is very dear. A slight knowledge of the language is also nearly as necessary—French and English being useless, except in a few of the principal hotels—and a courier, we can state from experience, is a very expensive nuisance; the charges are fully doubled if you have one, unless you happen to fall into the hands of those rare individuals who, however they may rob you themselves, have still honesty enough not to let others do so. There are plenty of travelling servants to be met with on the frontier, who are ready to accompany people through Spain, and are not sufficiently experienced in couriers' ways to have the bills doubled in order to fill their own pockets.

Tea is a useful article to take with one, and a bottle of spirits of wine, for boiling water, will often be found invaluable. A passport is useless, except for obtaining letters addressed *poste restante;* and that is so unsafe a direction, owing to the absurd mistakes they make in copying the names, which they then post up outside the office, that it is advisable to have them addressed to some one's care; a banker is the best; if sent to an hotel they are frequently mislaid, or refused altogether if not sufficiently pre-paid, though this is invariably most indignantly denied.

Money should not be changed in Spain, either on entering it or leaving it; in both cases it is best to change it at the frontier town in France, and you gain on the exchange from Spanish into French; but great care must be taken that no false Spanish coins are imposed on one, as it seems to be generally acknowledged that bad money is coined annually to a certain amount, and this is practically admitted by the Government, as they undertake to redeem false gold pieces, by paying on their presentation two-thirds of their value. The money is easily understood. An *Isabel* (worth a sovereign and tenpence) contains five *duros;* each *duro* five *pesetas* (each worth tenpence); a *peseta* contains four *reals*. Accounts are made out in *reals*.

The two worst things in Spain are her government and her laundresses; it is hard to say which does their work the worst, both are so abominably bad, and the people are the victims. Spain well governed what a country it might be! Very little is known of it beyond its own limits; and of the people still less. In the north, we think a Spaniard must be a *brigand;* or, at best, he is pictured with dagger in hand ready to attack the first comer. A Spanish lady in Madrid told us she had just returned from Paris, and that she had been frequently asked whether she did not always wear a dagger. That Spaniards fly to the knife in quarrels, and that their passions are easily roused, is true enough; but treat them courteously and kindly, and you will find them both ready and willing to serve you to the best of their power. There is a great deal of kind-heartedness about them, and they are especially gentle and tender with children. As a rule, they are honest and sober, and if one cannot add industrious, it is on account of their climate, and still more their oppressive government, that renders them heedless of the future. The beauty of the women is greatly exaggerated; you will see more beauty in one hour's walk in any English town than you will meet in a month's travels in Spain. They are clumsily made, and walk ungracefully; they have large hands, but—in Castile at any rate—beautiful feet; though, with their present fashion of long-training dresses, they are not seen. In the south, their teeth and hair are very fine; but they have unhealthy complexions. After twenty they lose all appearance of youth, and by five-and-twenty they become very stout and doubly ungraceful. Home life, as we understand it, they know nothing about; they are always either in their bed-rooms or out of doors; family gatherings hardly ever occur, nor is there sociability of any kind amongst them. They are great theatre goers; in almost every town there is a good theatre; their greatest entertainment, however, is within the bull-ring, but this cruel amusement is less frequented by ladies than of yore; by degrees, their eyes seem to be opening to the fact that bull-fights are brutalizing, and unfit for women to witness, and the majority are satisfied with going to see a sport where young bulls only fight, and where precautions are taken not only to prevent either man or beast from being killed, but even to protect them from injury.

Spaniards are inveterate smokers, from the beggar to the king; the cigarette is everlastingly in their mouths; even at dinner, between the courses, the cigarette is made and smoked, but they are not half the nuisance in consequence that one might expect; the tobacco is peculiarly mild, and, were it not for the results, one would care little for the actual smoke. What the cigar is to the man, the fan is to the woman. A lady is never without one; walking, driving, at home, in church, paying visits, even at meals, the fan will be in her hand, ever restless, opening and shutting it, occasionally making a pretence to fan herself, then talking with it to her opposite neighbour, for fans aided by bright eyes can say a great deal. Fans also do duty for a parasol, as with a mantilla parasols are not used; bonnets are, however, now beginning to be worn by a few ladies when driving; in Barcelona they are very general, but that is the only town in which they at present do not look singular. Till lately, ladies were not allowed in churches unless wearing a mantilla; now they may go in hats, if they like, or anything else, to almost all; but there are one or two churches where the mantilla is still enforced. Any lady intending to pass even only a few weeks in Spain, will find it advisable to adopt the fashion of the country, and wear this generally becoming head-dress; it will save an amount of mobbing by children little dreamt of, and they will be allowed to walk about in peace and unheeded, whereas with a bonnet, and still more so with a hat, everyone stares as if they had never seen such things before. Let them imagine the case reversed, and fancy what would be the result of a Spanish lady walking down Regent Street, or in the Park, with a mantilla. A bonnet in Spain is quite as uncommon; except, as we said before, in Barcelona, and by a very few in Seville and Madrid when driving.

Take as little luggage as possible; it hampers one's movements, and costs a great deal; but let a corner be found for a small medicine chest, as, except at Gibraltar, it is as wise to avoid chemists as it is prudent to keep clear of doctors.

Neutral tint, or blue glass spectacles will be found of great service.

CHAPTER I.

FROM LONDON TO BAYONNE.

WITH the prospect of encountering every conceivable horror, conjured up by the fertile brains of our friends and acquaintances, and portrayed in painfully vivid colours, and what we should have to endure on the one hand and forego on the other, if we persisted in our foolish resolve of spending a winter in Spain, we left London in October, resolutely determined to brave all, and make our way as rapidly as possible to Madrid, in order to see it thoroughly before the cold winds set in, which we were told—amongst other equally reliable information—froze people to death in the streets. You saw persons standing still, you spoke to them, but receiving no answer, you would look inquiringly and find them dead, stiff, and frozen!

In order to begin our journey quietly, children being of our party, we left London by a stupidly-slow train at 2·18 p.m. and reached Dover at 5·50 p.m., taking up our quarters for the night at the Lord Warden Hotel, where fortunately we had written to secure rooms, the rush being great to get in there, owing to people at the last moment resolving to take a look at the Grande Exposition of 1867 before it closed.

On to Paris the following day, and for a marvel the sea was calm and no one ill; for which reason people were in a condition to grumble, and not half so good-natured as they would have been had they undergone a certain amount of suffering. Paris was crowded to such an extent one could not help wondering where all the people found beds; yet it looked as bright and beautiful as usual, the weather clear and fresh, with a warm sun, rendering it doubly delightful after the yellow fogs we had been favoured with in London.

After a couple of days spent in gazing at the outdoor portion of the great fair in the Champ de Mars, we left for Bordeaux, going through in the day. We started by the 10·45 a.m. train, and arrived at 10·15 p.m.; a long journey, especially for the little travellers; but it is better than to divide it by sleeping at Tours, which is off the main line. The weather was beautiful, a little too warm for those who, like ourselves, were prepared for cold and not for heat. There is a capital table d'hôte dinner at Angoulême, which is reached at 7 p.m.

We were recommended the Hôtel de Paris, as being the best in Bordeaux; if so, there is ample room for better ones: we believe the Hôtel de la Paix is on a better scale.

Bordeaux is a very large but not very interesting town. The cathedral of St. André has two beautiful spires; the interior is a single nave, and is fifty-six feet wide. The Porte Royale was built by Henry 2nd of England and Queen Eleanor. The façade of the church of St. Croix is fine, as is also that of St. Michel; here are some fine painted windows, and a great collection of human remains, mummies, &c. The Palais Gallien is said to be the remains of a Roman amphitheatre. The bridge across the Garonne is fine; there are seventeen arches to it. The theatre is remarkably handsome, and is worth looking at outside if you do not care to go in. There is an English church and a tolerable number of English residents, wine merchants chiefly. We heard a very good sermon the Sunday we were there, and would afterwards have enjoyed a quiet walk, but for the fair then being held, which caused the whole town to be in a tumult. Articles were exposed for sale of every description, from rusty keys and iron bedsteads to *bonbons* and Dresden china. One great attraction seemed to be a gilt carriage, the body being panelled with looking glass, five musicians sitting on the roof, playing various instruments, and in front were two velvet-covered seats: a woman, gaudily dressed, and with gold beads and braid and feathers waving in her black hair, stood here inviting any one and every one to ascend and take a seat while she would extract their teeth, as many as they liked to part with, without pain. Several accepted her invitation, and calmly and quietly submitted to the operation, apparently without suffering; it was done rapidly and with seeming ease; still, on inquiring of one woman if it had not hurt her, she was incapable of answering, but her husband replied people must expect a little pain on such occasions. He clearly did not feel on the subject as she did. There was the ordinary exhibition of fat women, people with three legs and two heads, and the wild beast caravan.

Desiring to see Arcachon, the new *station d'hiver* now rising into renown, though very slowly, we devoted a day to it. At about thirty miles from Bordeaux, and reached by railway, situated amidst pine woods, and bordered on the west by a basin some miles in extent, which opens into the Bay of Biscay, it is one of the prettiest and most primitive looking little places possible. It is a village of châlets; the villas being all built in the Swiss style and studded about the pine forest, each having its own private garden; most of them are detached; here and there they may be seen in couplets. Living is extremely moderate, and house rent absurdly cheap. You may have a furnished house with seven or eight bedrooms and a proportionate number of sitting rooms for the six winter months for £10 a month; smaller, but very pretty and nice, from £4 a month. One benefit derived here by consumptive people is through the rain water which is caught from the fir trees that have their barks cut, it having imbibed a certain quantity of the turpentine. To produce enough for exportation, the plan they adopt is to cut a tree down, and allow water to pass slowly over the part where the tree is caused to bleed; this is caught in pails, then bottled off, and sent in large quantities to Paris and elsewhere. The right thing, however, is to drink it on the spot straight from the tree, after rain has fallen. Little pots or jars are fixed against the trees immediately below where they are cut to catch the turpentine; these also catch the water, which any one is allowed to pour off.

There is an English church and an English medical man at Arcachon. The Grand Hotel is the largest, newest, and best at present; it is very well managed, and the charges moderate. The *Times* is taken, and reaches there the morning after its publication, at nine o'clock. There is a Casino, admission free during the winter, but 50 centimes entrance fee is charged during the summer; a museum, and the celebrated Aquarium. It is also famous for oysters; small, green, uncomfortable looking oysters, but highly appreciated by many. For people of moderate incomes one can hardly imagine a better place for the winter, it is so easy of access, both in the way of distance and expense.

We left Bordeaux at 8 a.m. and reached Bayonne at 12·25, putting up at the Hôtel St. Etienne—the best. The cathedral, which we visited first, is a fine building, with some beautiful coloured windows and a magnificent organ. In a little quiet spot, about two miles out of Bayonne, lie the officers of the Coldstream Guards who fell on the 14th of April, 1814, at the *sortie* made by the garrison from the citadel. A marble tablet, erected in 1830 by their friend and companion, Captain J. O. Hervey (afterwards and for many years consul at Bayonne), is placed at the head and between two lines of flat grave stones; a border of cypress trees surrounds them, and a paling shuts out the public, but access is easily obtained from the people living in a cottage close by, who keep the key and the place in order.

From the citadel the view is magnificent; the two rivers, the Nive and Adour, join here and divide the town; they form a capital harbour, and being but a short distance from the Bay of Biscay, this is found of great convenience. A most intelligent man showed us over the citadel, and gave us a clear and distinct account of the famous night of the 14th April, 1814. The English coming from the Bay landed their men at the mouth of the Adour, and threw a bridge across the river, enabling them to place their troops on the right bank; their object being to join the Duke of Wellington then engaged against Soult before Toulouse. Knowing the citadel was garrisoned, they felt it necessary in self defence to attack it, so as to avoid themselves being attacked in the rear. The French however were before them. There were only 1500 men in the citadel, 1200 of these were passed through two gates, 600 by each; they moved quietly and stealthily onwards, and surprised the sentinels on watch in the British camp at eleven o'clock at night; they then forced on their way as silently as possible to the general's tent, took him prisoner, and carried him off to the citadel; by this time, however, it became known that something had happened; in a moment the alarm was given. It is said the French were betrayed, a man having informed an English officer high in command of the scanty number of troops in the citadel; the officer and his informer were killed by one ball a few minutes afterwards; the fight was now fearful, and of the 1200 men who left the citadel but 400 returned alive. Two days afterwards the English general was set at liberty, for news arrived that the empire, for the time being, was overthrown.

Bayonne is a bright, cheerful town; it is scarcely French, yet hardly Spanish, a mixture of the two in all things, habits, manners, dress, and indolence; the people are extremely obliging, will give you any information they can if you ask for it, but they are utterly devoid of curiosity; it would be too much trouble for them to meddle in or seek to know aught of others' affairs. For this reason, we were told, many English families made Bayonne their permanent residence; no one troubles to ask or inquire anything about them, or what object takes them there.

The bayonet was first made at about a couple of

miles out of the town, and derived its name from it in consequence. Bayonne has the sorry renown of being the place where Catherine de Medicis planned the massacre of St. Bartholomew.

CHAPTER II.

BIARRITZ—SAN SEBASTIAN.

WE spent a day at Biarritz; it is a charming place, in every sense; particularly clean and well-built, and the day so bright and lovely, that a July day in England could not compare with it. The Villa Eugénie is a large red brick building, something between a workhouse and a lunatic asylum in appearance, standing in a bare-looking park of no great dimensions, fir trees planted here and there, but at present so small that they in no way ornament the place. The little chapel, with its Moorish entrance, is extremely pretty, but, like the house, it stands too exposed. There are plenty of paths, broad and narrow, cut in all directions; looking like a mass of scars over the bare treeless land. The beautiful sea, the rocky, picturesque coast, and, above all, the bright deep-blue sky, all render it, however, an attractive spot. The sea, on this day, was like a lake, as unlike what the Bay of Biscay *ought* to be, as it is well possible. Hotels abound, as do "furnished apartments" and "houses to let." Already some fifteen or twenty English families had arrived for the winter, and the Hôtel d'Angleterre, which is considered the best, was quite full. A library with a good stock of books, and a *Cabinet de Lecture* is open to any one for 25 cents a day; there you can read the "Times" of the previous day; it reaches at 1 p.m.

The drive from Bayonne by the Adour and round by La Barre is very pretty; here there is a new lighthouse being built; further on, going by this route (which, however, is by far the longest) is the little village called La Chambre d'Amour, on account of a couple being drowned in a rocky cave on the coast just beneath it, where, after wandering about on the sands, they had sought rest and shade; they fell asleep, the tide rose, and they were awoke by the huge waves breaking nearly on them; there was no escape, the sea was up to the mouth of the cave, and so they fell asleep again, a long, last sleep. Soon after a village sprang up near the spot, and the romantic name of La Chambre d'Amour was given it. Before reaching it, we drove round to see the convent called La Refuge; it is about a mile from the village.

This convent receives all who seek its shelter, either from shame or sorrow; fallen women, called "penitents," are taken in, with or without a contribution of money: they have but to prove that they are in earnest. The sisters themselves are called "Servantes de Marie;" but the inmates altogether number 550. Their life is spent in working, either orders for trousseaux, or making clothes and embroidering them;

these are placed in a little room and exposed to visitors for sale. They keep and breed their own cows, bullocks, pigs, poultry, and rabbits; they grow the maize with which they make their own bread: the washing, no small labour, is done every week. They rise at 4 a.m., and go to bed at 9 p.m., summer and winter. They have three meals a-day, but meat only twice a week. They are always silent, except during two hours in the day, from noon to one, and from half-past three to four, and from half-past six to seven; then the noise of voices is almost deafening.

Beyond this convent, and situated in a flat but fir-clad piece of land, is the Convent of the Bernardines; it is under the same Superior as La Refuge. It is an Order amongst the severest that exist. They live in perpetual silence, *never* speaking, but at confession. Their dress entirely hides their faces from one another; they are not permitted by their vows to look on a human face, or be seen themselves; the large thick coarse white flannel cloak with the hood all in one which they wear, has an immense blue cross on the back, reaching from the neck to the heels, and from shoulder to shoulder. The hood comes completely over the entire head, a round hole being made over the mouth to admit sufficient air for them to breathe. They have one hour during the day for what is termed recreation; this is from noon to one; then they work in the garden, or in their cemetery. They were building a greenhouse when we were there. They live as the nuns at La Refuge; their food being sent to them from there. There are thirty-five of these poor misguided women in this Order, many of them ladies. They are obliged before entering to be postulants for two years, and novices for three or four, so that they may feel fully assured of their vocation: but all are free to leave if they like; indeed, as we saw, they have full liberty; but it is very safe to grant it, for where could they go, if they desired it? What other home would be opened to them? If one knew the bitter sorrow each carries in her heart, might we not, perhaps, think as they do? Better be there than spurned and sneered at by the world. It made one grieve, however, to see the soft, delicate-looking, white hands, which many had, doing coarse heavy work; one we saw bending over and trimming the flowers on the grave of one happier than herself; for *her* sorrows were over; none of them live very long—how could they?

The chapel belonging to this convent is very plain; on the altar was a life-sized image of the Virgin dressed in black: the old chapel, now only used for prayers, never for mass, has no flooring, and only a thatched roof. The Sister who accompanied us said that the Empress Eugénie, who frequently came here, always prayed in this chapel in preference to the more modern one. Their cells, arranged in two long straight rows, are each about six feet in height, the same in length, and four in breadth; in winter they must be intensely cold, for they are made of wood and have no flooring, nothing but the bare ground; they each contain a bed, a tiny stand which holds a brown earthenware jug and basin, a crucifix, and a piece of paper against the wall on which is written, "DIEU SEUL."

Their refectory has only a long table in it and wooden benches. On the table were standing some earthenware mugs and jugs, all of the coarsest kind and broken, the handles off all; of course, they drink nothing but water. At the Refuge there was nothing to depress one, but the visit to the Bernardines made one feel very sad; it left a weight on one's spirits; and for many a long day the thought of them arose, bringing with it anything but cheeriness.

We left Bayonne by the 12·40 train, and arrived at San Sebastian soon after three, having been detained an hour at Irun, the first Spanish town after crossing the frontier. All those who were bound direct for Madrid had their baggage searched here; ours was not looked at till we reached San Sebastian. At Irun we changed carriages; we found the Spanish ones large and roomy, but dirty; this is, unfortunately, the case with all of them, smoking being permitted in any of them; and as a Spaniard cannot possibly get on five minutes without a cigarette, no place (except churches) but what bears traces of tobacco. We were rarely troubled with fellow-passengers, our party nearly filling the compartment; but when one did get in, we had to bear with the smoking and what it entails without murmuring.

At Irun nothing struck us as peculiar in the people; but for the soldiers' uniform, we could have imagined ourselves still in France, the same tone seemed over all. We, however, remarked a great change the moment we entered San Sebastian; and the thing that seemed the most singular was the Mantilla, which, of course, every woman wore, from the poorest to the richest, rendering them to uneducated eyes like nuns. After a while, however, one sees how very little resemblance they bear to them, at any rate in manner.

The church of Santa Maria, which we reached just as vespers was over, was one living moving mass of black—almost all women—hardly a man amongst them. Being All Saints' Day, the crowd was immense, and candles were studded like stars all over the church. The building is heavy and massive, and the chapels with large and disproportioned gilt ornaments, reaching to the ceiling. The font is the same in which Ignatius Loyola was baptized. There is little to interest one inside or out; of the two, the latter is the most worthy of notice. The citadel is more interesting, to the English at any rate; from there a magnificent view is obtained, and the position seen which the English troops held during the famous siege of San Sebastian. The whole of this part of the country is fraught with interest; every spot has some tale attached to it. The graves of some of our brave men who fell during the siege, as also of others who were killed in the Don Carlos revolution, are studded about against the side of the rock, on the summit of which stands the citadel; some have mere tablets; others, crosses; others, but flat graves. Many of the stones are entirely broken away, and nothing but a mound of earth marks the spot where they rest.

In our descent from here we came on another convent of Bernardines, that terrible Order! The windows were not only barred so close as to admit of nothing larger than a bean between each bar, but there were outside this grating again thick iron bars, so that it seemed utterly impossible for either light or air to enter. This appeared far worse than what we saw at the convent near Biarritz, as there, at any rate, the poor nuns had God's beautiful blue sky above them to look at and enjoy.

San Sebastian, the Scarborough of the Madrilenians, has little to detain the traveller beyond a day. The scenery around is very fine; but to enjoy it, and the walks and drives, you must spend a month. The church and citadel are soon seen, and if time is to spare, then the admirers of St. Ignatius Loyola may drive through Cestona, where there are some celebrated mineral springs, and visit the college established by the famous founder of the Jesuits. The house was originally the home of his family, and he was himself born here in 1491.

San Sebastian has a fine bull ring; formerly the

bull fights were held in the Plaza Mayor, where the houses still bear the numbers on each story, which marked the various tiers of seats. We stopped at the Fonda Neuva de Beraza; it is the best, and comfortable enough; the rooms were good, and the dinners better than we had at Bayonne; even Bass's bitter ale was as good here as in Paris. The entrance to the house alone was objectionable; it seemed as if we were ascending from stables into a barn; as the horses occupy the rez-de-chaussée here. The bread we heard so much vaunted is certainly not Spanish at San Sebastian; it was both sour and coarse; and they have not the fashion of using saucers to their cups; there was not one in the house; plates did duty for them. The pretty waiting-maid at the Fonda was worth looking at; her bright face, her pale delicate complexion, her soft eyes, coral lips, and beautiful teeth, formed a picture very pleasant to dwell on.

CHAPTER III.

BURGOS.

WE left San Sebastian by the 8·17 a.m. train, and reached Burgos at 5·9 p.m. As far as Miranda the scenery was very grand and rich, but from there on to Burgos it was wild and desolate, and the soil poor and arid. At Tolosa, the façade of the church was good; but there is little inside to arrest the traveller on his road. As we went along we saw the most antiquated-looking carts, drawn by bullocks yoked at the head (as they are always throughout Spain), and with log wheels, one with the axle. At Miranda we stopped half an hour, where those who liked could dine at the table d'hôte at the station for fourteen reals, or take refreshments on a more moderate scale apart.

Pancorbo is worth putting one's head out of window to gaze at, if only to see what a perfect ruin an inhabited place can be; few houses had roofs, and those that had seemed devoid of frontage, having holes for windows, and ladders for stairs. One could not help wondering who were the people and what, that could exist amidst such desolation. At every station along the road, there always stood a small table covered with a clean white cloth, and on it bottles of water, lump sugar, and the *pan d'España*, the bread we had heard so much of; it is very good, and as nice to eat as it is to look at. From this onwards we never met with anything but this white delicious bread. By the side of the table, in a large deal box, lay a huge pig skin full of the *vino tinto* or red wine, drank by all the peasants of the country.

The best hotel at Burgos is now the Fonda de la Rafaela: there we stopped, having previously written for rooms, a precaution all travellers should take, as the comfort of finding everything ready, and the people prepared for the extra call on their larder, is by no means to be despised. We found good rooms and fires, and if not in their places, still there they were, standing in the middle of the room, or any other convenient spot, consisting of smouldering ash in a colossal copper soup plate; but these charcoal fires are abominations. All should avoid *braseros* in their rooms, if they would escape headache. We had as good a dinner as we could have got in any town in France—Paris always excepted. The attendance, however, was original, as was also the manner of serving the dinner; but that in no way deteriorated from the excellence of the dishes which were put on table altogether, and one plate to each person was considered sufficient; plates were clearly not plentiful, but we did get more. Potatoes were not to be had, but *garbanzos* seemed to take their place, as they do in many other parts of Spain. In appearance they are like large Indian corn, but they grow one seed in a pod, and are cultivated all over the country as potatoes are in England. The milk was very good, the *manteca* (butter) fully bore out its reputation; it was not alone uneatable, but objectionable in the room. However, with good bread and good milk the little people fared well enough. In the dining-room were hunting scenes framed on the wall; the subjects were described in French and English; the latter too amusing to pass unnoticed. "*Chasse au Buffle*" (Fox hunting to the wild ox). "*Chasse au Sanglier*" (Fox hunting to the wild boar). They were all equally well translated.

Early the next morning we went to the cathedral, said to be one of the finest in Spain, and it is wondrously beautiful. Fortunately it was Sunday, so we saw it stripped of its curtains and hiding draperies. We walked round it once or twice before attempting to see it in detail, in order to realize the reality of the fairy lace-like work which met us every way we turned. It seemed such a pity that the vista was destroyed by the *coro* cutting the centre nave in two; it would be as fine again if it were placed behind or right and left of the high altar. The seats, however, are richly carved, especially the archbishop's; the whole is in walnut wood. The high altar is very gorgeous, as are most of the chapels around, from the great quantity of gilding; this is especially the case in the Capilla de Santa Tecla, in which it is overdone; the ceiling of this chapel is very highly coloured, rendering the whole showy and gaudy. On the opposite side of the church to this chapel, and the second on the right hand as you enter the cathedral, is the Capilla del Santisimo Cristo; in it is the famous and miraculous Cristo de Burgos. As a work of art, it is very fine, painfully so; but it is impossible to look at it in that light, it is so dreadfully disfigured. In the first place it is covered over with real skin, and a great heavy mass of black hair hangs down all over the face and chest. From the waist to the ankles it is draped with a spangled tarlatan petticoat, the whole being the awful, caricatured. A broad massive frame is formed round it by *ex-votos*, some of them being thick plaits of hair. This crucifix is, according to "holy tradition," the work of Nicodemus, and was found by a native of Burgos floating alone in the Bay of Biscay; he brought it to land, and then wondrous miracles were wrought through it, which do not cease in the present day; it is an object of intense veneration to the people.

There is a great deal of very beautiful sculpture in many of the chapels; the finest is to be seen in the Capilla Real del Condestable; here are the tombs of the Velasco family, the hereditary Constables of Castile. In front of the altar the full-length figures of the founder, Pedro Hernandez de Velasco, and his wife, surmount the monuments erected over the place where their bodies lie; they are beautifully sculptured in Carrara marble; the hands of Mencia Lopez de Mendoza, the wife, are exquisitely done. The details of the whole are a marvel of art; they were carved in Italy three centuries ago. In this chapel is a Magdalen, said to be by Leonardo da Vinci; it is not possessed of that gentle penitent expression we are accustomed to see in her pictures. In the Sacristia are some little gems of work in gold and enamel, especially a tiny representation of the Virgin and Child seated on her lap; both figures are in ivory and beneath a canopy of richly wrought gold, the metal being some of the first brought to Spain from America by Christopher Colombus; also, of the same gold, a cup beautifully enamelled and studded with precious stones; and an exquisite cross. There is also a picture with folding panels of the Virgin and Child, by Albert Durer; it is much praised, but it appeared to us too hard in its outlines. In the chapel of Santa Ana is a group of the Holy Family, thought to be by Andrea del Sarto; it is in any case very beautiful. A picture less pleasing, yet more valued, is in the Capilla de la Presentacion; it represents the Virgin, larger than life, with the Saviour on her knee; it is ascribed to Michael Angelo. There is a fine crucifixion by Mateo Cerezo, in the Capilla del Cristo en Agonia. The curious and richly worked double staircase in the centre of the left side of the church, is by Diego de Siloe; it leads to a door, which however is never used, opening to the street, between thirty and forty feet above the pavement of the cathedral; it having been built on uneven ground, and instead of levelling it entirely, they dug down to make the building even, leaving an earth wall on this side of it. But one painted glass window remains in the whole church, but that is a very fine rose window; this gives ample light to see the exquisite lace work which abounds.

There are some pictures in the Sala Capitular; the finest, for few are good, is a Crucifixion by Domenico el Greco; it is very beautiful. The ceiling of the first room is very rich. Here, fixed against the wall, is the famous old chest of the Cid, *el Cofre del Cid*. This was the trunk he filled with rubbish and raised a loan on its weighty contents, which were passed off as jewels; it being stipulated that it was not to be opened. However, the Cid was honest, and the day came in which he redeemed his chest, paying, we are told, interest as well as principal. Amongst the relics in the Sacristia is the banner Alonso VIII. used at the battle of Las Navas de Tolosa.

The cloisters, always so still and seemingly so peaceful, are very beautiful; like the church, they are purely Gothic; there are many tombs here, all worthy of notice; some are as early as the 14th century. This cathedral was begun in 1221 by Bishop Maurice, an Englishman; the exterior, blocked up as it is by houses, is wondrously rich; the towers have spires, the stone work of which is so delicate and fragile looking, and so white, that it seems as if a breath of wind must shatter all to pieces. The effect of these pure lace-like tapering spires against the blue cloudless sky is lovely.

The Cid, the great hero of Spain, whose bones, together with those of his wife, we went to see in the town hall, where they are kept in a chest of walnut-wood, in shape very like an old fashioned wine cooler, was born in 1020. Great and glorious as the name of the Cid has become, his character was a strange mixture of good and evil, the latter predominating. He was a true Spaniard in his religion, showing devotion to the priest and worship to the Virgin, but little of either to God. He was intensely cruel, but daringly brave; rapacious and grasping, yet liberal to the church and the poor. The Cid's name had as many to curse it as to bless it; as many to rejoice at his downfall in court favour, as there were at his success at Valencia, which after capturing he ruled over. He died in 1099. His tomb—though his bones are not in it—still exists at San Pedro de Cardeña, an old convent now in ruins about eight miles out of Burgos. Over the entrance gate is a statue of the Cid mounted on his favourite horse, Babieca, which bore his dead body from Valencia to the grave; and when his master was laid in it, his own was prepared just in front of the Convent by Gil Diaz, a faithful and devoted friend of the dead warrior's.

It is hardly worth any one's while to go to Cardeña: the road to it is abominable, and therefore the drive takes a long time, besides there being positively nothing but the Cid's statue to see.

But every one must visit Miraflores, a now suppressed Carthusian convent, about two miles distant. It was built originally as a royal burial place by Juan II.; but being burnt in 1452, ten years only after its erection, his son Henrique IV. commenced rebuilding it; Isabella the Catholic finishing it in the Gothic style. She also raised the beautiful sepulchre, which stands in front of the high altar, and which caused Philip II. to exclaim when he saw it: "*We have done nothing at the Escorial.*" This monument to the memory of Juan II. and his wife Isabella, parents of Isabella the Catholic, is of alabaster, and the exquisite and marvellous work of the figures, the dress, the ornaments, the apostles and saints, the animals and flowers, is past description; it is impossible to do justice to it with the pen. Isabella's brother, who stood between her and the succession to the throne of Castile, the Infante Alonso, is also buried here. The monument is octagon; Juan and his wife reposing in the centre, the four Evangelists seated round, and every section, a mass of intricate sculpture, contains some scene from sacred history. The artist was Maestro Gil, father of Diego de Siloe, who designed the elaborate double staircase in the cathedral. It was completed in 1493. The *Altar Mayor* is very fine, the *retablo* is of carved wood. Brought to Spain by Christopher Columbus; it reaches to the roof, and is in tolerable order; whilst the sepulchre is unfortunately in many places very much injured.

Five old monks are the only inmates of this once famous convent; one of them took us over the entire building; there is little to see, as it is almost in ruins; but one can judge well enough what it must have been. The wealth and power of these institutions are even now very great in Spain, but they are but shadows of what was. The thousands of men who filled these magnificent monasteries always brought wealth with them; whilst the severity of their lives, solitary confinement, and perpetual silence, very soon killed them; they were thus removed, but their fortunes went to swell the treasury of these great societies.

The town of Burgos is a mass of tumble-down, quaint-looking houses; one gateway with a Moorish arch remains. The market place is large and open, with a colonnade running round it; every stall had a bountiful supply of the large red and green *pimientos* or capsicum; the Spaniards delight in them when made into salad. The common red pepper of the country is made from them, but they have neither taste nor smell. Acorns, the size of large filberts, are also sold in almost every town; the people eat them, both cooked and raw.

We found Burgos very cold, a sharp cutting wind

was blowing all the time we were there; it was therefore with little regret we bade it farewell. We were compelled to travel all night; the day trains being so slow that one can make no way in them at all. We were anxious also to push on at once to Madrid, in order to have a few weeks there before the winter set in. We left Burgos at 5.30 p.m. and reached the capital at 7·30 the following morning.

We unwisely divided our party in order to have more room for the night, and consequently had three vacant seats in our compartment, which at the first station we stopped at were filled by three Spaniards, two men and one woman, who remained till we reached Valladolid. Of course the cigarette was soon made and then smoked—it was a cold night and the windows shut—then followed what was far worse, a supper composed of a sausage savouring very strongly of garlic; after that the older man occupied himself by being sick; the window was quickly opened for him. The lady would talk, and being deaf would shout, consequently rest was utterly beyond one's power till they were gone; this was the more provoking, as one of our little travellers was very unwell and very suffering, and sleep was important; but it was little we got that night any way. It is a weary night to look back on even now.

The trains have an excessively bad habit of stopping everywhere—even these express trains do so, and the noise that is made of course wakes people up if they have the luck to be asleep; and they are not content with stopping only, but the porters open the doors of every carriage, shouting *diez minutos* in one's ears; often stopping longer, rarely less.

CHAPTER IV.

MADRID.

THE sandy hills and wild extensive uncultivated country around Madrid opened upon us in all the glory of the early morning, when Nature must indeed be ugly not to call forth some admiration, and so it was impossible, with the rosy tint that coloured all, not to feel that even that much abused, arid, wild land could be gazed on with a degree of pleasure. The character of this part of Spain reminds one of the mountain villages in Switzerland; there is such a hopeless look of misery, which one can understand in a country where never-ceasing dread and constant realization of avalanches exists; but here, where if solid buildings were raised they would remain, it seems utterly incomprehensible. Still the poverty and wretchedness of Castile, old and new, are so renowned, one ought not to be astonished.

We went to the Hotel de los Principes, on the Puerta del Sol. We found all ready and extremely comfortable. After a month's stay here we all agreed that nowhere, except in the best of the Paris hotels, had we ever found the same first-rate cooking, attendance, cleanliness, and general comfort. The manager, who speaks English thoroughly, has quite succeeded in his endeavour to make the house as good as an hotel can be. It is expensive, very; but so are the inferior ones.

The first impression Madrid made on us was that it was very French. It stands on an arid sandy plain 2400 feet above the level of the sea, and is about eight miles in circumference. The principal streets branch off from the Puerta del Sol; they are broad, and the buildings handsome. The public walks and gardens are numerous and very pleasant. The Prado, the "drive" of Madrid, is from three to six crowded with carriages; the horses are very fine; they are more generally used here than mules. Gentlemen ride, but few ladies; there is always a great crowd of pedestrians, who go, as all the rest do, to see and be seen. The "Buen Retiro" gardens are quiet and retired, but yet well peopled by nursery-maids and children, the little royalties included; they are driven here daily, and then get out and walk. The gardens are laid out in beds of box, cultivated so as to grow in all kinds of fantastical shapes, and then cut, rendering them still more quaint. In hot weather the walks in the wooded parts are very enjoyable, being sheltered from the sun and glare by dense foliage. These gardens were originally laid out for Philip IV., and a palace and theatre built near them. The palace was destroyed by fire, and with it many valuable works of art. Ferdinand VI. erected a new one, but it and the theatre were made a mere heap of ruins by the French. But these gardens and drives are only frequented for pleasure, whereas, for news-seekers and news-bearers the Puerta del Sol is the spot.

Here they gather in large groups, whether for discussing a change of ministry, a bull-fight, or the results of the lottery, that constant but only mode of gambling recognised and allowed in Spain. In every town, large or small, men, blind men generally, go about selling these tickets; half-a-dozen are always on the Puerta del Sol. From early morn till midnight is this place crowded. When ignorant of this propensity to congregate near the cool fountain, one asked, "What is this crowd assembled for?" but a few days teach one that all who can, place-seekers especially, make their way here till either the blazing midday sun or hunger drive them away. It is also the meeting-place for the ex-ministry. Fancy Russell, Gladstone, &c., &c., meeting daily in Trafalgar Square to talk over their chances of turning out Disraeli! Nine streets branch off from this *Plaza*, in which are the principal shops; but with all the bustle around this part of the town, little real business is done. The tradespeople seem utterly indifferent as to whether they sell their goods or not; you may take or leave, as you please. They close up their shops, some entirely, some only partially, during the middle of the day, either for eating or sleeping, or both. They have no thought for the morrow—few Spaniards but leave it to take care of itself. The women have a better idea of doing business than the men. There is little begging, very little compared with the rest of the country, and if they do ask for anything they accept a refusal at once. The very poorest have plenty of bread—they are never refused that when they ask for it, and it is all alike, no second quality, white as milk, close, but very light and sweet; no acidity is ever found in the *pan* of this country.

The Madrilenians have beautiful teeth and beautiful feet, small and well-shaped; their hands, however, are not so good; their thumbs are peculiarly long, and curl backwards in a way that is very ugly. As a rule, they are not handsome, though they are a strong healthy-looking race. This does not apply to the army; the men are under-sized and mean-looking. Troops are always marching about the town; it is thought advisable to keep them constantly before the people. There is a standing trumpeter at the barracks in the Puerta del Sol, and whenever soldiers march past, he trumpets till they are gone. This trumpetting goes on also every time any of the royal family drive by, and as they are constantly doing so, the trumpet is rarely still.

The Royal family, unlike our own, are easily seen; they are always driving out, or walking, or going to some church ceremony or some public amusement, and consequently they are never annoyed by a gaping, curious crowd. The Queen, though only thirty-seven years of age, looks much more, on account, no doubt, of her excessive size. She is heavy, awkward, and ungraceful in her movements; she looks best when seated, then there is a trifle of dignity in her appearance. She is utterly incapable, as all Spanish women are, of bowing; she will nod a recognition, but that is all. The King Consort is little and common looking, he is fair and foolish; some, however, think him as much of a knave as a fool. Princess Isabel,* the eldest daughter, now sixteen, has the beauty of youth; she is slight and tall, and gentle looking. The Prince of the Asturias, the Crown Prince, with his closely-cut hair and rather heavy features, is like a French college boy; the rest of the family are mere children.

With all her outward display of devotion, Queen Isabella has not the reputation amongst her loving (?) subjects of being over-pious. Monseigneur Claret, who rules the palace, has, since he has been her Majesty's confessor, been the cause of many strange rumours, and such as are not likely to help to increase the respect due to a queen. She always keeps near her the "Bleeding Nun," an object of adoration almost to herself, but of loathing and aversion to the educated populace.

The then prime minister, General Narvaez, was intensely feared and disliked; not so, however, his late

* Princess Isabel was married the other day to Count de Girgenti.

colleague, poor Marshal O'Donnell, who had just died at Biarritz, and whose magnificent funeral we witnessed. They brought his dead body, which, when living, was exiled, back to the country for funeral honours. It is astonishing how grateful we can feel to the dead. Narvaez was as bloodthirsty as any Spaniard can be, and that is not saying a little. A few years ago, in order to create terror, his only means of governing, he ordered women and children who were utterly innocent of any breach of law, or taking part in any way with those who were endeavouring to shake off his authority, to be shot down in the open plain, so that all might witness the awful sight. He succeeded in his object, which was to cow those he could not by other means bring under subjection, by slaughtering their wives and children. It is also told of him that one time having ordered a child to be shot in order to intimidate the father, and finding it impossible to keep him still, Narvaez desired an orange to be thrown him, and whilst the poor little fellow stooped to pick it up, he gave orders for them to fire; they say the men who had to obey these orders, accustomed as they were to the shedding of blood, were sickened at this. But it is by these means Spain is ruled, and no wonder, therefore, the people openly curse the Government, and lose no opportunity of endeavouring to free themselves from such a yoke.

For many long years Spain has had her towns protected at night by watchmen. It was quite a pretty sight to see them at Madrid every night at ten o'clock assemble in their cloaks, and holding their lanterns before them, preparatory to starting off for their various beats. They looked like a number of glow-worms in the distance. They are a useful body of men, if for nothing else than shouting out the hour, for the clocks in Spain have a bad habit of not going, or if they do, it is without due regard to time.

Water at one time was very scarce, but now it is both plentiful and good, though it has all to be fetched for household purposes from the fountains. The water carriers, as in Paris, are a numerous body, and a class not well to trifle with. They carry it in small barrels on their shoulders. There are sometimes as many as thirty or forty at one fountain filling their barrels. It is sold by tumblers full all over the streets, in the theatres, and at all the railway stations. The cry is "*Quien quiere agua fresca?*" Certainly, from one end of Spain to the other, bread and water are as good as can possibly be.

There are several cafés in Madrid, but no one is ever seen sitting outside them, and no ladies ever go into them. Spaniards don't seem to care much about either light or air; and if a breath of wind is blowing, the cloak is thrown round their shoulder so as completely to cover the mouth and part of the nose. Putting on the *capa* is quite an art, and one not very easily acquired. The very beggars in the street do it with such grace that an Englishman would gaze at them with admiration. It is their inordinate pride which shows itself in their every tone and movement, and which gives an air of decayed grandeur even to those who have never by fair means called a cuarto their own.

The system adopted here, and all over Spain, for obtaining letters addressed 'Poste Restante' is, though apparently good at first sight, most bewildering, and leads to endless loss of letters. Papers are posted up all round the entrance passage of the General Post Office, with the names of people for whom letters have arrived—not alphabetically, but according to the date they come on. To each name is a number affixed, which the claimant to the letter must copy and present at the bureau, with a passport or some proof of their identity, otherwise they will not be delivered. The writing of the names is sometimes very indistinct, and very often totally at variance with the original—in fact nothing can be worse than the working of this method; but the Spaniards are proud of it, and wonder how it is other countries are so stupid as not to adopt it. Letters insufficiently stamped are set aside altogether, and as a rule never heard of.

Doctors have a sorry reputation in Madrid, and no wonder; it was our misfortune to come in contact with three of them, an alarming number anywhere, but doubly so here. Dr. C., the first called in, frankly owned he could make nothing of his patient, one of the little people of our party; he thought it was gout, but it might be, and probably was, something else.

Under this unsatisfactory conclusion, it was suggested another doctor should be consulted; Dr. C. gladly agreed, but said it was the fashion to have three at a consultation; so it was settled a third should be present, Dr. C. of course making his own choice as to who they were to be. At the appointed hour these three men arrived, all dressed in the deepest mourning, and smoking cigars; it was a sight that was enough to frighten the strongest hearted invalid, and to send a timid one into fits, as it very nearly did the poor little child; however, she was quietly taken out of sight and hearing. Then, between puffs and spitting, they each delivered their opinion, which was worth as much as the smoke that came from their mouths. There was, first, the doctor who was the principal attendant at the palace, then the head of the hospital for children, and lastly, Dr. C. They all agreed that it might be one thing, or it might be another, and then they took their departure, and with them, each 200 reals; and being 600 reals out of pocket was the only fact we were made certain of by this consultation of Spanish doctors. Why does not some enterprising Englishman start forthwith for Madrid? If he wanted to make his fortune quickly and surely, it would be the best step he could take to insure success.

There is no opening, however, for a dentist. Mr. Mackeehan, an American, has resided there for upwards of twenty years, and is, like most of his countrymen in this branch of surgery, extremely clever. He is peculiar, not to say eccentric, in some things; for instance, he refused to take a fee for extracting a tooth; his reason for doing so was, he said, that he thought that any one who lost a tooth lost quite enough at one time without paying for it! Clever as he is, we doubt much his ever making his fortune. We still retain very vivid recollections of the pleasant cup of tea with which he welcomes every English patient in that tiny, cheery, sunny room overlooking the Alcala Street.

There are, however, other dentists to be found in Madrid besides Mr. Mackeehan; for one day as we were walking to the Plaza Mayor, we there saw a very well-dressed man on a fine horse, stooping over his neck and pulling out teeth by the dozen from people, who came forward amongst the crowd with open mouth and open hand, the latter containing a peseta. The horse never moved the whole time; he stood like a rock, and as only Spanish horses can and will stand.

The visiting cards of Spanish doctors are sufficient to produce fainting fits if you are not very strong minded. They are perfectly black—a dead black, and the name written in white letters. If the devil ever had visiting cards, these must surely be copies of them; that is, taking it for granted that all the doctors we saw in Spain—and they were not few—were not in black simply on account of the death of a relation, but from custom.

Madrid abounds in lodging and boarding houses; the

latter are called Casas de Huespedes. The lodging-houses are known by pieces of blank paper being tied over the iron railings of the balconies, and the boarding-houses by pieces of newspaper. These signs denote the same thing all over Spain. No fire-places are ever to be met with in these houses, but a *brasero* can always be obtained. At their evening parties, the Spaniards in cold weather place one of these horrid substitutes for fires under a table, and then sit round it.

There is not a great deal to see in Madrid in the way of sights. The great attraction, and it certainly is a host in itself, is the Gallery of Paintings. It is a magnificent collection, and the Spaniards may well be excused when they tell you it is the finest in the world. The building itself is very large, plain but handsome; the interior is strangely built, the rooms and galleries branching off from a common centre, others again branching off from them. This arrangement makes it sometimes difficult to find the room you want. The long gallery, facing the door as you enter, contains the finest pictures of the collection, though turn which way you will, the eye falls on some gem which will force you to pause; it is impossible thoroughly to see this gallery under several weeks.

Murillo, Velazquez, Ribera, Alonso Cano, Joanes, Raphael, Titian, Andrea del Sarto, Tintoretto, Paul Veronese, Guido Reni, Leonardo da Vinci, Claude Lorraine, Watteau, Poussin, Rubens, Rembrandt, Holbein, Van Dyck, and a host of others, whose names the lovers of art would be familiar with, can here be seen to perfection, and some of them here only. To begin with the Murillos, of which there are forty-six: the "Purísima Concepcion," numbered 229 in the catalogue, is exquisite; the marvellous purity, innocence, and beauty in the Virgin's face, and the holy submissive expression is so in keeping with her reply, "Be it unto me according to the word." The one at the Louvre cannot bear comparison with this. 202, the Child Jesus and St. John, is a lovely picture—the Saviour is giving St. John to drink, out of a shell. Also 46, the "Divine Shepherd:" the Child Jesus is seated, holding a staff in his hand, and a lamb at his feet; the child's position is so perfectly natural, and the expression of the face so holy and full of love. The "Asunto Místico," 315, the Vision of St. Bernard: the Virgin and Child on a cloudy throne, with angels about them, appear to St. Bernard; the saint is kneeling; the expression of his face is very fine; the whole picture is grand. Through every one of Murillo's paintings one might go, and to each give the praise due, but we must pass on to others.

Velazquez, the greatest of all Spanish painters, as most people say, though one is not bound to agree with them, can be better understood in the Madrid Gallery than elsewhere, as there are not only sixty-three of his paintings here, but they are his finest works. The best are his portraits, but those that show his power in portraying life are pictures like

"Las Meninas," perhaps his *chef d'œuvre*. It is a dull unpleasant-looking group, consisting of the Infanta Margarita of Austria being amused by her pages, whilst her dwarfs, two of them, are worrying a dog. The dwarfs are so intensely disagreeable looking, that one cannot give the admiration due to the painting as the marvellous work of art which it is. On the left hand, Velazquez is himself represented, with the pallet in his hand, finishing the portrait of Philip IV. This picture is numbered 155; next to it, 156, is the portrait of Philip IV., a splendid picture. The finest to our minds, being unable to tolerate the dwarfs, which mar all pleasure in looking at Velazquez's greatest productions, is "Nuestro Señor Crucificado," 51: it is a wonderful picture; and the agonized figure of our Lord stands out from its plain black background in terrible reality; the hair, long and dark, hangs over the face, as is seen in most crucifixion representations in Spain, whether in carving or painting. Velazquez was born at Seville in 1599; he founded the School of Painting in Madrid, in which place he died in 1660.

"Jesus and the Magdalen," 809, by Correggio, is exquisite: Mary's face of surprise, joy, and intense love on recognising her Lord in the garden, is so beautiful, that once seen it could never be forgotten; she is partially kneeling, and seems to have been suddenly stopped from approaching the Saviour by his command. Close to this picture is Rafael's Holy

Family, 726, called "La Perla;" it is very lovely; the colouring is both rich and soft. The infant Saviour is seated on the Virgin's lap, St. John offering him flowers and fruits; St. Ann is near the Virgin, and St. Joseph in the distance. This picture was sold to Charles I. of England; at his death it was bought with many others by Philip IV., who on seeing it for the first time exclaimed, "Ah, here is the pearl of my pictures." There are ten Rafaels in the gallery; one more we must mention, for it is considered as the best of all his pictures, "La Madonna del Spasimo." It must be familiar to all by the photographs that are to be seen of it in almost every shop window. Our Lord is borne down by the weight of the cross, and Simon is about to relieve him of it; the holy women are weeping around him, and he is saying, "Weep not for me, but weep for your children." A crowd on foot and soldiers on horseback, fill up the canvas; but the grand and noble figure of Our Saviour, with the sorrowing women, the bitter grief of the mother, the earnest, sad, beautiful face of Veronica with the napkin, form a splendid but terrible group.

There are forty-three Titians. The finest is a portrait of Charles V. on horseback, the emperor looks so thoroughly royal and kingly; he is supposed to be at the battle of Muehlberg; it is numbered 685. "Salome with John the Baptist's head" is very beautiful; it is said to be a portrait of Titian's daughter; it is 776. "The Victory of Lepanto" is wonderful, from having been painted when Titian was ninety-one years of age; 854.

Paul Veronese has twenty-eight pictures; 896 is well worth analyzing, "Cain the outcast with his wife and sons;" it all portrays gloomy despair.

Twenty-seven pictures by Tintoretto; ten by Claude Lorraine, all beautiful; twenty-one by Nicolas Poussin; sixty-two by Rubens, all coarse, unnatural, and with daubs of red and white for flesh. Eight by Alonso Cano; his "St. John in the Island of Patmos," writing the Revelations, 88, is very fine—St. John's head is beautiful; also 431, "Jesus at the Column," full of pathos and very impressive. There are fourteen Zurbarans, the truest portrayer of monks; hardly any of his best pictures but that one is in it; ten in this collection, however, represent Hercules in various scenes of his history. 40 and 317 are sacred subjects and very fine; the first is St. Peter crucified appearing to St. Peter Nolasco, and the latter, the Infant Saviour, sleeping peacefully on his cross; this is a charming picture; the perfect repose, the child so child-like, with the calm and holy expression that is rarely seen but in very young children, unconscious of wrong, or of sorrow, one feels inclined gently to lift the picture away and place it by itself in some quiet corner where no noise of footsteps or voices could disturb the sleeping child.

But we might fill a volume at this rate very quickly. It will not do to linger longer amidst these beautiful pictures, or the " Winter Tour in Spain " will be cut short at Madrid; yet it is a pleasant subject to dwell on; for we can almost whilst writing imagine ourselves once again surrounded by these great masters, which stretch of fancy will in all probability be our only means of ever again beholding them; the mind's eye will be the only eye with which we shall ever more see them.

We must not omit to mention two cases which stand in the centre of the long gallery, one containing some beautiful tazzas in lapis, agate, gold, enamel, and precious stones by Benvenuto Cellini, Beceriles, and others; in the second there are some fine specimens of Venetian and other glass.

The gallery is in the Prado.

CHAPTER V.

MADRID—*continued.*

THE "Academia," the Royal Academy, is in the Calle de Alcalá, and there is the same amount of envy, hatred, and malice amongst the R.A.'s as can be found elsewhere. It was founded a little more than a century ago. On the upper floor there is a very fine collection of natural history; and the pictures which are below are with few exceptions worth seeing, especially with the Museo so near at hand.

Murillo's grand picture called "El Tiñosa," in which Isabel of Hungary is washing the sore head of a poor child, and others standing by waiting for their turn, is too real to be pleasant; yet the face and expression of St. Isabel are exquisite. This picture was originally in the Caridad at Seville, and Soult took possession of it, but it was restored to Spain, though not to Seville, after the battle of Waterloo. There are two other Murillos, both of which had a journey to Paris from Seville, being taken from Santa Maria la Blanca, also by Soult; they represent the dreams of El Patricio Romano, which originated the building at Rome of the church of Santa Maria la Mayor; they are semi-circular, and are exquisite paintings. Some splendid monks, by Zurbaran, are in an adjoining room; his pictures certainly deserve more notice than they seem to attract. There are some of Rubens; and a beautiful picture of Our Saviour, by Alonso Cano.

There are some good bronzes studded about the principal rooms. Upstairs, the collection of Spanish minerals is very fine; there is, on a little stand amongst them, a loadstone, Piedra Iman, which weighs six pounds and holds sixty. The Spaniards have a kind of religious veneration for it; to the million it is miraculous, and therefore to them almost holy; this arises from their priestly education, the only kind they are permitted to receive.

Beyond this room are a number leading one out of the other, with stuffed animals and skeletons, one of a megatherium, found near Buenos Ayres, and said to be the largest and most perfect in existence. There is also the fossil skeleton of an animal, dug up near Madrid; it is enormous, and seems to have long broad fins of whalebone beneath the massive body.

The "Armeria" is close to the Royal Palace: the collection is said to be the finest in the world, but the recollection of the one at Dresden seems to be of a more pleasing nature; this one however is full of interest. All is collected in one room, 227 feet long; the centre of the hall is filled with equestrian figures, the sides are lined with armed knights, whilst the walls are hung with war implements and armour, and above these again are suspended the banners taken in war. The armour of Philip II. has the arms of England engraved on it. The armour of the Cid is preserved here and his saddle; his sword, called La Colada, 1727 in the catalogue, is the most interesting of all the relics exhibited here. The armour said to be worn by Isabella the Catholic at the siege of Granada has 'Isabel' worked on the vizor; her sword, 1705, is pretty and not unfitted for a queen, if she is to have one at all; it is a Valencian blade; 1696 is that of her husband Ferdinand, and was made at Toledo. 1702 is the sword of the Great Captain, the Wellington of Spain, Gonzalvo de Cordova: his arms are engraved on it in the centre, and on the hilt are the arms of Spain. There are two suits of armour which belonged to Boabdil el Chico, the last of the Moorish kings in Spain, also several Moorish saddles and shields; the latter are made of leather. 2364 is the armour of the Emperor Charles V., which Titian painted him in. 1632 is Jaime the Conqueror's helmet, and 1644 is his sword. Some of the armour is beautifully chased, and every object in the collection is worth examining.

At the end of the room, in a glass case, is a life-sized image of San Fernando; it is dressed in royal robes, has a crown on, and is seated on a gilt throne; in the left hand he holds a globe with a cross on it, and in the right a sword. On the 29th of May in each year this effigy is carried in procession to the Chapel Royal for a *neuvaine* in commemoration of the taking of Seville; formerly it was sufficient to look on this image only—with faith of course—to obtain indulgences.

The ancient armour preserved here is said to be invaluable, and the largest collection existing.

The Royal Palace, adjoining the Armeria almost, is very imposing looking, and magnificently situated, commanding the only fine view in Madrid, and that view, with the Sierra de Guadarrama towering in the distance, is splendid. The front looks on to the Plaza del Oriente, which is laid out as a garden, in the centre of which is the grand statue of Philip IV. on horseback; the model was carved by Montañes, and the bronze was cast in Florence; it is considered one of the finest equestrian statues in the world.

The palace occupies the site where stood the Moorish Alcazar, which was destroyed by fire on Christmas eve, 1734; then Philip V. caused a plan to be drawn for a new one, which bid fair to half ruin the country if it ever was carried out; a model was made, now in the Museo, which shows completely what it would have been; the Queen, however, had sense enough to make objections to such a huge pile being raised, when another architect was employed and the present palace built.

The interior, we were told, is very gorgeous, and really palatial; but the Queen being there it was not shown; the ceilings are well painted, the best are those done by Mengs. There is a fine collection of china, with some Capo di Monte ware among it. The Library is extremely valuable and very large, containing upwards of 100,000 volumes. Here is the beautifully illuminated missal which Louis XIV. presented on her marriage to one of the wives of Philip II.* The Royal Chapel, actually in the palace, is open every morning to the public; it is a handsome building, in the Corinthian style, and very richly decorated.

The stables are close to, though not joining the palace. They are greatly over-rated, and are badly kept, wanting in space, and ugly; they are much more like good livery stables. At the season we were there (November) the horses numbered only 128, and the mules 200. The usual annual sale had not long taken place, and the vacancies thus made are not filled up till the spring. The mules' stables are very inferior to the horses', because, one of the grooms said, "they did not care about it." With the exception of a few fine carriage horses, and four very pretty ponies that the Prince of Asturias drives, there is little to say in their praise. The horse ridden by the Empress Eugénie, and another by the King of Portugal, were trotted out to be admired. The Queen of Spain has not ridden for ten years, the reason why is self-evident.

* A copy was made of this missal the other day as a present for the Prince Impérial of France, on his making his first Communion.

The harness rooms are on a very superior scale, and well worth seeing; the state harness is splendid, and some of the saddles, especially the modern ones, deserve notice; the old are simply curious. There are several *sillas de manos*, which, as they all do, make one wonder how ladies with hoops ever got into them. They are used occasionally in church processions, otherwise never; they are very much gilt, and do not seem unfitted for such a purpose, though in what manner they are used was not stated; perhaps they put a saint inside, or they may carry them empty merely to swell the pageant.

There are one or two glass cases full of shabby old hats; ranged along one side of the room are the saddles used by the *picadores* when the Queen attends a bull-fight.

The carriages are very interesting; there are 146, and amongst them is the heavy sombre thing in which poor Crazy Jane drove about with the dead body of her handsome good-for-nothing husband, a ghastly load, but one the poor lady clung to with all the obstinacy of a weak mind; she never cared for him in life, but she loved him in death.

There is a small carriage, a kind of barouche with the front seat only, which was a gift from our Queen to the Queen of Spain; it is the only English carriage here, and certainly does not do us much credit; but then it is more than a quarter of a century old, having been presented twenty-six years ago. There are two heavy, lumbering carriages once belonging to Napoleon I.; another curiosity is a massive gilt car, which is used at coronations, royal weddings, or any other very grand or state occasions; then children, dressed like ballet girls, in gold and silver tissue and flowers, are placed in it, and one little child is perched up aloft with wings and a crown and other no-dress attire. But the carriage of all others is the Queen's own travelling carriage; it is like three in one: the front portion is like a chariot; this the King and Queen occupy; facing them is a recess which is made to hold the "Travelling Virgin;" in it is a small stand, fixed, on which the image is placed; this carved effigy of the Blessed Virgin is appointed to accompany her Most Catholic Majesty on all her journeys; excepting that she is placed back to the horses, her position is seemingly comfortable enough. The middle portion of the carriage is like a phaeton; here the lord and lady-in-waiting sit. And the third and back part is occupied by the immediate attendants. In this carriage is every imaginable convenience. Immediately outside the coach-house and near the stables is a large fresh-water bath, a luxury enjoyed by the royal horses only, as these are the only stables in Madrid where one exists.

They drive here as in England, on the left side of the road. ·Spaniards are first-rate horsemen and capital whips; and the horses, as a rule, are magnificent.

There are three houses in Madrid, or palaces, as they are called, and very justly, that certainly no one ought to leave without seeing; they are those of the Dukes of Albe, Osuna, and Salamanca. To begin with the last first, as being not only the most important, but also that there are two houses, a town and country one, both rich in works of art. Don José, Duke of Salamanca, though reputed to be of moderate fortune, has amassed such an amount of treasure that no English nobleman can boast of such a collection. His country villa is situated about three miles out of Madrid, and in such a sandy desert that it is in very truth an oasis. The gardens are beautifully laid out and well timbered; fountains abound; there are three immediately in front of the house, the others studded about so as to render them as effective as possible. The house is approached by a flight of broad marble steps, which lead to a verandah, and then very handsome carved doors, having sliding glass doors in front, admit you into the hall. The first thing the eye falls on is a card, on which is written, in large distinct letters, " No se permite fumar, escupir, sentarse, tocar ningun objeto, ni entrar con perros."* A not unnecessary prohibition to put up, we were told.

On entering you turn to the left; this room is Don José's bed-room, a splendid room, hung with rich silk, and furnished with beautifully carved chairs, tables, and bedstead. There were some curious old trunks or chests in the town palace as well as in this, which

* It is forbidden to smoke, spit, sit down, touch anything, or enter with dogs.

the Duke brought from Portugal, though they are Roman. On the writing table were some beautiful fittings of carnelian, malachite, and lapis lazuli. There are some fine paintings in this room. The adjoining room is the dressing-room, and excepting the bed, is in all respects the bed-room; this room opens into a gallery of the chapel. Passing along a corridor running parallel with the chapel, we come to the late Duchess's bed-room, the room in which a few months since she passed away from all worldly grandeur. The whole furniture of this room is buhl, and most gorgeous; the cheval glass, with a massive gold outer frame, holds within it one of Dresden china, which encircles the glass; there is a profusion of the most valuable Dresden china here, and of untold value. Passing through the son's, daughter's, and niece's rooms, we enter the reception rooms, which occupy the whole remainder of the floor; the house is built square, with a *patio* in the centre.

The drawing-rooms, picture gallery, boudoir, and dining-room, are all full of art treasures. The largest drawing-room of the suite has an Aubusson carpet over it, with views of the chief towns of Spain, executed as beautifully as paintings. Against the walls are ten Venetian looking-glasses, bordered with glass roses, and in the centre of each rose is a diamond; one glass alone has forty-five diamonds. In the centre of the room is a table of exquisite mosaic, and another that belonged to Louis XIV., both works of inestimable value. Amongst the sculpture are several pieces by Tadolini; perhaps the "Slave," and "Adam and Eve" are the most beautiful. There are paintings by all masters; one by Zurbaran, of the "Holy Family," most exquisitely conceived. The difference of age between Our Saviour and St. John is very marked. One might spend a week in wandering about these beautiful rooms and galleries, but so one may say of a great many places in this country; one feels so often there is not time enough to see all that has to be seen.

Don José has the most rare and valuable collection of Pompeian antiquities in the possession of any private individual. Owing to his having been either owner of the property about Pompeii where the railway was cut, or having contracted for all valuables that were discovered during the operation, he being a principal mover in the undertaking, he has amassed such a collection as rendered it necessary to arrange them into a museum, which he has done in the building that was the old residence till the present villa was erected. There are some six or seven rooms filled with these unearthed treasures; some of the vases are extremely beautiful and perfect, as also many bronze statuettes; others require the eye of the antiquary to appreciate—but take them as a whole they are worthy of being better known, and exhibited in a more recognized place for such objects, as here it is the palace that is spoken of, not the works of art and antiquity contained in it. The Spaniards indeed are so surrounded by them, that they do not know how to appreciate them as we northerners, who think nothing of paying a shilling to see a single picture, and that by a modern artist.

The town residence is still more magnificent, and is indeed quite worthy of being called a palace; every room is filled with gems of art. The dining-room is hung with pictures by De Vos; also the supper-room, which leads into a very fine and lofty conservatory, with three fountains at play; at night it is lighted up by gas from above, the jets forming stars. One of the prettiest of double staircases leads from a small inner hall up to the picture gallery; this staircase was designed by the Duke himself. The picture gallery runs along one entire side of the house, which, like the country palace, and indeed like all Spanish houses, great or small, is built square. There are some very fine paintings in the collection by Murillo, Zurbaran, Alonso Cano, Teniers, and many other masters whose names are household words. From the centre of this gallery you enter another, which runs round the principal *patio;* this is lined from the floor to the roof with antique china, placed in designs against the wall, with cabinets intersecting them at equal distances, containing precious tazzas, exquisite carvings in ivory and wood, antique crosses studded with fine stones, and other gems of various kinds.

The drawing-rooms, a magnificent suite, are gorgeously furnished; one set of chairs alone are said to have cost forty pounds each. The looking-glasses, the chandeliers, the rich silk hangings to the walls, each room having a distinct colour, the luxurious carpets, canopies and couches, the beautifully-painted ceilings, the Sèvres and Dresden china, the cabinet pictures, all form a mass of such wealth and grandeur, that one feels in a fairy palace, and not merely in a Spanish nobleman's house. Adjoining the first reception-room is what is called the armour room; dark and sombre, hung with green cloth, oak furniture, and well-executed oak carvings over each door. The gloomy but handsome decorations, all so thoroughly in keeping, form the attraction of the room, for the armour is more to ornament the apartment than for it to set off the armour; nor is there much of it, but as this leads into the brilliant reception-rooms, the contrast is so great that the one serves to set off the other. On the other side of the armour room is the billiard room.

On the landing at the head of the grand staircase, which is all of pure white marble, is a dog, cast in bronze, holding a dead pheasant in his mouth; both are wonderfully executed, but the bird is so perfect that one fancies one might blow the feathers apart. The artist's name was not on it.

The Duke of Salamanca's town residence is decidedly more worth seeing than his country villa, notwithstanding the relics of Pompeii.

The Duke of Albe's palace is a house full of all the comforts and luxuries that wealth can amass. Magnificent furniture, gorgeous gilding, loads of looking-glasses, carpets that refuse to permit a footstep to be heard; tapestry, china, and pretty ornamental objects; splendid suites of apartments; a ball-room, with a very handsome inlaid flooring, and everything that an English gentleman of fortune loves to see around him, and then all is told. No statuary, unless a portrait group of his children. No pictures, unless the picture of his sister-in-law, the Empress Eugénie, by Winterhalter, and here and there anyone's paintings to decorate an untapestried wall. The whole is seen in a few minutes, for there is nothing that requires one to pause, nothing to arrest the lover of art or antiquity, but it is handsome and very comfortable. The royal arms of England are to be seen quartered with the ducal arms of Albe, for the Duke of Albe is also Duke of Berwick, and his motto is "Honi soit qui mal y pense."

There is no portrait of any kind of the late Duchess to be seen. It is a Spanish fashion to remove altogether, or at least to curtain over, the likenesses of those members of the family who are dead, unless of a past generation.

The stables were in keeping with the rest, valuable good horses, and well-built handsome carriages.

The Duke of Osuna has two palaces—the one he occupies when in Madrid (at present he is ambassador at the court of Russia); and the other, close to it, containing his library and armoury, and the stables. There is nothing very remarkable in the former; it is a handsome, well-built house, with an air of comfort about it very English, as are many of the things in it. There is a very small private chapel leading out of a pretty morning room, with a " Conception," by Murillo; besides this, there are in one of the larger apartments two very fine Van Dycks; one the "Mater Dolorosa," the other a " Holy Family;" and these, with a very magnificent mosaic, are the chief works of art. There are other pictures, several good enough; amongst them some family portraits that are quite worth looking at. The rooms are very numerous, and handsomely furnished, but owing to the duke's absence, there was a put-in-order look over the whole that gave it a gloomy appearance.

There appears to be no great love felt for the present duke, who by the way unites seventeen Grandeeships in himself; but his brother, now dead, was spoken of with the greatest affection and devotion. The garden attached to the house is very nice, and the view from the upper terrace is magnificent, very much the same as that seen from the palace; the snowy capped Guadarrama, standing out so clearly and distinctly against the dark blue sky, and the vast plain around, arid and monotonous as it is, form no bad scene for the eye to rest on, and one not likely to weary. The cold winds, which in winter blow down from the

Guadarrama range, are so severe at times as frequently to freeze the sentinels on duty to death. Why don't they turn the back of the sentry boxes to these death blasts?

The other palace, on the opposite side of the road, Las Vistallas, the duke inherited from his uncle, the Duke of Infantado. It is like a vast barrack outside, and very little better in. Ferdinand and Isabella the Catholic occupied this palace; it was probably in a better condition then; now the whole of the lower part of the house is converted into stables. Horses are the duke's hobby. At the present moment, during his absence, twenty-eight carriage and saddle horses and six ponies are kept; some of them very fine. The harness-rooms are well worth seeing; there are three; they are so beautifully arranged, and the Gothic decorations of one of them deserve to be in a better place. Many of the saddles and sets of harness are English.

Ascending from the stables by a staircase twenty feet wide, only wood and whitewashed walls, which from the first landing branches out right and left, we came to the armoury, which contains the finest private collection in Europe. There is a set of armour which belonged to Charles V., another of Philip II., besides a host of others of great interest; they fill the centre and cover the walls of two long rooms. There are several guns of great antiquity, and a very curious and handsome bronze chandelier, made of pistols, daggers, cannon balls, shot, &c. &c. The library is on the same floor, and occupies the whole of the remaining rooms. It is the largest library in Spain, not excepting that in the palace or the public library. In the end room of all there is a very valuable collection of coins and medals; in short, the palace is far more of a museum than aught else. One old man has the charge of it; and as he is responsible for all the contents—not the stables—he keeps himself well armed; he showed us three holes in the large massive door through which he could fire in case of need. Blood shedding with the Spaniards, whether it be of man or beast, is lightly thought of; and yet withal they are a kindly, courteous race, and harmless enough if left alone.

We saw all these palaces in perfection; there was no uncovering, nothing to undo, no shutters to open, as is usually the case in our own country, when one is let in to a "show place." You see places here, if you see them at all, more as a guest than a sight-seer; you are not hurried through a certain number of curtainless, carpetless rooms by an independent housekeeper, with a few covered up pictures which are partially shown through the openings of one shutter. It is true that where a hundred go to see a Chatsworth or a Belvoir Castle, but one will request to see the Duke of Salamanca's or Duke of Albe's palaces; but that one is let see all there is to be seen, if he is admitted at all, and with every attention and courtesy.

What surprises an Englishman most in these foreign palaces is, that with all the great wealth, luxury, and taste that is shown to exist in them, there should be such utter disregard to actual solidity without; and in such portions of them as are not expected or supposed to be seen. The frontages are always very handsome, and kept in good repair, but the sides of the houses and the back parts are generally in a tumble down state, as well as dirty and untidy; instead of stone being used, as is for the façade, lath and plaster are thought to be good enough. You may enter a house with marble stairs, marble halls, and even marble walls, but the servants' entrance will be with thin doors that won't shut properly, staircases with the banisters giving way, and walls falling about from sheer neglect. This is the same in the Queen's palace as it is in other great houses; keep in front, and in those parts always visible, and all is solid and good; but diverge a little from the beaten track, and one is amazed at the seeming poverty.

CHAPTER VI.

MADRID—*continued.*—A BULL-FIGHT.

THERE are very few churches here of any interest whatever; indeed, one might also say that with one exception there are none. They are all large and dark, so dark, that except on festivals and Sundays, it is impossible to see anything; then, however, they are lighted up, and adorned with a multitude of ridiculously dressed Virgins, more resembling figures made as pincushion dolls than anything else; blue silk, tinsel, tarlatan, heavy gilt crowns, and white lace being the principal articles used in their decoration. The Virgins are many of them black and small; the infant Saviour is then, if there at all, merely seen by a head with a big crown on it issuing from beneath the stiff folds of the Virgin Mother's dress at the waist.

The one exception to these uninteresting churches is that of *Atocha;* and even then it is not the church, but the interest caused by the existence in it of two miraculous Virgins; the one black and small, the other white and large. The large one has the questionable honour of being appointed Mistress of the Robes to her Catholic Majesty, Isabella II.; and her perquisites consist in having the robes worn by the queen on the Feast of the Epiphany. Some of these are very costly and very gorgeous; there are already twenty-eight of them, no bad wardrobe for a lady who ever lays in a glass case, the lid of which is upheld by little gilt angels. This Virgin also possesses the magnificent state robes worn by the queen on that memorable day when, struck by the dagger of the assassin, Curé Merino, she nearly lost her life; the blow was warded off by the rich embroidery of the arms of Spain, over which the knife slipped, inflicting a slight wound only, not more than half an inch deep, instead of a death blow; the stain of her blood dyes the white silk lining of the crimson velvet robe. It is said the king was at the head of this conspiracy against the life of his wife; the occurrence took place in 1852, after the birth of her first living child, the present Infanta Isabel, which child he declared was not his. The Curé, by whose hand the plot was thus far carried into effect, was executed, and his body burnt to ashes; this was to avoid portraits being taken, or any trace of him left in this world.

It is, however, the little black Virgin perched up on high at the *Altar Mayor*, to which the greatest devotion is paid; this little image has jewels to the value of fourteen millions of reals; the crowns, armlets, necklaces, rings, stomachers, and belts being composed of precious stones; some of the diamonds, rubies, and sapphires, are very large. Every Saturday, soon after four o'clock, the king and queen, and some of the royal children, go in state to this church, and attend Benediction, and pay their homage to the Virgin of Atocha. She is said to be fifteen hundred years old, and the miracles attributed to her agency are so marvellous that one feels hardly disposed to relate them here. Ferdinand VII., the queen's father, is reputed to have embroidered a dress for her with his own hands; whether this is true or not, it is quite certain he paid her the same worship during his lifetime as his daughter does now. *Ex-votos* cover, literally cover, the walls on both sides of her. One day as we were leaving the church, and it was about to be closed, a woman with a child in her arms pressed by to get in; on being stopped, she pleaded hard she had a sick child with her, for whom she desired the Virgin of Atocha's intercession; however, she was not let pass, so for that day at least she was forced to remain unaided by the sacred image. There is a very fine dead Christ in the church, it is of coloured marble, the wounds are terribly natural, with the broken bruised knees, the blood running over the face from the torn brow; it is very awful, but as a work of art very beautiful. Horrible things must charm Spaniards, or why so many of these shocking representations? They are extremely fond of putting real hair on the images of our Lord, generally very long, thick, and black.

There is no Protestant church, none are allowed in Spain, but English service is performed every Sunday, at half-past eleven, at the British Embassy, in a small room capable of holding from eighty to a hundred people, but there is rarely more than a fourth of that number present. They have an odd habit here, as in other towns in Spain, where English service is read, of omitting the Communion service entirely, except on the Sunday appointed for the administration of the Holy Sacrament. The Rev. W. A. Campbell is the present chaplain.

All the shops are shut on Sundays and festivals, so this state of things happens twice and sometimes three times a week; the people are too glad of an excuse to be idle not to take advantage of it; even the water-carriers are fewer on fête days, and not to be seen at all on Sundays.

Madrid used to be extremely rich in convents, but since their suppression they have been pretty nearly decimated. One of the largest now existing is that of Santiago; it is situated in the old part of the town, and is an enormous, massive building, occupying almost the entire side of the street in which it stands. Like most things in Spain, it is of the past; here, where in days of yore there used to be between three and four hundred professed nuns, they have dwindled down to eight or nine and a few novices. An iron-barred door closes them up from the outer world; at this you knock, and then not the door, but a little square panel is opened: this is well guarded by closely webbed iron bars, and the nun on watch looks to see who asks admittance before she grants it. Within, it is bare and cheerless; over a *brasero* was sitting watch nun number two, for none are allowed to be alone; they are always in pairs, so that one is, in fact, a spy over the other. Upstairs it seemed a little more cheery, and the nuns seemed happy and contented; each has her separate sitting-room and bed-room; they might have a suite of apartments apiece as far as space went; however, they do have each a kitchen and a servant, and seem to live in comfort. The superior, a high bred charming person, still young, and with traces of beauty that sorrow or illness, but not age, has partially destroyed, has been but five years a nun, and three the head of this convent. Her predecessor was for seventy-three years an inmate here; she had been Maid of honour to the ill-fated Marie Antoinette, and on the death of her royal mistress she escaped to Spain, and shortly afterwards embraced a monastic life.

To become a member of this order is very difficult, inasmuch as, after the necessary permission has been obtained from the queen, the candidate is compelled to produce certificates of her nobility, which must be unmarred by ill-sorted marriages, or other flaws in the escutcheon, for four generations on both father's and mother's side. No wonder, therefore, in the present day there are less than a dozen within the walls. The knights of the order (it was through one of them who accompanied us to the convent we were enabled to see all over it) are elected only on the same conditions, but they are bound by no vows which forbid them to marry or enforce a cloistered life; they merely take solemn oaths to defend the dogma of the immaculate conception, and to take up arms in defence of their country should it ever again be attacked by the infidel. They hold Chapters of the order on certain days, when they wear a sort of priestly-looking garb. The nuns never leave the convent, on no pretence do they ever go out; they have what they call cloisters, which are simply large, wide, cold galleries, the windows looking into the court or *patio;* into this court they go occasionally, but it is little air or exercise that they get there; however, they evidently do not suffer for want of either, as they have good health and live long.

Since the suppression of convents, a community of Carmelite nuns has been allowed to reside in one portion of this house, their own having been done away with; their rules are much severer than those of the order of Santiago. The church is very spacious and lofty, and contains one or two good paintings, a few relics and other usual church appendages.

There are several good theatres in Madrid, they are all prettily decorated, clean, light looking, and extremely well ventilated; the principal ones are the Teatro Real, Teatro del Principe, La Zarzuela, Variedades, and Novedades. They are all very much about the same size, except the Teatro Real, and that, where Italian operas are performed, is considerably the largest. It is situated facing the palace, the gardens intervening; the queen is constantly present, and always when a new or favourite opera is given; the singing might be better; it might also be worse. The royal box is ornamented with crimson velvet across the front, and the arms of Spain embroidered in gold, all extremely dingy, and either wants cleaning or renewing; the interior is padded with quilted crimson silk, as is the box next to it, and the two facing it; it is not large, or indeed so large as those adjoining it; on state occasions the box in the centre of the house is used, which is very large.

Most of the theatres begin at half-past eight, the doors opening at a quarter past; and all is over by eleven, or very soon after. They waste a great deal of time between the acts, especially for those who have no acquaintances; as it is the fashion during these intervals for gentlemen to make a round of visits, and so, chatting with their friends, the time passes quickly away. Smoking is not usual within the house; but in the lobbies and *foyer*, between the acts, the air is thick with it, and this penetrates very quickly into the house itself, rendering the atmosphere hazy. With all their smoking, however, Spaniards are less objectionable than Germans, in this respect; the tobacco is so mild, that unless it is in very great quantities, it is not annoying; nor are the results of smoking so bad as we are led to believe; this, perhaps, may arise (in the streets at any rate) from the ladies, who wear their dresses so extremely long that they amount to trains, and never lift them up, dragging them over the ground, streets and roads, thus doing the work of a mop. It positively keeps the streets clean, and in all the towns of Spain this is the same: this dress-sweeping system has, therefore, advantages—if not to the ladies themselves.

There is a ruined bear-garden, fenced in by a handsome iron railing, which is called the "Botanical Garden." No name could be more misapplied, for there is positively nothing in it but a few ducks and goats and weeds; a hothouse, with a few flower-pots, and not larger than you see attached to a small country house in England; and then a species of museum, in a greenhouse, of stuffed birds, snakes in bottles, and human skeletons, sitting upright, and placed in groups; where the latter came from, or why they are there at all, no one seemed to know. The much-maligned climate of Madrid would, notwithstanding, allow of very fine botanical gardens, but there is no energy amongst the people; the great heat during the summer, which lasts fully seven months, renders them lazy for the remainder of the year. It can be very cold in Madrid, but the months of November and March are generally splendid, equal to our finest northern summers. Snow falls during the intervening months, but rarely remains; the sun soon melts it; the winds are what the people have most to contend with; and, coming straight from those snowy mountains, they should be carefully guarded against; for it must be remembered that Madrid is on an elevated plain, and very elevated, and so, exposed in all directions to the heat in summer, as it is to the cold in winter.

Madrid is the only town in Spain where bull-fights take place in winter; therefore, if we were to see one at all, we had to see it here; moreover, they are supposed to be first-rate. They take place on Sundays, in the afternoon; occasionally, but very rarely, on a Thursday, and then they are not so good. With all one has heard of the horrors of these barbarous exhibitions, nothing that can be said or written can give a real notion of the disgusting cruelty of this national sport. Unwisely, we determined to go, as probably every one will who has the opportunity; people do not care to accept the opinions of others, they prefer judging for themselves. We secured an entire box on the shady side of the arena, a very necessary precaution, as the intense heat of the sun, even in November, is blinding and scorching to northerners.

The Madrid arena holds 12,000 spectators, and could it hold double that number it would doubtless be full, as we saw hundreds endeavouring, vainly, to get in, notwithstanding the counter attraction of poor O'Donnell's funeral, which took place the same afternoon, with all military honours, and at the expense of government. Thousands seemed to follow him with mournful countenances. He was but fifty-nine years of age, and his country's loss is great. Narvaez, his friend and some time colleague, yet rival, was his chief mourner. He, too, has now passed away, having outlived the Duke of Tetuan but five months. The crowd of carriages and people was so dense, we, who were bound for the bull-fight, were stopped short about ten minutes' distance from the arena, and told we must walk, only such carriages as were going to the funeral service at the Atocha church could be allowed to proceed. The heat was intense, the dust suffocating. The building, both outside and in, is shabby and dirty, and apparently run up as a temporary building only, so flimsy does it appear; but this is not the case; it clearly is more substantial than it looks, for no part of it has ever given way during the years it has been standing. The programmes, of which there are always plenty placarded in the most frequented streets, gave glowing accounts of the exhibition that was to take place, "weather permitting." There were to be so many bulls of one breed, and so many of another, and one a special one, of a very favourite and fine breed, and dogs, *perros de presa*, bull-dogs, and a seal; also the names were given of the various performers who act in this tragedy, for that is truly what it too often turns out. The public have their favourites amongst these men; the most reckless and daring always winning applause.

It was to begin at three; we were in our places by half-past two (and out of them by twenty minutes past three—but of that further on); the half hour before the horrible scene that followed, was extremely entertaining. The arena was then occupied by sellers of oranges, who threw them in the most dexterous manner to the purchasers, whether they were far or near; the payment for them was equally well managed; if a single coin had to be given, it was easy enough, but when change had to be returned, the money was placed in a pocket-handkerchief, which, being tied into a ball, the orange vendor caught, returning the change in the same manner. Then the multitudinous and varied specimens of man and womankind around us, all eagerly watching for the moment when their day's pleasure was to begin; young women, handsome women, old women, women of all grades, had assembled; the poor with their infants in their arms, the rich and medium class with their fans. The men by no means outnumbered the women; clearly the taste for such exhibitions is universal.

As three o'clock neared, the impatience of the mass of living beings around began to manifest itself very much in the same way as the gallery at an English theatre expresses its desire for the performance to commence. A band played at intervals. But now the wished-for trumpet was sounded, the sign that business was about to begin, which it does by a procession of the actors (all but the bulls) in the coming scene walking right across the arena and bowing to the president, whose box faces the royal box, he then presents the key, or rather throws it, of the cell in which the bull is. Two horsemen, dressed in black, with feathered hats, well mounted—these horses are not destined for the arena — head the procession; then follow the *picadores*,—they are mounted on the doomed horses, and carry spears; then come the *chulos*,—these men carry the red cloaks which they throw towards the bull to anger him; then the *banderilleros*,—they carry the arrows, which, with their barbed points, are planted in the poor beast's neck; then follow the *matadores*, with their swords,— they are the actual slayers of the bull; four bull-dogs were led by cords; and lastly came *el tiro*, which is a team of mules, gaily harnessed and abreast, with bells tinkling, and small flags waving from their heads,— these drag the dead bodies from the arena at the end of each part of the performance.

When these had all retired, three *picadores*, with ten or twelve *chulos*, returned to the arena. The *chulos* are dressed in the gay, bright costume of the south, like the *majos;* they wear breeches and stockings, the former decorated with silver buttons, as are also their velvet jackets; their hair is tied with a knot at the back, and put into a net; their whole costume, enlivened with the crimson cloak, is very picturesque; they are extremely graceful in their movements; active of course they must be—they bound like deer, and spring like monkeys. The horses are all blindfolded; poor, wretched, worn-out animals, that are considered fit for nothing but death; they are thus condemned to act out their last scene in life in tortures most frightful for the *amusement* of society. Their riders are as well protected as they can be, by wearing iron casings over their legs and a kind of armour over their bodies: nothing of this is visible, however.

Now the bull was let in, and his first bellow, low and deep, seemed almost to electrify the thousands who were so eagerly looking for him; there was an instantaneous silence, singularly strange amidst such a vast multitude. The bull wore floating green ribbons from his neck,—this, to the learned, denoted his breed. Now began the real work: for a moment, the bull was allowed to look around him, and then, as he did not seem disposed to be the aggressor, and the audience not being a patient one, a *picador* rode up to him at a foot's pace, and then, standing still, pricked him with his spear; thus goaded, the bull made a lunge at the poor horse, who being blindfolded, had not even the chance of escape; a fearful wound was inflicted, and he staggered back a few paces; in the meanwhile the *chulos*, right and left, threw out their red cloaks, both to irritate the bull and for the moment to draw him off his bleeding victim: this went on, in a still, almost motionless, manner, for the bull did not rush and tear about as we expected him to do; he seemed to us but too willing to remain at peace with all around if they would but let him. However, a few more painful stabs from the *picador*, and the bull made another attack on the horse, which this time fell over, and, with one death struggle, the poor beast remained motionless on the ground. The *picador* extricated himself with wonderful rapidity and tact from the dead body, bounding over the ledge which forms a barrier between the arena and the people. In this manner was another and another horse killed, but neither of them so rapidly as the first; they were longer dying; and one continued going round the ring for several minutes with its inside trailing out on the ground: the sight was so sickening, so horrible, that no words can express the feeling it produced.

The next act or part was to place the arrows or *banderillas* in the bull's neck; six are thus placed, two at a time; they are decorated with coloured ribbons and cut paper, and the thrusting them in is attended with some danger. The *chulo* seemed to rush at the bull, and at the moment of his lowering his head to toss him, he dexterously plants a couple at the back of his neck, and with a bound was beyond his reach: the bull seemed half wild with the pain inflicted, the blood streaming down from the wounds; it was with these six torturing instruments sticking in him, and that he had endeavoured—vainly, of course, from their barbed points—to shake off by furious plunging and tossing of his head, that he made for the barrier. A man—one amongst several, who are placed about on the inner side in case of accident and need—prevented the maddened brute from leaping over, and then the poor bull, with an expression in his eyes we shall never forget, stood and moaned, rather than bellowed, as if pleading for assistance to save him from his merciless tormentors. But pity for animals is unknown in a Spaniard's heart; their natures are so brutalised by these scenes, which from their infancy they are accustomed to witness, that nothing in the way of cruelty in the slightest degree touches them. They would as soon hand over a horse they had perhaps ridden for years, if he was past work, to be tortured in the bull-ring, as not; and moreover, they would, and witness his death; so it is no wonder that in this instance the man so appealed to, drove the torn and bleeding animal away.

Now came the last act: the trumpet sounded, which announced the president's pleasure that the *coup de grace* should be given: this is not done without great risk, and is the most dangerous part to perform. Two *matadores*, or slayers, each armed with a finely-pointed spear, about the length of an ordinary sword, entered the arena: one only attacks the bull, the other is there in case the first fails, which simply means, in case the bull kills him instead of he the bull. The *matador* advanced steadily, and faced the bull; every now and then the bull seemed as if he was going to attack his antagonist, and the moment he actually made the rush to do so, the *matador* made a plunge, and in went his spear up to the hilt: for a second the bull stood motionless, then staggered and fell down dead; hardly a struggle was visible. The *matador* then drew out the sword—which is always driven in at the shoulder,—and the *chulos* advanced and forced out the *banderillas*, the blood flowing in all directions; then the mules came in with their gay coloured trappings and tinkling bells: first, one by one the bodies of the dead horses were attached by a great iron hook to what is, we believe, called a swing-tree or bar, and dragged out at a rapid rate; the mules were lashed into a wild gallop. Last of all, the bull was taken. All this time the shouts, and even screams, of the audience at their admiration of the courage displayed either by man or beast, were both deafening and bewildering. Even the mules received applause when taking off the bull, for they tore across the arena, and it was a heavy load they dragged behind them.

Immediately after the arena was cleared, men began to rake up the gravel so as to cover the pools of blood that were in several places, and thus to prepare it for the next fight.

What we were present at, and what we have endeavoured to describe, occupied but twenty minutes from first to last; the actual bull-fight certainly not more than twelve or fifteen; yet this slaughter-house exhibition was to continue till six o'clock, when the fading light would put an end to further displays for the day. Men are but too frequently killed in these terrible scenes, and if they are killed on the spot, they are denied Christian burial, as not having confessed; but we were told that a priest is always present in the arena, so that if an unfortunate man was gored and had a few minutes' life and power of speech left him, he might confess and receive absolution.

Will these bull-fights ever be put a stop to? Surely if people want to see animals killed they can gratify their taste by attending a slaughter-house, for it is no *fight;* it is folly to call it such. The poor animal is goaded on till he defends himself by attacking his tormentors; the horses are blindfolded, and the men make their living by risking their lives, like fools, to gratify a national taste which might be directed into another and less barbarous channel, if the rulers of the country would only set the example; but as long as the queen sanctions these bull-fights by her presence, they will continue; yet they do nothing but harm. We feel perfectly sure that we but waste words in recommending no woman to attend one of these scenes of butchery, as they are as certain, just as we did ourselves, to go. But we paid dearly for it. For days, the horrors of those few minutes, during which we witnessed barbarous, cold blooded cruelty and torture inflicted on defenceless animals, were never absent from our mind's eye; and even now it is with a shudder of horror that we recall the scene.

It was with no little difficulty that we managed to get out of the building, for to remain to witness more was impossible. The rush of people endeavouring to force their way in was so great, that the *Salida* gate had been given up for an *Entrada*. However, by dint of patience and perseverance we succeeded in making our way through the mob; but outside we met with another stoppage: the dead bodies of the bull and horses had been dragged out here in the open space before the principal entrance, that, by the ghastly spectacle they presented, more people might be induced to pay their money and enter on the chance of finding standing room only. Clearly, the sight of blood has a marvellous effect on a Spaniard. It seemed to make them wild; and with shouts of delight they rushed forward towards the arena to witness that which as yet they had but seen the shadow of. But enough of bull-fights. It is a sickening subject; and we can only hope that in a few years those who now drive to these scenes in their carriage and four may have found out some other entertainment more beneficial and improving and less demoralizing and brutalizing.

Charles I. of England was present at one given in his honour by Philip IV. in the Plaza Mayor, where they used to take place till the arena was built. The house the English king occupied during his stay here is still in existence. It was built by Herrera, the architect of the Escorial.

CHAPTER VII.

THE ESCORIAL.

We left Madrid by the 8·20 a.m. train one lovely morning to visit the Escorial; we reached the station, which is not more than half a mile from it, at 10·10, taking nearly two hours to travel twenty-three miles and a half. The road the whole way was barren and wild, but very grand, especially as we neared our destination.

The Escorial is a monastery, palace, mausoleum, and college, all in one. A huge massive pile of granite, built at an elevation of 2700 feet on a far stretching plain, amidst rocks and desolation; there is nothing about it to charm the eye or cheer the heart; all is gloomy, harsh, and dreary in it and around it, and yet it is one of the wonders of the world, and so must be seen, and ought to be seen.

Philip II., after his marriage with Mary of England, managed to drag our country together with his own, into a war with France, in 1557; on the 10th of August in the same year the battle of St. Quentin was fought and won by Philip, by the English army, and by way of showing his gratitude for this event, at which however he was not present, he vowed to St. Lawrence, whose martyrdom in the third century is supposed to have taken place on the day of the same month on which the battle was fought, to build a monastery, which vow he fulfilled by erecting this superb palace. It was then Philip II. transferred the government from Toledo to Madrid, which henceforth became the capital, the better to suit his own convenience, for he lived a sort of monastic life in the Escorial.

On the 23rd of April, 1563, the first stone was laid by Juan Bautista de Toledo, a native of Madrid, but it was completed by Juan de Herrera, who was in fact the real architect, in September, 1584, though he was compelled by Philip to carry out the absurd plan which he himself gave in the form of a gridiron, out of respect to the broiled Saint Lawrence. From north to south it occupies 744 feet, and 580 from east to west, the whole ground it covers being 431,520 square feet. The handle of the gridiron forms the portion called the palace, and is occupied by the royal family *when* they go there, but Queen Isabella has been but once during the last six years, and no wonder. The towers at the four corners make the four feet; the whole is constructed in granite, some of the blocks being so colossal that one cannot understand how they were ever placed in the position they are in. The cost of the whole is said to have been upwards of ten millions. There are sixteen *patios* or courts, eighty staircases, and eleven thousand windows, in memory of the eleven thousand martyred virgins of Cologne; some are extremely small, and all with few exceptions barricaded by iron gratings. The interior is intersected by cloisters or arched passages (many of them decorated with frescoes, representing biblical and historical events), so as to form the bars of the gridiron.

The most interesting part of the building is the *panteon*, or royal tomb. We descended by a marble staircase into a vault placed immediately beneath the high altar in the church. Two closed doors on the right and left mid-way down, lead to the burying places of the Infantes; at the bottom of the stairs you enter at once through very fine bronze gilt gates into the mausoleum. In shape it is octagon, thirty-eight feet high, and thirty-six in diameter. The walls and columns are of Toledo and Tarragona marbles, the former are very much injured from water, which is constantly dripping down them. In each of the eight sides are niches for the sarcophagi, seventeen are occupied, nine still remain empty. That intended for the last resting-place of the present queen, stands immediately beneath her father's remains, Ferdinand VII. When Marie-Louise, mother of Charles IV., came to see this royal tomb, and her own was pointed out to her, she took a pair of scissors and scratched her name on it. She died in Rome towards the latter end of last century, but was brought here to be buried. Only kings and queens in their own right, or the mothers of reigning sovereigns, are buried in this dark, gloomy vault; the only light that ever reaches it is from the candles carried by the guide and visitors who descend to see it, or when it is a blaze of wax tapers for a funeral.

From here we went through the *ante sacristia*, to the *sacristia*, with their beautiful arabesque ceilings, the colours all so bright and fresh, one could better believe they were executed three weeks ago instead of three centuries; they were painted by Granelo. The sacristy is a long low room; at the end of it, over the altar, is the beautiful painting by Claudio Coello, called the Apotheosis of the Wafer; all the faces are portraits. Charles II. is kneeling and worshipping the *Forma*. This picture forms a screen to the miraculous wafer, which is kept behind it. It is exposed for worship on the 29th of September and 28th of October in every year. It is forbidden to be shown to any but Roman Catholics. This wafer is said to have bled when trampled on by the Zuinglian heretics in 1525. It was given to Philip II. by Rudolph II., of Germany. The picture represents the apotheosis of the wafer as it actually took place in this sacristy. Very few of the magnificent vestments formerly belonging to the Jeronimite monks remain, but those we saw are rich and gorgeous in the extreme, the heads embroidered on them resembling enamel paintings more than anything else. In the prior's room are the first frescoes ever done here; the date is on the centre one, 1581, and the subject is the Judgment of Solomon; nothing can exceed this rich colouring.

The church is very fine, and like the rest of the building is in the Doric order, but perhaps more of interest exists in the choir than elsewhere. Ascending the principal staircase, each step of which is formed by one solid piece of granite, fourteen feet in length, the roof decorated by magnificent frescoes, by Giordano, we entered the *coro*. Here are to be seen the beautifully illuminated choral books, in parchment, and of an enormous size; formerly, in Philip II.'s time, there were 216, now but 140 exist. In one corner Philip's seat is shown, where he sat during mass with the other monks; a secret door let him pass a private way to his own apartments. He was kneeling here when the news was brought to him of the victory gained at Lepanto. The stalls are of various woods, but richly carved; in the centre is a huge stand for the choral books; notwithstanding some unheard of weight, it turns round with the gentlest touch. Above it hangs a magnificent rock crystal chandelier, formed of birds and flowers. Passing out behind the *coro* is a small recess, in which is placed the marble Christ, by Benvenuto Cellini, a wonderful piece of sculpture; it was in one piece, but the French, those destroyers and appropriators of the beautiful and valuable in Spain, broke off the arms; they are joined on, but then there is the join.

We now returned to the church; there are a few good paintings, several of them by the dumb painter, Juan Fernandez Navarrete, but the light is dreadful, in fact there is hardly any. There are forty small chapels, all having a painted *retablo*. The high altar, like most in Spain, is ornamented by carved figures and gilding up to the very roof, the Virgin crowning the whole; on the right side of it is a group of figures, portraits of Philip II., and three of his wives, the first, third and fourth, our queen does not swell the group; on the opposite side is a similar one of Charles V., his wife, daughter, and two sisters; beneath Philip's own effigy is a wicket, which led to his cell, a small dark room where he lived more a monk than a king, for fourteen years, and there he died in the most horrible state, having been for fifty-three days without leaving it, or its being touched, thus the state both he and the cell itself were in was revolting and disgusting. He died with the crucifix in his hand which Charles V. held when dying, and he crawled up to the wicket to be in sight of the altar, and in this position he died on the 15th September, 1598. He suffered greatly from gout, and the stools on which he rested his leg and foot are still in the cell, a stuffed cloth one for winter, and one of horse hair for summer; the blotting book is also preserved on which he signed the treaty after the battle of St. Quentin.

The church used to be extremely rich in relics, and is so still. St. Lawrence's bones were the first to be placed here, they were followed by others very rapidly and in great numbers, Philip II. alone having accumulated between seven and eight thousand. Amongst them was a bar from the veritable gridiron on which San Lorenzo is said, when being broiled, to request his torturers to turn him! This bar was placed in the hand of a silver effigy of the saint. The saint was taken by the French, but they left the bar, which is one of their most precious and prized relics.

The library is an arched room, nearly 200 feet long, and between thirty and forty in height and width; the ceilings are painted in frescoes, the colours being gaudily bright, too much so for a library. The books are all turned with their gilded leaves to the front, for the sake of harmony, as the gay colouring of the frescoes and gildings of the book cases would be too abruptly cut off if it were continued by the dark sombre binding only. There is a portrait here of Herrera, the architect of this monastic-tomb-palace. Many abstractions took place in 1808, of valuable manuscripts and books, but the catalogue never having been found since that period, what really is gone cannot be ascertained. In a glass case on a table in the centre of the room are some illuminated missals of the 16th century, and a Koran, in Arabic, taken at the battle of Lepanto, but some doubt is cast on its authenticity, as *on dit*, the real one was given away, and that this one actually bears a later date than the battle.

In the Chapter House, besides the frescoes, which all here are very fine, there are some good paintings by Giordano, Ribera, Titian, and Tintoretto; two by the latter artist belonged to Charles I., of England, the subjects are, Mary Magdalen washing Our Saviour's feet, and Queen Esther fainting; as also eight small pictures of flowers. At either end of the room, let into the walls, are *basso relievos,* in porphyry, one represents the Virgin and Child, the other the head of Our Lord.

We now visited the handle of the gridiron, the royal apartments; beyond the tapestry there is little of art, or interest either; but that is wonderfully beautiful, and with the exception of one or two Flemish specimens, it is all of Spanish manufacture, and executed at Madrid. The establishment does not exist any longer. The subjects are chiefly from Teniers, Wouvermann, and Goya. Two pieces were interesting, apart from the merit of their execution, on account of the subjects: the one is a portrait of the late Duchess of Albe, sister to the Empress Eugénie, dressed as a Sevillian *maja*, and standing with her arm within that of a Spanish noble, dressed *á lo majo;* they are talking with some bull fighters, a *picador*, and *matador;* the other is a group of children playing at bull fighting, one boy having an imitation of a bull's head on his own, others either with horses' heads or representing the *matadores*, *chulos*, and *picadores*, to perfection; the whole is admirably executed, the merriment and excitement all so well displayed.

In one of these rooms is a mahogany table, something like a bagatelle board, only instead of being covered with cloth, it is padded and covered with silk;

on this the newly-born royal infants are laid to be dressed. Clocks abound in every room, in some there are even three, and in most of them two; these clocks were a weakness of Ferdinand VII.; it is the same in the palace at Madrid, clocks are everywhere. The walls of the queen's own private rooms are very handsomely inlaid, as is also the flooring. The locks and handles to the doors are of polished iron, and as bright as steel, but the rooms are extremely small and wanting in comfort; the chairs are hard, the sofas straight and stiff, no foot stools, nor anything else inviting; no wonder she prefers her palace in Madrid, or the sunny slopes of Aranjuez and La Granja, to this cold, gloomy, dismal place. Even the gardens, formed by quantities of box cut out in all manner of shapes, with small fountains, one pipe to each, shooting a thin line of water straight up ungracefully in the air, in the centre of each design, breathe solitude and dreariness; the desolation around, the arid rocks, the uncultivated plain, all is more suited to birds and beasts of prey than to man. The whole is vast, heavy, and unbeautiful, and a morbid unhealthy mind alone could have imagined and then enforced the carrying out of such a sponge-for-money.

There is a wonderful echo across a large tank which is in the garden; a double echo, almost painful to hear in such a land of the dead, for the voice answers, truly as if from another world.

There are now but thirty-five priests in the Escorial,

and about 230 scholars in the college; all that was once in it has sadly dwindled away. The world of treasure it contained was almost all removed early in the present century to Madrid, for safety, and what was not so removed, was destroyed by the lawless French soldiers under Houssaye. There is little else that we can recollect worth noting, unless the curious paintings in what is called the "Battle Gallery," representing scenes from the great wars of Spain; they are frescoes, and were done in the sixteenth century. In another of these cloisters or galleries, the frescoes represent scenes from the life of Our Lord, one showing the "miraculous draught of fishes," has the Saviour standing by the edge of the sea, and with three feet, two feet only however bearing the print of the nails.

Leading out of the main road, about ten minutes' distance from the Escorial, is the shooting box of the Infante; it was originally built for Charles IV. There is little in it deserving notice, but it is pretty; there are a few pictures and some ivory carvings; but the great attraction in this barren spot, is the avenues and trees, which are really pleasant to the eye after the arid rocks and bare mountains around, it is like an oasis in the desert. We were very near seeing more of it than we should have cared for, as by some mistake we were locked up in the grounds, and both gate-keepers had gone. It was only when the prospect of having to pass the night there was clearly developed, and that the hour was fast approaching when the train would be due by which we were to return to Madrid, that we made up our minds to climb the stone wall which enclosed us, and make our escape; if it was not done easily, it was done effectually, for we reached the station just in time to catch the train. We left at 6·12 p.m., and reached Madrid at 8·30, longer by half an hour than we were going. However, if Spanish railways are slow, they are very sure: they are punctual always to a minute.

The Fonda de Miranda is by no means a bad substitute for an hotel. Though the Escorial season is pretty well over, we had a very good *déjeûner à la fourchette*, and some capital Valdepeñas wine, which, as a rule, is good throughout Spain.

La Granja, the Versailles of Spain, we did not go and see, as it would have entailed three days absence from Madrid, and also that the coaches which run in the summer time between the railway station and the palace (some twenty miles), cannot go in the winter on account of the roads, which at this season are generally impassable; it also requires summer weather and summer heat to see it in, being at an elevation of nearly 4000 feet. All these drawbacks considered, we thought it wisest to give up the idea of attempting it.

CHAPTER VIII.

TOLEDO.

To go to Toledo, which of course every one *must* do, requires nevertheless a certain amount of moral courage; you must either go over night, and sleep in a first-rate *posada*, or atrociously vile *fonda*,—you may call it either you like, it amounts to one and the same thing,—or else leave by 7 a.m. from the station, necessitating the unpleasant proceeding of getting up at 5. That step once taken, however, to see the sun rise very nearly repays one for all disagreeables; the purple gilt sky, the fringe of gold that borders the horizon, and that seems to hang over the far distant snow-capped Guadarrama mountains, is a grand sight, and one begins to wonder why one does not *always* get up early; this feeling, however, invariably dies out by the following morning.

In about an hour after leaving Madrid, we lost sight of everything, the whole country was enveloped in a dense white mist, and so it remained till we reached Toledo. At Castillejo we changed carriages, from dirty to dirtier. We arrived at 10, the hour we were due. The approach to Toledo is very fine; the fog cleared off just at the right moment to enable us to enjoy the view. The town rises up on an almost perpendicular hill, the Tagus rushing rapidly through the valley below, with granite walls on either side. Though perched on a hill, Toledo is twelve feet lower than Madrid. Seen from a little distance, it looks like a dark ruined tower; on a nearer approach you are undeceived as to its form only, it is dark, and is ruined.

We drove up the winding road in the station omnibus, not a handsome one, not too luxurious; still, it might have been worse. As we entered the town, all fear of being overturned was dispelled, for the four mules that galloped and kicked their way along had now no further chance of playing more tricks, as we had not more than three or four inches on either side between the wheels and the walls. We were turned out in the yard of the Fonda (?) de Lino, and having, in stupid ignorance, ordered a chicken, we set out at once for the cathedral. It is situated in the centre of the town, and all but one side is blocked up by wretched buildings; from the small Plaza de San Yuste only is a view obtained, and from this point the tower—one alone is finished—is well seen. The several entrances are all extremely fine, the bronze doors are lined inside with carved wooden ones. The principal entrance, nearly opposite to the archbishop's palace, is only opened on rare and special occasions: these magnificent large doors swing on their hinges for crowned heads, but for little short of them.

The interior of this Gothic cathedral is beautiful,

and exceeds in richness of detail that of Burgos. The *coup d'œil* is, however, destroyed by the *coro* being in the centre of the church, but this is the case in almost all the cathedrals of Spain. According to tradition, this church was built and dedicated to the Virgin in her lifetime, and it has ever been under her especial care; notwithstanding this, however, it was converted by the Moors into a mosque, and so remained until re-converted by Alonso VI. into a Christian temple. Ferdinand, however, destroyed the original building, believing that what had once been defiled by the Moors could never be thoroughly purified; and in 1226 he himself laid the first stone of the present edifice, but it was not completed till nearly the end of the fifteenth century. In 1808, it was robbed by the French—under that lover of art and wealth, General le Houssaye—of such treasure as seems to have been accumulated in no other church to the same extent as here. Paintings by the finest artists were, if they could not be carried off, torn to pieces or burnt; the church plate melted down the better to remove it; the jewelled ornaments taken; nothing, in short, slipped through their fingers that once touched their hands. The only thing they did not destroy were the windows: they had much to do, and perhaps had no time to waste at the last, so these still remain. And what glorious windows they are! What exquisite colouring, what softness, and depth of richness! Nowhere can these windows be surpassed.

There are five naves, supported, perhaps, by too many pillars, for they were almost clustered together, and the choir and high altar occupying the entire centre of the church, gives the whole an over-crowded appearance. The *coro* is one mass of exquisite sculpture, stone and wood. The stalls, of which there are seventy, represent the victories gained by Ferdinand and Isabella over the Moors, especially the conquest of Granada. In one the keys of that city are being handed to the catholic monarch, and Isabella is seated on her horse, astride, and wearing armour. The arms and under-ledge of the stalls are likewise carved, the subjects chosen being light and frivolous. One not quite unfamiliar to us is two children: one on his knees and hands, not over draped, with another astride on his back with his face turned to his companion's feet, and his right hand uplifted. We had this sculptured in marble in the International Exhibition of 1862, and called "Children at Play."* The stalls are separated by red marble columns, the marble carvings above representing the genealogy of our Saviour. The beautiful tracery work around each figure deserves careful inspection; there is not an inch of the whole choir, outside and in, that does not call forth expressions of admiration. Facing the reading-desk is a black marble Virgin of great antiquity, but it is dressed up with silk, and crape, and other

* By Manfredini.

hideous drapery, that its beauty, as a work of art, is utterly destroyed.

Between the *coros* are two pulpits of gilt metal, very beautifully executed. The high altar is a mass of gilding, and represents scenes from the lives of our Lord and the Blessed Virgin. To the right are the tombs of some of the ancient kings, and to the left is the tomb of Cardinal Mendoza, who, in order to have himself buried in this spot, and an elaborate monument erected to his memory, caused the exquisite side tracery, which existed similar to that still on the opposite side, to be removed. Mendoza was the celebrated minister-prelate in the time of Isabella the Catholic; but he must have been a Goth as well.

Behind the high altar is a mass of awkward-looking people sprawling about amongst clouds and suns, which is thought extremely fine. High up as it is, it is an ungainly-looking object, and would be better veiled off, as, however remarkable it may be as a work of art, it is unsuited to the place it is in.

Chapels completely line the church, every one containing something of interest. In San Eugenio is a fine bit of Moorish workmanship; in Santiago are the tombs of the family of Alvaro de Luna: the High Constable of that name, whose tomb is magnificent, was executed by the orders of his king at Valladolid, in 1451: but there are other monuments here besides his of great interest. In the Capilla de los Reyes Nuevos, where lie a whole heap of kings and queens (it will be remembered that Toledo was formerly the capital), are the bodies of Henrique III. and his wife Catalina, who was the daughter of John of Gaunt of England: she died in 1419. In San Ildefonso, tradition says, the Virgin appeared one morning and attended matins, sitting in the saint's seat; he had written a work in defence of her being "ever virgin." Since that moment the seat has been held sacred, and of course made an object of worship, no one daring to occupy it; but one day, some faithless, unbelieving person attempted to do so, when he was instantly ejected by unseen hands. At the conclusion of matins, the Virgin, to show she had not come for nothing, decorated Ildefonso with the *casulla*. This stone seat, whereon the mother of our Lord is said to have alighted, works wonderful miracles, and faith in its agency is as strong to-day as ever it could have been in times past. The *people* of Spain believe anything told them by the priests; and how can it be otherwise, when they are taught to look on them, not as men, but as gods, and moreover are never taught anything else. There is not one educated man or woman in all Spain that is a Roman Catholic. But they dare not avow the contempt and indignation they feel against the priesthood (who barely endeavour to hide their lying and treachery), because the Queen and Government uphold them. The mass—the uneducated mass—on the other hand, blind and ignorant, are steeped to the verge of insanity in superstition.

There is less religion in Spain, less worship of God and our Saviour, with all its church ceremonies and—notwithstanding the way the French relieved them—church wealth, and monasteries and nunneries, and other so-called religious institutions, than exists in the heathen parts of Africa and Asia. The time must come when a mighty reformation will take place, and at no distant period. As yet, however, the country is not ripe for it; the fire smoulders and spreads, but the flames will not burst forth just yet; but when they do, it will be to burn rapidly and surely, and idolatry will be destroyed before the priests can stay its destruction.

A very interesting chapel is the one called Muzarabic, where the so-called ritual is still used. It is simple in its decorations, as it is in its forms, which are said to be as near, and nearer, to those handed down by our Lord than any other extant. There is a painting over the altar, and a fresco covers one side wall, but there are no images, no confessional boxes, for auricular confession is not used (here, however, they make the people confess just the same in the confessionals of the cathedral), and the Host is not retained. Many of the collects in the English Prayer-book are taken from those used in this church. In six other churches in Toledo do they observe the Muzarabic ritual; but of course the officiating priests are Roman Catholics, and observe all its forms and ceremonies outside of these little chapels.

There are portions of the cathedral still retaining many

Moorish remains, as may be seen in the Winter Chapter-house, where, besides the architecture, are some finely carved doors, and a wonderful ceiling. In the sacristy is still a marvellous collection of treasure, as well as a few good paintings. In a glass case is a statuette of San Francisco, carved by Alonso Cano; the saint, dressed as a monk, seems to be in a state of starvation, but it is valuable as a work of art, if not agreeable to look at. In the same case are the virgin's jewels and jewelled robes, literally stiff with gold and pearls. Her crown, armlets, and stomacher, are masses of precious stones, some of rare size and value. The image intended to represent the meek and modest virgin, on which all these gorgeous clothes and ornaments are placed, is of black wood, life size, and seated on a throne of partly silver, partly gold, the metal being brought by Columbus from America. Her wardrobe, which is very extensive and magnificent, is kept in a separate room, where the priests' robes are also kept. The number of these latter may be imagined when we repeat what the sacristan told us, that there are eighty vestments for each service which is performed in the church, and we could well believe it by what we ourselves saw.

The reliquary is very rich in its contents: amongst the most precious are a piece of the cross; some of the Virgin's milk; a bible, beautifully illuminated, which belonged to St. Louis of France; and the cross of Cardinal Mendoza, which was elevated at the Alhambra when it capitulated to the Christian army. The entire room is lined with cases containing relics of saints. The *custodia* is very gorgeous, and is of silver gilt. The sword of Alonso VI. is also here.

As we passed through the church to visit the cloisters, we were much struck by the peculiar way Spanish women squat themselves down, they neither kneel nor sit; seats there are none as a rule, anywhere; mats are placed in various parts, and on these they plant themselves. Dressed in black, with their mantillas and restless fans, they look studded all over the building like nothing we ever saw before.

The cloisters are very fine, and there is a bright cheerful look about them not often seen. They are of Gothic architecture, and the walls painted with frescoes.

The next point of interest lies in the ruins of the Franciscan Convent, San Juan de los Reyes, and there we went from the cathedral. The convent was erected by Isabella and Ferdinand, in commemoration of their victory over the Portuguese, in 1475, at Toro. Outside of the church, and over the doors, hang some chains, which are said to have been fastened on the Christians when they were delivered from their infidel oppressors. Within is beauty and desolation wonderfully blended; the beauty above, the desolation below; the latter the result of the work of those destroyers of everything, the French; the former, the remains of what was, and what was beyond their reach. Not a pane of glass is left; stones reached them and did their work, which, however, fortunately did not injure the beautiful Gothic carvings yet there to show what the church once must have been. One or two pictures in the side chapels, a statue here and a statue there, and nothing else is left within the walls. A portion of the convent has been sufficiently restored to make it into a kind of museum; a room, formerly the refectory, is lined with bad paintings: they are hardly worth the space they occupy. Leading out from here are the cloisters, the most beautiful specimen of Gothic architecture that can be seen anywhere; one may stand beneath their shelter from the burning sun and dream dreams of other days, of days when they were peopled by those whose minds then swayed the world. As yet we have seen nothing anywhere to come up to them, and yet here the destroyers' hands went cruelly to work; the French soldiers, under their lawless commander, set fire to them, and for thirty days the flames raged, utterly annihilating one side, and leaving several portions of the remainder partially ruined.

From the upper story a good view is obtained of the site where stood the palace of Don Rodorigue, also the place where stood the house of Toledo's friend, Wamba. Such a city of the past! First peopled by Goths, then by Moors, then by Spaniards, then the Goths returned in the shape of French soldiers.

From here we went to see the churches that were formerly synagogues. The first, La Santa Maria la

Blanca, was for five centuries a place of worship for the Jews; then it was turned into a Christian church, which for four centuries more it remained; then it was turned into a stable by the French. It is very plain; it has three aisles, divided by pillars, having the horse-shoe arch to connect them; there are bits of Moorish work about it, but nothing very remarkable. The ceiling is made from cedars brought from Lebanon, and the earth beneath the pavement is said to have been brought from Mount Sion.

The other church, called "El Transito," is much more perfect; it was built in the fourteenth century, by the Jew treasurer of Don Pedro the Cruel, who had the poor man tortured and put to death when he wanted his money, and no longer required his services. The upper windows, looking out from a gallery, with an entrance apart, were for the women, then never publicly seen in a place of worship. There is a great deal of Moorish lace work, in stucco, against the walls, which fortunately escaped destruction. This church is still used for worship, Christian worship of course, as no Jews even are allowed in Spain; if there are any (and there are plenty) they are compelled to call themselves Roman Catholics, and make a semblance of being such.

The Alcazar, the great palace or fortress of Toledo, is worth seeing, were it only for its associations; but besides, the patio, with its fine granite columns, is magnificent; the staircase, also, is very grand. Beyond these it is a colossal ruin, being converted into infantry barracks, the queen having given it up for that purpose. It is here that the widow of Philip IV. was confined; the rooms may still be seen, but with no little risk of having one's head broken, for stones are falling in all directions, portions being pulled down and others being built up, and the dust and dirt blinding.

The bridges across the Tagus, and the gates—entrances into the town—are all worth seeing; the Moorish archways are very fine. The Puerta Lodada, now blocked up, is shortly to be opened, and a road made through it; it is sunk now in a kind of sand pit.

The Zocodover, a very Moorish Plaza, is the resort of the Toledians in the evening, and then it is crowded by the high and low, rich and poor. Formerly this was their Plaza de Torros, now one has been expressly built, and bull fighting goes on during nine months of the year. On the opposite side of the Tagus stands the famous sword manufactory, an uninteresting looking red brick building, from whence it is said finer blades are sent forth to the world than from any other manufactory in Europe.

There are many little spots worth visiting in this old town, where may be seen Moorish doors, bits of Moorish buildings, to which modern ones have been added, here and there a ceiling, an archway, a patio. Two days here are better than one, for to see all in a day, though it can be done, is very fatiguing, still the night comes so awkwardly in the way, that had we to do it over again, we should prefer anything to sleeping in the town. No one should dream of asking for a *pollo*, chicken; the thing they gave us for one would have been disowned in any poultry yard. Partridges, when in season, are very good here; bread and water capital, the coffee and milk barely drinkable, but still we have had worse. A short time since the Grand Duke Constantine of Russia came here with his suite, and breakfast was ordered at the Fonda de Lino; there were twenty-seven to partake of it, and the modest charge made for a *déjeûner*, that, however good it may have been for Toledo, would have been a disgrace to a decent hotel, was 7000 reals; however, they were induced to accept three thousand; that was at the rate of more than a guinea a head.

The return train for Madrid not leaving till 8 p.m., we began to find the long narrow dining room, with doors that would not shut, very chilly. There was what is called a "chimney" in the room, so we insisted on lighting a fire, nearly driving the landlady mad with fright: she could not understand a fire anywhere but in the kitchen, and the servants of the house flocked in to look at it. They were all exceedingly relieved when we left, and before our backs were turned began to reduce the flames that threatened, they thought, to burn their house down.

Spaniards have little idea of small comforts, or else not sufficient energy to insist on having them. Or else why no fire-places? Why should trains run at such unreasonable hours? Why no order in anything? Everything takes its chance: it is a happy-go-lucky sort of country, and more frequently the luck does go, and one finds oneself left in the lurch. But a Spaniard does not seem to care about it; doors will be closed when they ought to be open; appointments made will be postponed; promises given will be sure to be broken: but this won't disturb a Spaniard; gently and gracefully throwing his cloak over his shoulder—always his left—he will say, "*Bueno, esta por la mañana,*" and walks away. To-day or to-morrow, it is invariably one to him.

We reached Madrid a little before midnight, not a little tired with our long day. Pleasure is a very wearying business, when a great deal has to be seen in a short space of time.

Aranjuez, a summer palace, where the royal family always pass Easter, is about an hour from Madrid by railway; we did not go to see it, as it is purely for summer weather, the gardens being the great attraction. We passed through it going to Toledo, stopping about ten minutes, just time enough to be able to judge what the place might be under a June or July atmosphere, with the fountains all playing. There are some very fine elm trees, brought by Philip II. from England.

CHAPTER IX.

CORDOVA.

To get away from Madrid is quite as difficult as it is to reach it, even more so. As, to Cordova, whither we were next bound, there is but the choice of two trains: one leaving at 7 a.m., and not arriving till 1·35 in the middle of the night—worse could not be; and the other leaving at 8 p.m., and reaching Cordova the next day, at 11·40 a.m.; decidedly this was the best, and so by it we left. It is only in Spain this prodigious time would be taken to go over 150 miles. Setting aside church matters, nothing in the whole country is so open to reform as the railways, and yet no improvement is likely to take place, for they do not pay; and how should they? The directors will do nothing for the public, and so the public won't go by railroad if they can help it.

At Cordova, however, we arrived to the moment: they certainly are punctual. We went to the Fonda Suiza, where rooms were all ready for us, and very nice ones, only—no fireplaces, a want which, in the chilly evening, proved great; those horrid *braseros*, which give out more headache than heat, were had recourse to.

But, after all, one cannot travel and see the world without coming across many disagreeables, and to see the "Mezquita" something must be paid; but surely that again repays one cent. per cent., to say nothing of that payment being durable and for ever, and the outlay is over soon, and forgotten as quickly.

Cordova, a city of the past, like all others worth seeing in Spain, contains many and very beautiful Moorish remains; at each turn something greets the eye that tells of their former rule and greatness, and of the marvellous refinement of their taste. The cathedral, or " Mezquita," as it is still commonly called, is the great wonder and attraction; it stands more alone than most cathedrals in Spain are allowed to do, perhaps because the exterior is so simple that space around it is really of no great moment, and so from pure contradiction it is not built round. We entered by the Puerta del Perdon into the *patio* of oranges, containing some magnificent trees, together with palms, both being laden with fruit. In the centre, the cistern placed by the Moors in 945, is still there. To the left of this court is the belfry tower, a magnificent view is obtained from the top; on the right is the mosque. Formerly there were nineteen entrances, now there are but two, the rest are all closed; one is in the centre, and the other to the right at the furthest end.

It is difficult to give an idea of the impression produced on first entering this wondrous building; it certainly does not give one the faintest idea of being a church; with a low roof not exceeding thirty-six feet in height, amidst a very forest of columns, you find yourself in a space which takes time to discover the extent of, apparently very nearly square, being both ways upwards of 360 feet, with the columns forming nineteen aisles one way, and twenty-nine the other, the whole being lined on the four sides by chapels. The pillars are none alike, either in size, height, or marble, —some with capitals, others without, some of jasper, verd-antique, porphyry, and other valuable marbles; one was shown us as being sulphur, which the guide scraped in order that we might test the truth of his statement by its strong smell. It is a pity this is allowed, as the dilapidated state of the pillar proves how common the practice of "testing" is. On two other of the columns are small crucifixions scratched, hardly visible without the light of a candle; one is said to have been done by a Christian prisoner, who was chained by his neck to the pillar, the places where the chains were fixed being visible enough, but it seems difficult to understand how he could scratch a crucifix in that position, and just where his shoulders would be against the column; and to increase the marvel, he is said to have done it with his nail; if by this was meant, as it clearly was, his finger-nail, it becomes simply ridiculous. The other is much more perfect and slightly larger; it is railed over, the better to preserve it; the figure of a saint in relievo, kneeling, is on the wall close by it.

In all there are 850 columns, formerly there were more, but the *coro*, which was unfortunately added in 1523, necessitated the removal of many. The retablo of the high altar is very fine, and the dome elaborate and delicate, with its white and gold ornamentation, but it looks so thoroughly out of place, and much as one must admire the exquisite carvings of the " sillas," one feels at every moment that *there* the whole thing is a mistake, and spoils itself, as well as this the finest specimen of a Moorish temple in Europe.

The Capilla de Villaviciosa, to reach which we had to pass through another chapel, having been built against on either side, is rich in beautiful Moorish work, and looks as if hung all round with fine lace; those horse-shoe arches, one succeeding the other, yet forming in a whole one perfect one, are marvels of architecture. The *azulejos*, or tiles, are very fine. San Fernando is placed in the recess, where the Alcoran was formerly; he is painted in bright colours, and as he is generally represented, holding in his hand a globe with the cross on it. The large window of this chapel is where the kalif prayed in public; it faces the *Ceca*, the Holiest of Holies. In this portion of the building, the part leading to the *Ceca*, is such mosaic work as is not rivalled at Rome, as indeed may be said of the whole; the roof, the beautiful arches, and the brilliancy of colouring rendering this Mezquita a thing apart. A railing separates the " Ceca " from the tomb of the Conde de Oropesa, who rescued Cordova from an attack of the Moors; the monument is perfectly plain, with a badge lying across, cut into the stone, indicative of his profession; not even his name is recorded on it, but that is not required, it is in every one's mouth that you ask.

The "Ceca" is octagon shaped and richly inlaid; the roof is formed by a solid piece of white marble, in the shape of a scollop-shell. All the inscriptions are in Cuphic. Pilgrims who came here walked seven times round this Ceca, and the pavement shows evident marks of many feet. This mosque ranked second only to that of Mecca, and a pilgrimage to it was thought as much of by the Spanish Moors, as one to Mecca by those who were better able to reach that place. St. Ferdinand first converted this mosque into a Christian church; it is fortunate he did not think it necessary to rase it to the ground, in order to purify it, as he did that of Toledo. Double rows of arches, one over the other, support the columns, and the fret-work on some of them is delicate and beautiful beyond description. The church plate is now of little value :·Dupont and his troops admired it all too much to leave it; the custodia is, however, rich, it is silver gilt, of Gothic design, and executed in 1517 by Henrique de Arphe; it, together with a few other things, was hidden, and thus escaped the marauders.

Leaving the Mezquita as we entered it, by the Court of Oranges, the bishop's palace, a dreary sombre-looking building, stands on the right. The garden is famous for its lemon-trees, the fruit being peculiarly fine; the house is famous for nothing but as having been the prison of Ferdinand VII., in 1823, and from where he made a vain attempt to escape. Further on is the bridge over the Guadalquiver; it is of great width, and has sixteen arches, varying in size and architecture: to reach it you pass under a fine old gateway, built by Herrera, for Philip II.; the relievos on it, now much destroyed, still bear proof of great merit: they are said to be by Torrigiano. Not far from this gate is a gorgeous elevation to San Rafael, the patron saint of the town, whose effigy tops the whole; a little further on, on a stone let into the wall, is a request that he will *Ora pro nobis*.

Following the road by the river, we came upon some Moorish mills, which, if not very picturesque, are certainly interesting enough to walk through; they are still worked for grinding corn; many of the arches about them are blocked up. Towering high above, on the opposite side of the road, are the gardens of the Alcazar; we walked round to them. The building itself was formerly the Inquisition, now it is a college; there is nothing to see in it, the gardens are pleasant. We went over several churches, but except the mosque, there is nothing to see in them that cannot be seen anywhere, but at every turn in the town something is sure to be met, reminding one of those days when the Moors ruled here with eastern magnificence.

Almost every house has a *patio*, more or less pretty. All arrangements here are for coolness: thus the streets are very narrow, to exclude the sun; the floorings of the rooms are either marble or brick tiles, and a fireplace is a thing unknown in Cordova. The town is extremely clean, but oh! the pain of walking in it! The stones are so uneven and sharp, that if one filled one's shoes with marbles, walking would hardly become more difficult. No wonder the Spanish women are remarkable for a peculiarity in their walk: how could anyone get along without an odd gait? It is anything but graceful: they walk like ducks, slowly and heavily, and with a decided waddle, but one cannot be astonished, nor surprised that they never walk at all if they can help it.

The Fonda Suiza, though the best hotel Cordova has ever known, would bear improvement; the attendance is bad and the food not over good; and the cold inside the house is unbearable, at this season, of course.

From Cordova to Seville, as from Madrid to Cordova, there is little to interest. The scenery is not quite so monotonous; it is relieved by mountains in the distance, and by olive-trees near. These trees bear the large green olive, the size of an Orleans plum; they are not quite so highly flavoured as the smaller kind. The olives in all Andalucia are triturated in the same simple, primitive manner, as along the north coast of the Mediterranean in the Maritime Alps.

From Cordova to Seville it is but four hours, and, as we picked up the night express train from Madrid, we left at a reasonable hour, starting at noon and arriving at Seville at 4 p.m.

CHAPTER X.

SEVILLE.

SEVILLE, a city of beauty and romance, as we had always pictured it to our mind, very much disappointed us at first sight. Instead of being situated amidst beautiful scenery, and intersected by groves of oranges, we found it a commonplace-looking town on the banks of an unornamental but useful-looking river; no country about, the land around looking like many ploughed fields; and the orange-groves away from the town, and most of them walled in and quite hidden. Yet all this disappointment completely wore away at the end of a few days, and at the end of a fortnight we were ready to agree with its most wildly-enthusiastic admirers. There is an indescribable charm in it, but it must be well known to be appreciated.

We were at the Fonda de Londres on the Plaza Nueva. The house was dirty and dear, and we would not advise any one to try it if they can get into the Madrid or Paris. The weather, during the five weeks we were in Seville, was, with three or four days' exception, magnificent; soft and warm as a fine English summer. We began our sight-seeing with the Alcazar. This palace was built in the eleventh century, but has undergone many changes. It was completely restored by Don Pedro El Cruel, by whom the beautiful frontage was built, as an inscription in Spanish bears record : this is written in Gothic letters, and round the upper portion of the façade. The workmen employed were Moorish, having been borrowed from the king, Yusuf I. of Granada, who had just completed the Alhambra. The principal *patio* is splendid : one feels it almost impossible to realize the reality that surrounds one ; the brilliant colouring, the delicate lace-like work ; the minute patterns, all so perfectly executed ; the immense time it has remained, many portions untouched for five centuries ; all render it marvellous to behold. The apartments, as in all modern as well as ancient Spanish palaces, surround the *patios*. In the one leading from that called the Hall of the Ambassadors, we were shown the spot, stained, it is said, with blood, where Don Pedro so treacherously murdered his half-brother, Don Fadrique, from jealousy, because he suspected him of being in love with his queen, Blanche of Bourbon ; and he caused her to be cruelly murdered at Chiclana, not far from Cadiz, in 1361. Fadrique's death was amply revenged by his own brother, Henry of Transtamare ; these two brothers were the sons of Alonso XI. and Leonora de Guzman—but all this is history, and too well known to need recording here.

The Patio de las Doncellas is very magnificent ; it is so called from having been the court where the

Moorish kings caused the virgins, always a hundred in number, to pass before them, being the yearly tribute imposed on their vassals, till Alphonso, surnamed the Chaste, delivered them from this thraldom. The Patio de los Muñecas* is exquisitely delicate in its decorations; the slender marble columns, the lacework arches, are so fine and pure-looking, it seems impossible to believe that all this fairy-looking building is of a substance as hard and durable as stone. Above the first is a second tier of pillars, and again another range of arches. The lower part is very ancient; the upper part was added in the time of Ferdinand and Isabella. But it is impossible to give a description of this Moorish architecture and do it justice; it is so elegant in design, so intricate in its patterns, and so minute, that it is unlike anything we ever saw before. The lower portion of the vestibules and the floorings are of azulejos, the difference between the ancient and the modern tiles being that the former were worked out with their patterns in mosaic and raised work, whilst the latter are in square or long pieces, and the pattern and colouring stamped on them; thus the one is very easily distinguished from the other.

On the upper story is a little chapel, erected by desire of Isabella the Catholic. The altar is entirely of azulejos, representing the Annunciation and Visitation of the Virgin, and the initials of Ferdinand and

* Dolls.

Isabella with the Tanto Monta, meaning, *Tanto Monta Isabel como Fernando;* that is, The queen was equal to the king, and they shared all honours alike. Beyond this chapel is the Cuarto del Principe, a magnificent Moorish apartment; further on, after passing several ordinary rooms, is the bedroom of Don Pedro, from whence, through a private door, he had access to the apartments of Maria Padilla, the only being who ever exercised the smallest influence over him, so far as making him occasionally human (one can hardly say humane). Her gentle nature, her real love for this brutal man, enabled her to mould him at times to her will, and that will was always exerted for some good purpose. It is said that she knew of, and by offering no opposition tacitly sanctioned, the murder of the unfortunate and innocent queen; but that is not so, and none deplored the horrible deed more than the king's mistress.

In the gardens—magnificent as they are, still only the reflection of bygone grandeur and beauty—is the long bath used by Maria Padilla: formerly it was that of the sultanas. It is now walled up on either side; then it was bordered with orange-trees. Here the real queen of the Alcazar received her king and court, whilst in the enjoyment of her bath. There are some orange-trees of enormous size and age in the gardens, one which existed in Maria's time, and which is now laden with its golden fruit. Myrtle-trees abound; they line the paths, and in some places are formed into hedges, and so trained and at such a height that a perfect maze exists of them. There are fountains in all directions; one plays along the terrace fronting the bath, and up two side walks, causing an extremely pretty effect. Summer-houses are studded about; one is built entirely of magnificent azulejos, by Charles V., and is the principal one in the gardens. Charles V. was married, at the Alcazar, to Isabel of Portugal, in 1526, and it was on this occasion that the Emperor granted freedom to his royal prisoner, Francis I. of France, who, since the battle of Pavia, had been kept at Madrid. One of the large basins here has an anecdote attached to it in connection with Don Pedro. He was one day in great perplexity as to the choice of a judge who should decide a very important matter then in agitation; and walking up and down near this water, he picked up an orange, cut it in two, and throwing half away, threw the other half into it, the cut side downwards. Then the king sent for one of the judges, and asked him what was in the water. He replied, it was an orange. The king, vexed, dismissed him and sent for another, and so on for several more, each having given the same answer. At last one, before answering, took the branch of a tree and drew the orange towards him, took it out, and said it was "half an orange," upon which the king at once appointed him judge over the pending matter.

Nothing is more delightful than sitting, during the heat of the day, beneath the shade of these almost forest trees. We made friends with the old man who keeps the rusty keys of the rusty lock that prevents the mob from intruding, and many an hour have we passed, lazily dreaming ot those great, grand old bygone times we may read of, but which will never come again. We have surely lived two or three centuries too late for real enjoyment of life, or—too soon.

If the spirits of those that are gone ever revisit their old haunts, what can they think of these magnificent places being allowed to go to ruin! The Duke of Montpensier has won well-deserved thanks for the time and money spent in endeavouring to restore the Alcazar; but these places can rarely be brought back to their original perfection if once allowed to decay.

The cathedral is not far from the Alcazar, and coming from the palace, the best view of the exterior is seen. It is a magnificent building, and after seeing the principal churches of Spain we have come to the conclusion that, taking this all and all, it is the most beautiful of any, and we recall it to our recollection with greater pleasure than either that of Burgos or Toledo.

It is far larger and loftier, and of finer proportions than any in Spain, and is built on the site and in the form of the original mosque, nothing of which now remains but the beautiful Giralda tower, so called because on its summit is a colossal weathercock, in bronze, and in the shape of a woman, representing

Faith; it is fourteen feet in height, and weighs nearly three hundred pounds, yet it spins round with every changing wind. Entering, by the beautiful filagree-worked Moorish gate, into the Court of Oranges, the Giralda rises up, straight and stately, to the left. In the centre of this court is the original fountain which existed in the time of the Moors. To the right is the *Sagrario*, the parish church which really forms a portion of the whole building. Facing it is the stone pulpit where St. Vincent Ferrer preached, advocating *autos da fé*, and other iniquitous proceedings. The entrance to the tower is not in the court, but in the outer plaza; the ascent is easy, it being a broad path on an incline, and no steps till within a short distance of the summit, from whence the view is magnificent, the mountains of Ronda towering to the east; the Guadalquiver winding in and out amidst now well seen orange groves; the white town glistening in the sunshine; the innumerable and picturesque church towers and spires; the bull-ring, the Alcazar, and the cathedral itself, at our very feet, rendering the whole a scene once looked on, never to be forgotten. The clock in the tower is thought much of, probably because a monk's hands made it; the bells are numerous, colossal, and as unmusical as they are big. On great festivals the tower is illuminated, and the effect extremely striking and pretty. Our guide to the tower, a young, intelligent man, but totally blind, though he pointed out correctly each object in the distance of any note, was very curious about our King Henry VIII. and Katherine of Arragon, the wife of two brothers. He clearly thought a greater wrong was inflicted on her by the divorce than was done by marrying her to her dead husband's brother.

We entered the church at all entrânces, on all and almost every day, and all hours, for we were never weary of that beautiful building. Even the old sacristan used to exclaim, when he saw us, "How you must admire it to come so often!" And so we did. However, to give some account of it, it is better to commence by the fine Moorish arched doorway, with delicate lace-work decorations, every atom of which will bear close examination. At first, all is gloomy and dark within, till the eye becomes accustomed to the *demi-jour*. Unfortunately, the two *coros* are placed in the body of the church, spoiling the view by blocking it up through the centre; thus it is difficult to realize the great size of the church. The best way to do this is to go at night, and then stand at the extremity of one of the aisles, looking straight down, and, by the dim light of the candles which are placed against each column, one can perceive the immense distance it is to the opposite end. Taking the lateral chapels first and turning to the right, is, in a small capilla, an exquisite painting of the "Virgin and Child," by Alonso Cano, a gem that one can never tire of looking at. Here is the Virgin truly pourtrayed in her meekness and simplicity. Next, in the Capilla de

Santiago, is a grand picture by Roelas; the saint is represented as riding over the Moors: the frame is worth noticing, not alone for its workmanship, but for its great size. In the end chapel on this side, where the christening font stands, is Murillo's great picture of "San Antonio," thought by the Sevillians to be his greatest work; but, beautiful as it is, and marvellous as the representation is of the Infant Saviour standing in mid air, few will agree in this opinion after they have seen those exquisite paintings in the Museum. In the nearest of the two chapels at the western end, is a "Holy Family," by Murillo's pupil, Alonso Miguel de Tobar: it is a fine painting, and, but for its proximity to the "Guardian Angel," by the great master himself, would attract much more attention. The "Guardian Angel" is a holy-looking picture. The drapery of the little child is so wondrously transparent, as he moves on led by the angel, the breeze seems to be gently moving it. It is an exquisite painting. One can never tire of it; on the contrary, the oftener we saw it, the more we desired to see it again.

Facing these chapels, at the western end, beneath the pavement, between them and the *coro*, is buried the son of Christopher Columbus, Fernando. On the large flat stone which covers his remains, are told, in a few short words, the great deeds of his father: "*A Castilla y a Leon Mundo Nuevo dió Colon.*" There are ships engraved on the stones on both sides of the grave.

Continuing up the south side in the chapel of Santa Ana, is a picture of that saint, by Zurbaran, and a finely-painted "Crucifixion," by a Mexican negro. This was brought to Seville by a bishop sent out from there to Mexico, and was justly considered worthy of a place in the cathedral: the man was never known to paint any other subject. Most Spanish artists paint Crucifixions with three nails, and the Italian and other schools with four; they also place the wound on the left side, and the Spanish on the right. In the Capilla de la Santa Cruz, is a very fine "Descent," by Pedro Guadalupe; and in the Sacristia de los Calices are several beautiful pictures. Amongst them is a nun, "Dorothea," by Murillo; a beautiful "Christ," by Roelas; and a "San Pedro," by Herrera el Viejo: there is also a crucifix by Montañes. Painted on the side wall, outside the chapel, is a huge fresco of "San Christobal" with the Infant Saviour in his arms, holding the globe. This fresco is thirty-two feet high. One sees this saint in almost all cathedrals. Beyond are two enormous-looking cupboards, with a great deal of good carving about them. Passing by the sacristy, which we will return to presently, is, facing the east, the high altar. The retablo is very grand, and thought to be the finest in Spain: there are forty-four compartments, each representing a scene from the New Testament, chiefly those in which the Virgin plays a part. At the gospel side of the altar is the stand for the "Cirio Pasqual," which now weighs ten arrobas,—250 lbs.—but formerly, in more flourishing days, it weighed eighty, and even ninety arrobas, and towered up to the very summit of the cathedral. This is only used at Easter, and every year there is a fresh candle. At the foot of the marble steps leading to the altar, is a natural stain in the stone so exactly resembling a parrot that it appears to be inlaid. On the upper portion of the iron gate that rails off the *coro* is a figure representing Adam in a recumbent posture, with a tree sprouting out of his side, and Eve growing out of the top of that.

The *coro* is very fine, the carving of the stalls and the whole interior is magnificent; there are 117 " sillas," and in the centre is the archbishop's seat. The marbles outside the choir are hardly in keeping with the rest of the church, they are too rich and gaudy in their colours, some being of a deep orange and red. Continuing the round, now nearly completed, of the chapels, we come, after the altar mayor, to the Capilla de San Pedro, rich in fine paintings, by Zurbaran, all treating of the life of the apostle. To the iron gates of this chapel is a marvellous bolt, in one piece of iron, and of immense weight, yet it slides with the greatest ease by the lightest touch; an offer was made to present a duplicate bolt in silver, if this one would be given up, but the offer was declined. This is the last of the lateral chapels, but around the choir are several others; one contains the Virgin of Montañes, famous as one of his finest carvings; the expression is soft and beautiful; the robes on it destroy its otherwise sweet simplicity. This image was, on the day that the Bull of the Immaculate Conception was issued, taken to the Infanta's palace, and she then and there decorated it with a diamond ornament for the neck, an amethyst bracelet on each arm, and rings on her fingers; these are always left on the figure.

Behind the altar mayor is the Capilla Real, where San Fernando, the conqueror of Seville, is buried; his body is in a silver coffin, richly embossed, standing immediately over the altar, and in front of the miraculous Virgin, "de los Reyes." St. Ferdinand's body is exposed three times in the year to the faithful, when a military mass is performed; the body is in a very perfect state. The silver coffin was given by Felipe V., four years after he abdicated; it cost 71,000 duros. In the centre is a large gold medallion, with a representation of the keys of Seville being handed to him after the conquest. Right and left of the chapel, as you enter, are the tombs containing the bodies of Alonso el Sabio, St. Ferdinand's son, and Queen Beatrix. The "Virgen de los Reyes," *the* Virgin of Seville, was given to St. Ferdinand by his cousin, St. Louis of France; the miracles she works are marvellous. The Duchess de Montpensier is her mistress of the robes, reversing the order of things as they stand at Madrid. On all great festivals, the Infanta is in attendance, and directs and helps the dressing of the Queen of the Sevillians. Passing behind the altar is a quiet peaceful little chapel, which is under the especial care of the Infanta; as in a recess, leading out of it, lined with crimson velvet, are two little coffins containing the remains of her youngest children. The open-worked or-molu doors which enclose these coffins have the arms of Spain and France on them in medallions. In the same chapel, but in a vault in front of the altar, Don Pedro the Cruel, and Maria Padilla are buried: on the altar, lies San Fernando's sword.

The Capilla Real has its own sacristy; there are some pictures, but the light is so bad we were obliged to have candles, and then one could see them a little better. Here are kept *the* Virgin's jewels. The diamond necklace alone is worth 90,000 duros; it belonged to Doña Berenguela, the mother of St. Ferdinand; the crown she wears is the same wherewith the saint-king was crowned. Her wardrobe is very extensive and very gorgeous.

It was some time before we succeeded in obtaining an order to see the sacristy and reliquary; there are always some difficulties raised, and day after day we were put off with one excuse or another. You may always see the sacristy by being at the cathedral early in the morning, but you will see nothing in it; and, unless by special order, they will not show the relics.

The interior of the sacristy is very rich; it was built a few years only after the cathedral. Here are contained all the treasures of the church, and the dresses of the clergy; the latter are gorgeous in the extreme, and wonderfully numerous; the weight of some of them is so great, that it is a wonder how any man can bear to carry them on his shoulders, still less how he can move about with them. The "relicario" is at the end the room; it is very plain, and like a cupboard outside; when the doors are unlocked, the relics are seen through glass. There are some magnificent ornaments and cases with relics :—The pix, used on great festivals, has 1300 diamonds in it, and two pearls, each the size of a small nut. A massive gold ornament, made from gold brought by Columbus from America, consisting of two figures, holding a globe, the globe alone weighing fifteen pounds. A small gold "custodia," with precious stones. A beautiful gold mounting to a circular crystal case, in which is placed a thorn from *the* Crown of Thorns. An ornament, equally valuable, containing a piece of wood of the Cross. The keys that were presented to St. Ferdinand when he took Seville. A small wooden cross, wonderfully minutely carved, representing, on the stand, scenes from the Old Testament, and on the actual cross scenes from the New. A diamond cross, presented to one of the archbishops of Seville ; it is placed here on account of its great value. There are, besides these we have named, armbones, legs, fingers, and other relics of saints, all handsomely mounted in silver or gold.

At the other end of the room is kept the heavy and massive silver altar which is erected over the retablo of the High Altar on great festivals. The silver custodia is of an enormous size, and solid silver; it is the work of a Spaniard named Arfe; the candlesticks are so massive, that it is all one man can do to raise one; the intrinsic value of this colossal mass of silver is almost fabulous, for all is solid; the altar, when up, is twelve yards high, and one figure alone, which is placed with others at various points, that of St. Rosalie, weighs nine arrobas and a half; her relics are let into, and seen through a piece of glass in the breast. The *tenebrario* stands here, it is an enormous bronze candelabra, twenty-five feet high; during Passion week it is lighted by thirteen candles; one after the other are extinguished till only one is left burning, typical of the desertion of our Lord by the Apostles, and the fidelity of the Virgin.

Above the press containing the relics is a "Descent," by Campana, thought at the time it was painted so true to life that the people looked on it with awe and fear; it was painted in 1548. Murillo was never weary of looking at it, and at his own request he was buried before it in the church of Santa Cruz; this church was pulled down by Soult, Murillo's grave destroyed, his remains cast away, and this picture cut up into several pieces; fortunately it was not past restoration, but it took three months to do it. To the right of it is a beautiful saint-like picture, by Zurbaran, of "St. Theresa;" and, on the other side, "San Lorenzo," by Mulato, a pupil of Murillo's. But the finest pictures are two by Murillo himself, hanging right and left in the centre of the walls, and with a good light on them; the one is "San Leandro," and the other "San Isidoro," both full length, and magnificent paintings; the rich stiff silk robes of Isidoro are wonderful.

We obtained permission to ascend to the galleries of the cathedral; from there a good idea may be formed of its size, and the beautiful windows are also seen from them. Outside on the roof is like walking over hilly land, the ups and downs are so frequent; here the enormous size of the exquisitely painted rose window over the western entrance can be seen; it is fourteen yards in diameter.

The ceremonies attached to the church of Rome are performed here, on the various festivities, with as much pomp and display as at Rome itself; and the rush of visitors during the holy week is so immense that fabulous charges are made for apartments, whether in hotels or private houses,—in fact, you pay by the hour. A curious custom prevails at Seville during the octave of the Feast of the Immaculate Conception,—it is of dancing before the altar every evening at benediction service. We went twice to see it.

The "altar mayor" was adorned with its massive silver altar and retablo, brilliantly illuminated; the Virgin's image in the centre gorgeously attired, wearing a massive gold and jewelled crown; above all, and in the centre of a gilt glory, was the precious pix, with the Host exposed. The service was performed to a certain point as usual; the singing was beautiful, and the organs sounded rich and full. All the clergy of the town were present, the cardinal archbishop officiating. Just before the time when, on other occasions, the blessing would be given, a band of musicians entered from behind the altar, and took up their places on the right; the priests who, with the exception of those officiating, were in the choir, now advanced in a body to the altar, passing in between the dancers, who appeared, like the musicians, from behind, at the same moment. The priests placed themselves right and left, and as far back and as close together as they could. The dancers, ten in number, were young boys between twelve and fifteen years of age; they were fantastically dressed in yellow, blue, and white silk jackets and breeches, slashed; white stockings and white shoes, white hat and feathers. They seated themselves on benches, five on each side, till the signal was given for the band to play; the music was light and pretty, and operatic; the boys now rose and sang to the music, and then, still singing, began to dance, a slow measured dance, more like the *Minuet de la Cour* than any dance of the present day; after a little they ceased singing, and played the castanets; then again they sang, but all the while dancing and the band playing; this lasted for about a quarter of an hour, when the boys, having finished their part of the performance, ran up the altar steps and disappeared behind it, followed by the orchestra. During this *ballet* the cardinal archbishop, and his assisting priests, stood by the altar; the people in the church were, the women sitting on their heels, and the men standing; but now all knelt, and the cardinal gave the benediction: the Host, however, was not taken down for the purpose, it was understood just the same, and in sign of all being finished a curtain was drawn over it. Then the priests, preceded by the choir, walked from the altar across the church; the cardinal was the last; his train was held up, and as he passed the kneeling multitude, he gave his blessing with his scarlet-gloved and ringed hand. Passed out well into the church, he entered his gilt sedan chair, and was carried off home; fortunately for his bearers he had not far to go, for the night was very bad, the rain pouring down, as it can do in these latitudes.

The first night we witnessed this extraordinary ceremony, the Duke and Duchess of Montpensier, the Count and Countess of Paris, and two younger daughters of the duke were present, and sat within the altar rails.

There is something more heathenish than Christian in exhibitions of this sort.

CHAPTER XI.

SEVILLE—*continued.*

LEAVING the cathedral by the north door, a beautiful Moorish horse-shoe arch, you pass beneath an extremely ungainly looking alligator. This was sent as a present to Alonso el Sabio from the Sultan, at the same time requesting the hand of the wise king's daughter in marriage; this was declined; the alligator remained all the same. Straight along the covered way, at the opposite corner, is the Chapter Library. It contains 35,000 books, left to the town by Fernando, Columbus' son. Above the books in the first room hang the portraits of all the great men Seville has given birth to; amongst them is that of Cardinal Wiseman: the house he was born in, overlooking the cathedral, has a tablet erected, commemorating the fact. His father was consul here. In the adjoining room are all the cardinals, archbishops, and bishops of Seville. At the end is Murillo's beautiful picture of "St. Ferdinand." Facing, as you enter, is the portrait of a younger son of Charles III., who, at fourteen years of age, was appointed by his father Archbishop of Toledo and Seville. At the age of thirty, this youthful church dignitary chose to throw aside his clerical habit and cast his vows to the wind, and in exchange took a wife. A son of this marriage was made Bishop of Seville; his portrait, a perfect Bourbon face, hangs next but one to his archiepiscopal father.

Amongst the books are two in Latin, on various scientific subjects, with notes on the margin written by Columbus, also in Latin. There is also a most interesting manuscript written by himself, proving the discovery of America was foretold in Scripture; the quotations he gives from the Bible are so numerous, that there is an index to them at the end. The handwriting is small but extremely distinct; it is in Spanish, and was drawn up by him when in prison, to lay before the Inquisition. There is also a manuscript account of his travels written by his son; little care seems to be taken of these precious relics; they were locked up in a table drawer, in no covering or case of any kind, and we were permitted to handle them as we liked. The sword presented to Varas, St. Ferdinand's captain, at the taking of Seville, is preserved here. This sword is said to have been buried for three centuries, and was found when tardy honour was about to be paid to the remains of its former owner, Fernan Gonzalez. The number of Moors this sword has slain is unknown, but it is stated that to the execution it did, the taking of Seville was due.

The Lonja—the Exchange—is an important building standing on the south side of the cathedral square; it was built by Herrera, and very much like the Escorial in outward design. The *patio*, surrounded by Doric pillars, is very fine. A magnificent marble staircase leads to the rooms containing the archives of South America; there are upwards of 3000 of these documents arranged in mahogany bookcases. In the entrance room is a vile painting of Christopher Columbus: the last room of all has four maps, by Arrowsmith, of the four quarters of the globe; and a portrait of Fernan Cortes.

Seville is a city of churches, all of them having something to see in them. Foremost in interest is La Caridad; the origin of this hospital was to give burial to the poor; now it is for the support of infirm old men. In the chapel are six grand Murillos; two of them are very large, and painted expressly for the places they occupy. They are called "El Pan y Peces," and "La Sed;" the first is "The Miracle of our Lord Feeding the Multitude," and the last, "Moses Striking the Rock;" they are both magnificent paintings, the expression of the faces so full of life; the eagerness of the thirsty groups, especially the anxiety of one child to get his turn, pushing forward and watching till another should finish drinking from the shell. In the other picture, Peter seems to be bargaining for the few fishes, whilst the Saviour, seated a little back, has the loaves of bread before him, apparently blessing them; the hungry multitude is in the background. Of two small pictures beneath these large ones, "The Infant

Saviour" and "The Infant St. John," the latter is far away the finest picture; the Child Christ seems either unfinished or injured,—nor is the colouring good. The other two are "The Annunciation," and "An Angel's Visit;" the light of these two beautiful pictures is so bad, that unless the large doors near them are thrown open, it is impossible to see them. Over the principal entrance is "The Triumph of Time;" it is a fine picture; another, by the same artist, is "A Dead Cardinal," so horrible that it is sickening to look at; he must have been dead too long when this painting was done of him; others in the background are nearly as offensive. Over the high altar is a carved and painted "Descent;" it is wonderfully executed, the figures around the Crucified Saviour being full of expression and life; it is by Pedro Roldan and considered his *chef d'œuvre*. The hospital itself has not much to see in it; it is very clean and airy, and the old men, just now 140 in number, seem to be well cared for by the nuns who superintend the management of the institution. The *patio* is very fine, and has some well grown orange-trees in it.

There is a Moorish *patio* to the church of San Salvador full of orange-trees. In this court is a little chapel, which was built to contain what is considered a miraculous crucifix; it is perfectly imbedded in *ex-votos* in all shapes; pictures, wax figures, wax limbs, hair, crutches, and even entire wax babies. The church itself, is laden with heavy massive gilding.

San Pablo is a very fine church; it is very large, with a great quantity of decoration about it. From the opposite side of the river the ruined exterior is very picturesque. San Lorenzo has some good paintings, and the retablo and the figure of the saint holding a large silver gridiron are both by Montañes. The carved larch-wood roof of San Clemente is beautiful; and the azulejos on either side of the high altar are extremely fine specimens of the genuine ancient tile. This chapel is attached to a convent, and a very curious old door leads out of it into the convent, through which the nuns pass. The tower of San Pedro is Moorish; the roof is handsome. There is a good picture here by Roelas of "Peter being Delivered from Prison." The retablo of the high altar is heavy; in a side chapel is a virgin, celebrated as being her of Saragossa. San Juan de la Palma was a Moorish temple. San Diego is curiously built; the church being divided by a wall going up the entire centre, communication is obtained at both ends, but it has the appearance of being two churches. There is a very beautifully illuminated missal here of 1642.

San Bernardo has little to recommend it beyond a painting of "The Last Judgment," by Herrera el Viejo, in one of the side chapels. San Felipe Neri is an extremely pretty church, with a great deal of gilding and rich ornaments, and some good pictures. San Esteban was formerly a Muzarabic church; the retablo is by Zurbaran. Santa Maria la Blanca, once a synagogue, contains some old Roman granite columns, and one or two good pictures; one, said to be by Murillo, of "The Last Supper;" but we should think it very doubtful. San Nicolas, with its many beautiful marble columns, looks like a miniature copy of the Mezquita at Cordova. Santa Paula, a beautiful little church with azulejos as fine as those in the Alcazar, and paintings and carvings by Alonzo Cano; the azulejos at the entrance are magnificent. This chapel is attached to a convent of a very strict order. Santa Catalina has a miraculous virgin, and a velvet banner, embroidered with a Virgin and Child, the faces painted, worth alone going to see. San Louis, the Jesuits' church; San Marcos, San Geronimo, and several others, may all be visited, and in each will be found something to repay the trouble.

The Muséo is a large plain building, with many *patios*, and little to recommend it for architectural beauty; but it contains such gems of Murillo's that, on entering the room to which the name of the great master has been given, one has to pause and resolve, if possible, to study one at a time quietly—for one's inclination is to do as one frequently does with an interesting book, running the eye from page to page, galloping through to see the end; and it is difficult to keep from glancing on in this way till the eye has rested on all these exquisite paintings, that cannot be equalled in any other gallery.

It would be perplexing to say which delights one most, they are all so beautiful. All but two are large paintings; but these small ones are perfect gems; the one is "The Virgin and Child," called "La Servilleta," from having first been sketched on a napkin; the child is marvellous, it is leaping with life; the other is a "Conception," which formerly belonged to the Capuchin convent. The others are, two of "San Antonio," one with the Infant Saviour standing on the book before the kneeling monk, and the other with him sitting on it—the latter is the finest, though both are beautiful; "The Annunciation," "The Nativity," "The Adoration of the Shepherds," "The Virgin and Angels with the Dead Saviour;" "San Felix de Cantalicio," called by himself *his own picture;* besides several others: one feels overwhelmed with such works around one, and day after day did we return and feast our eyes without ever feeling we had seen them sufficiently. There are several pictures by Juan de Castillo, Murillo's master; but the master could not compete with the pupil. Velazquez's master, Herrera el Viejo, has one or two pictures in this room; through his "San Hermenegildo" his life was spared; he having been condemned to death for forgery, Philip IV., seeing the picture, and learning who it was by, sent for the artist and pardoned him. Though Velazquez was a Sevillian, there are none of his paintings here. Zurbaran, so little known in England, yet a great master, and with none to equal him in painting monks, is seen here to perfection; amongst the finest is "The Apotheosis of Thomas Aquinas." There are some works of Roelas,

Pacheo, and Valdes; but with such a collection of Murillos, one does not seem to want more. There is a fine " San Geronimo," in *terra-cotta*, by Torrigiano; and a beautifully carved " San Domingo," by Montañes.

In the *patios* are some interesting remains of sculpture found at Italica; also a very ancient filigree iron cross, which formerly stood in the Calle de la Sierpe, and was removed when improvements were being made. In front of the Muséo, in the centre of the plaza, is a very fine bronze statue of Murillo, who was born in Seville, and died there.

The next best pictures are at the Universidad. It was formerly a convent belonging to the Jesuits, but suppressed by Charles III. in 1767, and converted into a college. There are some fine paintings by Roelas in the church; and two, very beautiful, by Alonso Cano, " St. John the Evangelist," and "St. John the Baptist." The two large figures above the retablo of the high altar are by Montañes; and to the right and left of the altar are images of San Francisco de Borga and San Ignacio, by the same artist; the latter is said to be the best portrait of the founder of the Jesuits in existence, and if it is, his looks belie him, for his countenance is not only honest-looking, but has a thoroughly good expression, and he must have been extremely handsome. Here are the tombs of the Ribera family, removed by the Duke of Medina Celi from the Cartuja, when that convent was suppressed;

the sculpture of the marble is very fine. Two of these ancestors of the Duke of Medina Celi, having each had two wives, are buried with the effigies of both lying on either side of them. In some of the side chapels are some good paintings, and a carved "Conception," by Montañes. In a small room, used as a kind of secretary's room, is a fine painting on wood, by Albert Durer. In the council hall are a whole string of worthless portraits, with one of the present queen worse than the rest.

The palace of the Duke de Montpensier was formerly a naval college, founded by Fernando, son of Christopher Columbus. The duke bought the building when the college was removed to Cadiz. The exterior and façade are extremely handsome; the house, a large, spreading, rambling place, is out of character with it. The interior is like any other gentleman's house; it is handsomely furnished, yet with utter disregard to uniformity. For example, in the ball-room, a looking-glass is let into the wall, on one side, and à propos of nothing; it is framed with badly-joined marble; on the opposite side it has no match, and it seems placed where it is without any reason. The room when lighted up looks extremely pretty; glass stars line it, with jets of gas at each point. There are some fine pictures in some of the other rooms. Amongst the Murillos, of which there are two or three, is "The Virgin with the Sash;" Louis Philippe paid 6000*l*. for it. There are several by Zurbaran, and the famous picture, by Ary Scheffer, of "Monica and St. Augustin." Many of the paintings are modern, but all are good. The gardens, if they can be called such, are very extensive, but they are a mixture of park, zoological gardens, and botanical gardens. The ground is very flat, with carriage roads intersecting it. There is a great variety of trees, a large range of greenhouses, and a pinery; here and there aviaries, large and small, with all kinds of foreign birds, from parrots to an owl, and a very spiteful fellow he is. There is a little island, and two boats on the water; not far from it is a spiral staircase under a net-work of wire, which ascends to some height; from the summit a tolerable view is obtained. One side of the gardens is skirted by the Paséo de las Delicias; the other extends to the tobacco manufactory.

This Tobacco Manufactory is a wonderful establishment, and the largest in Spain. It is a colossal square building, containing thirty-seven *patios;* this alone may give an idea of its size. Five thousand women are employed in it, in the manufacture of tobacco and snuff of all kinds, good, bad, and indifferent: their pay, according to their capabilities, varies from one real to eight a day. They find themselves in board and lodging. When we went in the first time, and looked down from one end to the other of one of the many galleries, it seemed as if we were suddenly transported into a lunatic asylum;—the dirt, the squalid-looking misery, mixed up with tawdry finery and flowers; their talking, laughing, screaming; the different attitudes they were in; the overseers—men and women—walking to and fro, to keep a certain amount of order; the bare walls, or else draped with skeleton crinolines, which they take off for convenience; the wild looks, the sullen manner;—the whole scene resembled more what one might expect to see in a madhouse, rather than a manufactory, where wives, mothers, and daughters, were working for their daily bread. The cigars of Virginian tobacco, which are made for selling in the streets, are sold at a cuarto, or farthing each; cigarettes for the streets, of Manilla tobacco, are sold twenty for a cuarto. The Havana tobacco is the best; the cigars made from it are one real each. The smell is very slight, and new hands only perceive it for a few days; it produces a slight drowsiness. They are all allowed to smoke as much as they like, but they are not allowed to take any away. Many of them use the privilege very freely. The snuff is made less noisily, and fewer hands are employed in it, as a great deal of rolling is done by a machine; the smell is so slight one can hardly believe the hills of brown stuff around are all snuff. It is a dirty, nasty place to visit, still it ought to be seen.

Many are the interesting houses in Seville, either from their architecture or associations; amongst the latter is Murillo's. Here he was born, and here he died. It is a large house, in the Plaza de Alfaro; one side of it is so near to the old city walls that they seem to form a portion of it. The *patio* is hung all round with pictures, not, alas! Murillo's. Rooms lead off from it, all filled with worthless copies; upstairs the same; every room is lined from the ceiling to the floor. Out of the whole mass there are not more than half a dozen decent pictures. The house now belongs to two brothers, nephews of a late canon of the cathedral, Dean Cepero, by whom the collection was made, and which once was really valuable, but everything worth buying was bought. All the rubbish now here is to be sold, house and all, if anyone wished for it. It is said that there is nothing in Spain that cannot be bought, provided only the price is paid. In the long drawing-room, under a little glass case, was a minutely carved crucifix, with the Virgin Mother standing at the foot of the cross; the whole was not longer than an inch; it was wonderfully done. There was also a painted glass worth seeing; it was the shape of a soda-water glass, very ancient. This is highly prized by the owner.

The archbishop's palace, Cardinal Louis de la Lastra, is on the plaza, close to the cathedral, with a very massive and elaborate stone-worked entrance leading into the first *patio*, and then under arches into another. Between the two is a magnificent marble staircase, which goes up to the reception rooms, the chapel, and the cardinal's private apartments. Notwithstanding our being heretics, we were received by him most graciously, and he conducted us himself through all the rooms. There are a few tolerable paintings, and the ceiling of the long room is beautifully painted with subjects from the Old and New Testaments. In this room, he said, he took exercise in bad weather. There were—a rare sight in Spain —two large fireplaces in it, both tightly fastened up. On asking him if he never had fires, he replied, never, as, if ever he felt cold, he thought he must be ill, and at once sent for the doctor. His bedroom and dressing-room were large and lofty, but so devoid of comfort; there was a hard, stiff look about them, and not the symptom of a bath. The secretary's room looked more homely than any other part of the palace, but he had a suffocating *brasero* in it, rendering the atmosphere unbearable. The chapel has not much in it, its chief recommendation being to the cardinal that it is in the house. There, unless ill, he offers up mass daily. We had a long talk on politics; he was well up in all the questions of the day. He spoke highly of Lord Derby, and thought Mr. Disraeli had a great mind, and was a great man. He denounced the Fenians, and said no good Catholic would countenance them for a moment. Everything he said showed him to be tolerant and liberal minded—qualities rarely met with amongst the priesthood of Spain. At parting he gave us his cross to kiss, and blessed us, urging us to return for the Holy week, which, he said, every one should see once, for it is a grand sight, and offering us every facility to see it thoroughly if we would; but it was not a question of would, but could.

The house called La Casa de Pilatos was built by a gentleman named Ribera, in 1533, on his return from a pilgrimage to Jerusalem, and is supposed to be an exact copy of Pontius Pilate's house in that city. It is a perfect Moorish building, and the engraved work very beautiful. The *patio*, decidedly the handsomest portion of the whole, has not two arches around it of the same proportions; thus the marble columns that support them are irregularly placed, some being far apart, others close together. The chapel is entered from the *patio*. In it there is a large black cross, from where the "Stations of the Cross" are commenced, which lead up to the Cruz del Campo, about a mile and a half out of the town, close to the great aqueduct. The stations are still made by the people, but more especially at Easter. A grand staircase, the walls lined with azulejos, leads to rooms now turned into offices, but which formerly were copies of those in which Pilate lived. Against a well is a cock, with an iron grating before it. The garden is a perfect bed of weeds and rubbish, broken columns, broken statues; bits—heads, legs, and arms —lay about in all directions. A grotto—or rather what once was one—is called Susanna's grotto. The house is the property of the Duke of Medina Celi, and he has moved, to his palace in Madrid, many of the works of art which were formerly here.

At the Casa O'Lea is one large room, with Moorish work in it; it might be a stable (which Soult really did turn it into) or a barrack, for all there is to see in it; but the embroidered arches and lace-work around the walls is, as all of the same description—very beautiful.

The house in which Lord Holland lived, belonging to the Duke of Alba, has a great deal of Moorish work about it, but it is in a sadly dilapidated state. The gardens and the once fountains—now a desert, with ruin on all sides—show what the palace was, and what perhaps it might be if restored; but it is getting very nearly past the possibility of it. The *patios*, of which there are several, are very handsome, and the azulejos are ancient; but so little care seems taken of anything, that even they will soon cease to exist; for if one falls out it is kicked aside, without any thought of replacing it. The myrtles in the garden are quite trees; and the *padre* of the orange-trees is said to be 1100 years old. The stem is very large, but hollow. The tree was, however, when we saw it, laden with fruit.

The Marquis de Mantilla's house, as a specimen of a modern Spanish residence, is very good; it is extremely handsome. It has some pretty Moorish work about it—all modern, of course. It is within a door or two of La Cuna, the Foundling Hospital; it is a good institution, and in great request. There is a small door in the centre wall as you enter, with a kind of portico; on knocking, this is opened, and the poor little unknown is taken in without question or inquiry.

CHAPTER XII.

SEVILLE—*continued.*

THERE is a very large cannon foundry, and a copper foundry, here; both worth a visit. The former is a very extensive building; it belongs to the Government, and no cannons are made for exportation. There are some magnificent lions being cast, which are to adorn the Cortes at Madrid; they are as superior to those at the foot of the Nelson column as gold is to brass; they are made from cannons taken during the late war in Africa. The details are perfect; every hair is worked artistically. The artist is a Spanish sculptor. The copper foundry is at no great distance from the cannon foundry; the copper is brought from Rio Tinto, and made into caps and other articles required for guns. The building is not large. English vessels are used for making the explosive matter. Continuing along the Carmona Road, where these foundries are, by the old Moorish city walls, many portions of which are very perfect about here, we reach La Sangre, an enormous hospital, with a façade of 600 feet. It was erected in 1546. Notwithstanding its size, it is generally well tenanted. The *patio* is fine; the church, a handsome edifice, stands in it. There are some paintings here by Zurbaran.

Very nearly facing La Sangre, on the opposite side of the river, rise the sugarloaf-shaped chimneys of the pottery belonging to Mr. Pickman, once the famous Cartuja convent. To get to it you have to cross the bridge and drive through the suburb called the Triana, a populous portion of the town, the inhabitants being gypsies, bull-fighters, and any other class of a lower grade that may exist. A rough road soon brings you to the hospitable gates that lead to the wide spreading building, where the kind-hearted, generous Englishman, has formed a little world of his own around him. The long ranges of rooms, filled with pottery, are alone sufficient to show the immense business done here. In fact, Mr. Pickman supplies all Spain with earthenware. A new showroom, now nearly completed, is entered by two magnificently carved doors, 500 years old. There were two chapels to this convent; one is still retained as such, and mass is performed there on Sundays and festivals, when the family, and those employed on the premises, attend. In it is a beautifully-carved Virgin, and the stalls are magnificent. Only half of them, however, are there, the other half having been taken by the government, before the property was sold, for the cathedral at Cadiz. An Englishman lately offered Mr. Pickman 500*l*. for those in his chapel, which offer, it need hardly be said, he declined. On the stairs which lead round to the back of the upper portion of the altar, is a mark showing to what an enormous height the water rose in 1784. These water-marks are to be seen in many parts of Seville, where floodings are very frequent. Lately precautions have been taken to guard against them. The old chapel is used as a work-room; there is a rose window in it surrounded with some fine azulejos. The ceiling of the refectory is of carved cedar. What would the poor monks think—for they have all died off—if they could look down and see what their grand old convent was converted into? The prior's house and private garden prove him to have been a man of taste. In the latter stands a magnificent pipless-orange tree. The oranges and sweet lemons here are celebrated, and they well deserve their fame. The flavour of the sweet lemon is so very delicate that nothing should be eaten before them. The smell of the peel is like bergamot, and is very powerful; it is nice to place amongst wearing apparel. The groves and groves of these orange and lemon-trees occupy upwards of thirty acres, and is a sight worth seeing, when either laden with their rich-coloured fruit, or covered with their beautiful blossom.

Mr. Pickman purchased the whole property from the government immediately after it was sequestered, and he has resided there ever since 1839, honoured, esteemed, and loved by all. At first he employed English workmen only in the pottery, on account of the utter ignorance of the Spaniards, but very soon he found that drink was ruining one half and killing the other; so by degrees he introduced Spaniards, teaching them the business, till now, with the exception of his own family, he has none but Spaniards in the manufactory; their wages are high, and so they remain; some have been there five-and-twenty years. Of the produce of the pottery it is hardly necessary to say that it cannot compare with that produced in England; yet there were some Moorish-patterned jars that could not be matched in our country for richness of design and beauty of shape. Mr. Pickman sent two pairs to the International Exhibition held in Paris last year, and as they have been seen by all the world, very probably we may soon have their duplicates produced.

The most interesting excursion out of Seville is to the ruins of Italica. They are about six or seven miles distant, and on the same side of the river as the Cartuja; after passing the bad road through Triana, a good carriage-road takes you to within a few hundred yards of these ruins; but every one should make a point of getting down to walk before passing through the turnpike, as the toll is thirty-two reals, nearly seven shillings, and as the previous toll close to the town is eight reals, it is enough, without the exorbitant charge of the second.

There is interest attached to every step one takes: to be standing on the spot that gave birth to the great Emperors Trajan and Adrian is alone sufficient; but the whole history of this place is fraught with interest, and more especially to those who can visit it. The excavations made, for it has been treated simply as a quarry by the matter-of-fact Sevillians, have brought to light a great deal of sculpture, mosaic pavement, bits of mosaic, and many coins : these excavations are only made when material is wanted; there is no thought of digging for the hidden treasure. The arena, still perfect enough to mark its size, shows also the tiers of galleries as they existed, the entrance of the gladiators, and that for the wild beasts, also the place they were taken through from the arena when dead. It held 23,000 spectators. A marble tablet, hitched on to one of the old walls, records a visit from Queen Isabel II. on the 23rd of September, 1862.

The old guide, who looks eighty, though it will take twenty years more, according to his own reckoning, before he reaches that age, showed us his own dwelling, close on to the ruins; it was more curious, decidedly, if not so interesting as the grand old relics he guards. It is made of mud, which is plastered in amongst and against a few huge stones, one of which juts inwardly and forms his pillow; a long flat stone, over which he threw a piece of matting, being his bed; his covering a manta, that is, a sort of coarse scarf worn by the peasants as a cloak. There was no window, a low door; the roof, cane, inside black from smoke; a hole in the ground, his kitchen fire; a wooden table and a broken chair, his furniture; three spoons and a knife, pushed into the cane roof, his plate; a brown earthenware dish, his crockery. He had, however, a good supply of arms and ammunition, and a couple of dogs. He had a wife, but she was ill, and so was down in the village being looked after. No wonder the poor woman moved her quarters, if here her pillow was of stone, and her bed the same. The man said he slept little—a fact not likely to create surprise. He had meat for dinner once a week, fish and vegetables on other days.

On our way back we stopped at the fine old convent of San Isidoro, close to the village of Santiponze. It was built in 1301 by Alonso Perez de Guzman, who is distinguished in history for his defence of Tarifa, and which cost him his boy's life, which event, according to tradition, he thought little of, having saved the town from the Moors. The Guzman's family house is still in existence in the Plaza del Duque at Seville. The convent of San Isidoro was destroyed by Soult and turned into a prison, but is now once again a convent with 230 nuns in it. The chapel, and all near and about it, tell of devastation and destruction. There are two fine images of San Isidoro and San Geronimo by Montañes. The tombs and effigies of Guzman and his wife are near the high altar. There is also the tomb and effigy of Uraca Osorio. It is related of this poor woman that she was condemned to be burnt to death because she refused to listen to the addresses of Don Pedro el Cruel, and that she was to be exposed to the fire uncovered; her maid, Leonora Davalos, seeing her mistress suffering from modesty more than from the flames, sprang towards her and concealed her by her own person, and thus they perished together, and now lie in the tomb side by side.

Continuing along the Badajoz road towards Seville till it divides, and by taking the narrower one to the right, you reach Castilleja by an easy winding ascent, for the little town is situated on the summit of the low range of hills which skirt Seville on this side. Castilleja is celebrated as the place where Fernan Cortes, on the 2nd December, 1547, died. The house this event took place in has been bought by the Duke de Montpensier, and by him converted into a pretty Moorish-looking summer palace. The room Cortes died in is filled with pictures relating to his great deeds in Mexico, and sadly blended with those of the ill-fated Maximilian, whose portrait on a gold medal hangs against the wall. The room also contains a very fine ivory crucifix, and in consequence claims the privilege of being entered by visitors "uncovered." The remainder of the house is most comfortably and prettily furnished, with a great deal of English taste, and many English things. From the tower the view over the country is very fine. Cortes was buried at first at the convent of San Isidoro, but his remains were afterwards taken to Mexico, where they were left in peace till 1823, when they were once again moved, but where to does not seem to be clearly known.

The only other excursion is to San Juan de Alfarache. The view from the heights of the still existing Moorish wall fronting the convent is very fine. Seville looks better from here than from any other point, and the winding river adds considerably to the beauty of the scene. Sunset is the right moment for this view. Little of interest now remains in the ruined convent; the chapel has a *retablo* by Zurbaran, and the christening font is curious; in the time of the Moors it was a drinking place for horses—the excavation for the horse's neck is there in the centre of the font; a natural spring used to fill it. The story told is, that every Holy Thursday this font was miraculously supplied with water, being probably turned on for the occasion; but, any way, it has given up the practice. The twin wells in the *patio*, with their healing properties, still draw many of the sick and suffering to test their efficacy. One priest alone resides here now; he is paid by government, his parishioners being neither rich nor numerous.

In the village is a large licorice manufactory; to those who care for such sights it is a curiosity, as the licorice may be seen in all its stages, from the raw root to the thick hard substance, packed in wooden cases ready for exportation. They manufacture thirty *arrobas* a day. An arroba is twenty-five pounds. Only the scrapings are made up into sticks here, and so the sticks sold in Spain are not so good, nor are they considered the best licorice. The process it goes through after cooking is very much like the trituration of the olive. It is sent by river to Cadiz, and from there anywhere and everywhere. There is a scent manufactory and a pottery in the village.

There are a great many olive farms about here, some of them on a very extensive scale, and producing enormous crops. Almost in all the olive woods the licorice grows, and the produce of ten acres is considered worth 100*l.* a year; it grows uncultivated. The olives are the large green eating olive, the size of walnuts, and the small black olive, used chiefly for oil, though they, too, are sometimes eaten.

There is no doubt Seville should be seen in spring, that is, at Easter, when the *Feria*, a sight that cannot be seen elsewhere in the same perfection, and the bull-fights, and every description of gaiety, gives a bright holiday look to everything. The Plaza de Toros is a large building, and can hold 13,000 spectators; the bull-fights go on during the whole summer. But Christmas is not a bad season to spend here; the town is gay with turkeys, which stand in flocks at various points of the town for sale: every one has a turkey for dinner on Christmas Day. There is also a fair held for about ten days on the banks of the river, near the bridge, where stalls and stalls sell nothing but sweetmeat made with almonds: there are also plenty of toys, and very noisy ones, especially the *zambomba*, which is a flower-pot with a piece of parchment stretched over the top and a piece of cane running through it in the centre; the children wet their hands and draw the cane through their fingers: the noise is awful. There is no wintry look in any part of Andalucia during the early winter, or till the end of January; for, besides the evergreens, which abound, the leaves do not fall from the trees till the middle of January; the consequence is spring is very late, and when trees will be in leaf in the south of France, in the south of Spain they will not show a symptom of them.

The Paséo de las Delicias is a beautiful sight on Christmas Day. It is the drive of Seville, and all the world comes here in gala dress; the road is filled with carriages and riders, and the paths at either side with pedestrians. Mules are generally used in carriages. The Duke de Montpensier and the Infanta, with their son and daughters, are always amongst the crowd; they are much liked, and always receive a sincere welcome. But it is amongst those who are walking that to the foreigner the most amusement is to be found—to see the ladies, their long dresses raising such clouds of dust, that one must be partially choked, their restless fans sometimes sheltering their bright eyes from the sun, sometimes conveying more meaning than their words, but rarely fanning themselves; the graceful mantilla, which on these occasions is usually of lace only, and therefore shows the whole figure, is all so unique and charming, that one never wearies of sitting here and watching them. They have summer fans and winter fans, morning fans, and evening fans;

you rarely see a lady use the same two days running. In the evening the theatre, the Teatro Real de San Fernando, is full; on Sundays and festivals the people dress a little more: as a rule, only morning dress is worn. This is the principal, and may be called the only theatre. Italian operas are given on alternate nights. It is open all the year round. Most of the residents have their private box, which they take like an empty house and furnish according to their fancy; this gives an odd look to it, some being fitted up one way, and some another. All is open as in the dress circle of an English theatre, only with low divisions, so the interior is plainly seen. The house is large, well ventilated, well lighted, and extremely clean; the decorations are white and gold; the boxes have an open-work balcony in front of them so that the ladies' entire dresses are seen, which gives a gay appearance to the house. The stalls occupy the entire body of the house; there is no pit at all.

Besides this theatre there are two places where the Andalucian dances are given, but these are nothing more than large rooms, dirty, and ill-lighted; the men and women who perform dance in the centre, the spectators, never very numerous, and always composed of foreigners and the lower class of Spaniards, line the room. The dancers are heavy and ungraceful; one alone did we see that had any pretensions to be called a dancer; then the castanettes or clapping of hands, one of which is always used as an accompaniment, is so noisy and so very unmusical, that, except out of curiosity, no one would dream of going to these places. There were between eighteen and twenty dances with different names, and they seemed very nearly their only distinction. The orchestra consisted of a guitar and a violin. These dances are best seen during the Carnival and La Feria; the dresses are fresh then, and the whole thing is on a better scale.

Seville is a very clean town; the streets are, as a rule, narrow, for the sake of shade; some of the new Plazas, however, render the houses so exposed that, however agreeable in winter, in summer the heat must be unbearable. Every house, even the very meanest, has a *patio*, varying in size and beauty of decoration according to its importance. The door is always open into the entrance-hall, then a light open-worked iron gate admits to the *patio;* this gate is of course closed. They are extremely pretty all over Seville; some of the designs are beautiful. The lower rooms all open on to the *patio*, which has usually a fountain in the centre, and flowers; around, beneath the gallery, sometimes pictures are hung. This portion of the house is occupied in summer, in winter the entire furniture is removed to the upper floors; thus the people convert one house into two residences. The hall or outer door is usually ornamented with large bronze nails; some of the ancient ones are very handsome, especially those on the doors of public buildings. The shops are very oriental in their bazaar-like appearance, having no windows and being entirely open; a marble pillar is usually in the centre, against which the large doors are closed when the shop is shut. The pavement of the streets is quite in a position to bear improvement: it is impossible to understand how the horses keep their feet in some places. In some of the streets they have put the large flat stone common in Italian towns; but on these they slip instead of stumble. In the old parts of the town the carriages nearly scrape the walls. This is especially the case about the Juderia, or Jews' quarters. Here there is a sort of fair held every Thursday, it is called "Of Antiquities;" but it would be more properly termed a Rag Fair, as these antiquities consist of rusty locks, keys, fire-irons, hats, boots, chestnuts, and cotton goods. Yet in the early part of the day the place is thronged; some quaint things may, perhaps, occasionally be picked up, but we saw nothing, and felt rather injured at having been induced to waste half a day in going there, for we were long before our coachman could find out this Feria.

These narrow streets are extremely good for setting off processions, of which there are so many in superstitious Spain; they are usually so poor that in a wide street their banners and candles, few in number and mean in appearance, would look ridiculous. Dogs, cats, and watchmen are a nuisance in Seville. The former abound, looking half-starved, and apparently belonging to no one, but always fighting. The cats are often to be seen in churches, frequently springing through the iron gates and across the altars. The watchmen are worse in Seville than anywhere else; they shout out, " *Ave Maria Purissima, las diez* " (or whatever the time may be) " *han dado* " every hour and half hour, from ten at night till six in the morning. This is extremely annoying, for if it happens to be beneath your window, it must awake you; and they manage so that once or twice during the night no one shall escape hearing them. Beggars are also very trying; they waylay you at every corner, and frequently exhibit some fearful malformation, that sometimes one will give, to be delivered from the sight; but this is an extremely unwise plan, as you are sure to be seen, and in a few minutes you are surrounded by them. Blindness and diseases of the eye are very common in and around Seville amongst all classes.

Cock-fighting is a favourite sport amongst the inhabitants of Triana, where a Sunday or feast-day never passes without this cruel amusement going on in the centre of the street. This Triana is thought to be the artist's paradise; and we doubt much if any one after seeing it would dispute it with them; dirt on canvas may be very picturesque, but dirt in nature is most repulsive. Those groups, sitting on the pavement outside of their houses—mothers with curly-headed, black-eyed, brown-skinned, half-naked urchins, busy in removing what is easily imagined by the diligence with which the duty is being performed; young girls, half-lying, half-sitting on the ground, doing some lazy kind of work; men, in their short embroidered trousers, leather gaiters, red sashes, velvet coats, and quaintly shaped hats, are charming when painted, but when seen in all their living dirt, they become so repulsive that the picturesque is all lost, and what is disgusting alone visible.

As the cock-fighting is especially for the lowest class, so is the "Sociedad Filarmonica" for the highest; it is peculiarly select, and strict rules maintained as regards those admitted. The Infanta and family are always present; the performance is by amateurs, and, though not perfect, is extremely good. Concerts are given about once a month, from October to May. It is a pleasant place for meeting friends, and talking is carried on with lips and eyes and fans; and the beauty of Seville is seen here better than anywhere else. Evening dress is *de rigueur*, which it is not at the Opera. Small réunions also take place in the winter, when dancing is in the open air. We were present at one of these entertainments on the day after Christmas Day, given at a little country house at the end of the Paséo de las Delicias. It was a pretty sight and very novel; the ladies all wore lace mantillas and thin light dresses; their fans sheltered them from the sun, for there was no awning; it was a magnificent day, but too hot till about four, when it became delightful—there was every kind of refreshment and wines. The "Villa Nueva," or "Vino de la Tierra," is a delicious rich sweet wine, something like Tent, though it is nothing but the wine made in the neighbourhood of Villa Nueva, from whence it derives its name, and is very cheap. We were told it would not bear exporting.

English service is performed in a room in the house of the British Consul, Mr. Williams, who is a Roman Catholic married to a Spaniard, and is half a Spaniard himself, his mother having been Spanish, and he born and bred here. Thus every sort of difficulty is raised, and it has frequently happened that no service has taken place at all; amongst other trifling annoyances, singing is not permitted. The Rev. L. Tugwell is now doing duty there, but it is a hard task; he has much to contend against, and no means to do it with. There are 300 Spanish Protestants in Seville, but there is no toleration for them; the government hardly permits business residents to be of any persuasion but their own; or if they are, they find they must cease their occupation. There are many English families amongst the working class; but they have all been received into the Church of Rome. There is an English priest here, whose labour of love it is to make smooth the rough path of the Protestant till he is a Romanist; then he passes on and goes and does the same charitable deed for the next. Many debts are paid for heretics that the papist may pay for himself.

Mr. Williams's father, who is still living, but resides

out of Seville, was celebrated for his fine collection of pictures, china, and antiquities; almost all are now dispersed, the principal part having been sold.

Many anecdotes are related here by old residents of the eccentricities of the late Mr. Richard Ford. We will repeat a harmless one, which, however, proves him to have been peculiar in some of his ways. He one day issued invitations for a dinner to the leading people of Seville, amongst them the Captain-General of the Province. On their sitting down to table they found the entire dinner was served up in the great, heavy, coarse earthenware dishes made in Triana; hideous to look at, and enough to prevent any one eating the most tasty dishes off them; they have to be seen really to be understood. Mr. Ford's guests were naturally extremely indignant, and considered they had received an insult not easy to forgive.

The Barber of Seville's house still stands, but it is no longer a barber's shop; a tailor has got possession of the celebrated premises, but there are plenty of "Barbers of Seville" to be seen.

CHAPTER XIII.

JEREZ DE LA FRONTERA.—SHERRY.

From Seville to Jerez de la Frontera (it is called de la Frontera, because there is another Jerez to the north-west) is three hours over an uninteresting country, and as usual the trains start at inconvenient times. A closed carriage, except private ones, are not to be found in this town; the carriages used are waggonettes, with a water-proof covering over the top and sides, clean and roomy, and pleasant enough if it does not blow and does not rain and is not cold. The best hotel is the Fonda de Jerez; the rooms are good and nicely furnished, but all the rest is very bad; cooking bad, attendance worse, everything done without system or order; gas burnt that gave no light and sent forth instead such an atrocious smell, that one wished it had never seen the inside of the house. Outside the atmosphere was very warm and heavy, but inside the house it was like a well: we tried a *brasero*, but were compelled to send it away; the horrid smell rendered cold preferable to such heat. We asked for a warming pan, the sheets seeming to be rather damp; they did not own one, so they brought us a wine bottle with hot water in it as a substitute.

Jerez is an extremely clean town, very white-looking from the white-washed houses; the streets are tolerably well paved, and not so narrow as in most purely Spanish towns; almost all being traversable with a carriage. The watchmen are a wonderful improvement on Seville; instead of shouting out the "*Ave*" and time, they simply whistle it in a soft melodious tone, a whistle for each hour, quite loud enough to hear it if you are awake, but not sufficient to awake you.

Jerez stands amidst undulating lands, covered with the famous vines producing the sherry grape. The wine vaults are of course what people go to see at Jerez; amongst the largest and finest are those belonging to Señors Gonzalez, Domeck, and Garvey;* but in visiting one *bodega* you see all. The forests of casks, numbered according to their flavour, value, and age, are alike in each of them, as is the courtesy and hospitality proffered by their owners. The way the wine is made is very interesting to learn; when out of the vaults we tasted the famous Pedro Jimenez, a wine hardly known in England; it is made from the muscat sherry grape, and is more of a liqueur than wine.

A visit to the vineyards in winter is utter waste of time, as it neither gratifies nor edifies, the buildings being deserted, and the vines black-looking, leafless roots.

* This latter gentleman is an Irishman.

It is better to spend one's time in seeing all that is left of the once famous Cartuja Convent, though now little but memories of the past is left to create enthusiasm. Here, as elsewhere in Spain, the churches are fine and their decorations showy, from the mass of gilding there always is lavished in every available part of them. The exterior of San Miguel is very fine. The Alcazar is Moorish and interesting; there are one or two other specimens of Moorish work, that have fortunately been permitted to remain, without their entire beauty being effaced with that eternal whitewashing, which is always going on all over Spain. The Spaniards have certainly been sadly maligned in being called dirty; in one respect only is the accusation true; and that results from an utter disregard to the use of combs and brushes. This of course only applies to the very lowest classes.

CHAPTER XIV.

CADIZ.

FROM Jerez to Cadiz is two hours; the road is interesting enough. The first station is Puerta Santa Maria, on the Bay of Cadiz; it is the principal port from whence the wine is exported, and here there are, as at Jerez, very large *bodegas*. A little further on is the place where Lord Essex landed in 1596. The last station is San Fernando. Salt is made here in enormous quantities; the pyramids of it that cover the ground on all sides, make the place look like a large camp: the process is very simple, narrow canals are cut in lines from the sea, and the water is allowed to evaporate. When the evaporation first begins the much appreciated fish, called Lissa, is caught, and then they are much more delicate than when taken in the open sea; crabs are also caught in these canals, a small kind, but very nice. Cadiz is about six or seven miles further on.

Cadiz is built on a peninsula, and seems as if it rose out of the sea. The pure white look of the town, with the deep blue setting around it and above it, renders it extremely pretty from a little distance; the innumerable towers (almost every house has one) add very much to its picturesque appearance. The streets are very clean, well paved, and wide enough for carriages. It is famous for guitars, gloves, prawns, and cream; the latter like Devonshire cream, but made from goat's milk. No other milk is to be had as a rule in all Spain. The prawns are from seven to eight inches long; their flavour is not so good as the smaller ones, which are sold here as shrimps. No one should omit to send to the Pescaderia, to the "Casa del freidor" for the Pescadillo; it is pieces of fish cooked, and easily warmed up, without soddening or in any way being spoilt: it is most delicious, and quite a thing of Cadiz. The Fish-Market is a disgusting sight, and enough to prevent one eating fish to see it. There is a fish, called here the Choco, an iron-grey scaleless fish, with a round body and numerous snake-like legs. By some it is called Calamar; it is disgusting to look at, but is thought much of in Andalucia. It is very plentiful, and tastes something like lobster. Every thing is good that is caught here, hence the most obnoxious looking things are eaten. Nothing but rain-water is to be had; but you get it filtered for drinking if you ask for it; it has a brackish, disagreeable taste if it is not, and then not wholesome. It is frequently so scarce that it has to be bought; it is then brought from Puerta Santa Maria, and sold at one real the *arroba*. There is an English company now in

Cadiz, endeavouring to enter on an agreement for supplying the town with spring water; it is proposed to bring it from Santa Maria by an aqueduct. When there is a water famine, such houses as have tanks are compelled to give a certain quantity from their store to the poor of the town.

The vegetable market is very fine. In the middle of January we saw new potatoes, green peas, bananas, and pines in abundance. The radishes are a sight from their great size—they are twelve and fourteen inches long; turnips like beet root in size, but very delicately flavoured, are much eaten here, so is the oak-apple. Partridges, plovers, quail, woodcock, and hares in quantities, and all very moderate in price, but they don't understand cooking them. The shops are very good, especially the silversmiths; the Calle Ancha is considered the best street for shops, but the Calle San Francisco is the Oxford Street of Cadiz. The hotels are vile. We were at La Vista Alegre; and the Vista was the only Alegre thing about it; it was dreadfully wanting in common necessaries, marble floors without carpets or matting; a palace of a house, but nothing in it, not even food. It was here General Solano was killed in 1811. He was Captain-General of Andalucia; the recesses in which he hid himself, now converted into cupboards, are still shown. He attempted to make his escape by the roof, but a ball struck him down and killed him. Beggars are fewer and less importunate than at Seville; here they wear a badge, showing themselves licensed to beg; if they do not wear this, a word sends them off.

The sights of Cadiz are limited. The cathedral, La Nueva, so called to distinguish it from La Vieja, is a very handsome massive building—too massive; the pillars are formed by eight marble columns grouped into one. The *coro* has the beautiful carved stalls taken from the Cartuja at Seville. In the *sacristia* is a "Conception," said to be by Murillo; but M. Blasco, a very good authority, told us that it was by Clemente de Torres, born in Cadiz in 1665, a pupil of Valdes Leal.

Beneath the chapel del Rosario is a vaulted chapel, where penitents go three times a week to pray and do penance; they used formerly to inflict on themselves corporeal punishment; the disciplines were provided by the church. This practice has very lately been given up. Men only are admitted, even to see the chapel, but with silver keys, and being accompanied by one having both power and influence, we were allowed to enter—not that it really repaid one the trouble. The altar has a finely carved "Calvary" over it. At the opposite end of the church is the seat of the priest, who presides during the performance of penances.

At the Capuchinos' convent of San Francisco, occupied by Lord Essex in 1596, and now converted into a lunatic asylum, is Murillo's celebrated picture of "Santa Catalina"—the marriage of St. Catherine. Apart from the exquisite beauty of the painting, a sad interest is attached to it, as being the last he ever painted, and the cause of his death. He was on a scaffolding working at it over the altar, where it still remains, and stepping back a little to contemplate what he had just done, he lost his balance and fell on the marble pavement within the altar rails; he was carried home to Seville, and died very shortly after. This picture, not quite completed, was, however, so far near it, that none ever dared put a brush to it; whilst the subjects around it—separate pictures, but forming a sort of frame to it—and which are together so large that they entirely cover the wall, were finished by his pupil, Meneses. The subjects are, "San Francisco," and the "Guardian Angel" on the right side; above it the "Eternal Father," and on the left, Michael the Archangel, and St. Joseph leading the Saviour by the hand. In a side chapel is San Francisco receiving the Stigmata; it is by Murillo, but there is no light at all to see it by. There is also a "Conception" by him—very beautiful. Opposite to it is a portrait of a "Principal of the Capucines," by Vandyke. In the centre aisle is a very fine "Mater Dolorosa," by Zurbaran. This church is by far the most interesting object in all Cadiz.

The Museum ranks next, but falls terribly short of it. There is only one Murillo here, an "Ecce Homo," but very fine. There is a good copy of his "Virgin de la Faja," by Tovar. The Saviour is seated on the Virgin's lap, distributing small loaves of bread to the venerable doctors. The original belongs to the Duke de Montpensier. A grand "San Bruno," by Zurbaran. A head by Alonso Cano. A very fine "Crucifixion," by Montañes. "Michael the Archangel," by Rubens, and a "Last Judgment," by Michael Angelo, but not a pleasant picture at all. Most of the other pictures are modern; one a very pretty landscape, by Belmonte. Two represent the fall of Murillo at the Capuchinos.

Señor Blasco, 17, Calle Jardanille, has a small collection of good pictures; the finest is by Murillo, of the Infant Jesus lying asleep, his left hand resting on a skull, and his right doubled in, as children are apt to place it; three angels are looking down at him, raising a curtain to do so: it is a lovely picture. The child asleep is perfect. Señor Blasco obtained it from a relative who was superior at a convent which was suppressed. He asks 2,000*l.* for it. He told us he was then in treaty with the authorities of the Kensington Museum, who wished to purchase it.[*] There is a fine old work by Zurbaran; a head by Velazquez, and two "bocetas"—original sketches; one by Murillo, of a lamb, the wool of which one fancies one might bury one's hand in; and the other by Velazquez, of his famous picture in the Madrid Gallery, of "Las Meninas." There is a head by Goya; a Jan Steen,

---

[*] Señor Blasco is now in London, and has brought this painting with him; it may be seen at his residence.

and a few others, more valuable perhaps than pleasing; but it is, for a private collection, a very fair one. All, or any of them, are for sale.

At the Hospital for Women, in the Calle del Hospital de Mugeres, is a very fine *patio*, and a singularly handsome staircase; the latter is built like an open plait, four flights of stairs branching off from the first landing, and again four above that; the arches entwining themselves cross ways above. This hospital is one of the finest institutions in Cadiz; it is entirely supported by voluntary contributions, which, judging by the manner it is kept, cannot be small. Nothing can exceed the neatness and cleanliness. The dormitories are large and airy; the beds well apart; the sitting-up rooms supplied with all comforts; the kitchen a perfect sight for such a country, and indeed could not be better anywhere; a nice little garden, bright with flowers; and the *patio*, with fine banana-trees, the broad green leaves always affording a cheery lookout for the poor sick and suffering ones within.

There is but one theatre here of any pretensions, or that is at all frequented by the Gaditanos, and that is El Principal. It is open the whole year round, in winter for the residents, and in summer for the visitors, who flock here in numbers for sea bathing and sea breezes. It is the first theatre that was built in Spain; and though in appearance and size it cannot vie with that of Seville, in point of performances it greatly excels it. The sisters Marchissio and Emma Lagrua, star it here, and certainly well deserve the praise and applause accorded them. Bottessini leads the orchestra, which is first-rate. A little romance is attached to him as the husband of a lady known as La Florentina on the stage, daughter of the late, and sister of the present English consul at Seville. At the minor theatre El Balon—something between a circus and a theatre, and where they frequently have dancing—the *people* only are ever seen.

The cemetery lies at some little distance, close to the church of San José, which looks from afar like a miniature St. Paul's. Within the church there is little to admire, but outside it looks very imposing; the Plaza de Toros and the prison are passed on the road to San José. Close by here is also the plot of ground where English and other heretics are buried. The first person ever laid here was the late consul's mother. At the church of San Felipe Neri, a small plain building, is where the Cortes sat during the War of Independence. There is a " Conception " here by Murillo, and a " Padre Eterno " by Clemente Torres. Near here is a bureau for the sale of indulgences, as there is in most of the principal towns of Spain.

There is no English chaplain. Mr. Dunlop, the consul, reads the service every Sunday morning at half-past ten in his own house in the Calle Ahumada, near to the Alameda. There are plenty of protesting Spaniards, but they dare not admit their disbelief in the practices of the Romish church. In almost all the churches are English clocks—those old-fashioned hall or kitchen clocks—upright square columns.

At the pretty little town of Rota in the Bay of Cadiz, the Tent wine is made that is used in our church—a rich sweet dark red wine—called here Tintillo de Rota. The grapes grow on the sloping hills around the town. 70,000 butts of sherry were exported from Cadiz during the year 1867; the grapes producing it grown almost within sight of Cadiz; each butt paying at the lowest 30*l*. The Vino del Campo de Cariñena is extremely nice, and it may be had at six reals the bottle. Señor Moreno de Mora, the owner of extensive vineyards at Jerez, and whose *bodejas* at Santa Maria are worth seeing, if none have been visited at Jerez, has one of the handsomest houses in Cadiz. It is built, furnished, and decorated from materials brought entirely from Paris or London. The cost of it was immense. The house door alone, of rosewood, made in England, cost 300*l*., and all other things are in proportion. It is more like a palace than a private gentleman's house. He has a relative that for forty years has been subject to sleeps, lasting sometimes two or three days, and sometimes five and six weeks. They cannot be called trances, for she eats and drinks during this strange state, merely opening her mouth as a sign. When she awakes she is utterly unconscious of anything that has happened, or how long she has been sleeping. She is generally aware when the attack is coming on, by a sensation of uneasiness all over her. Nothing has ever done her the least good, though the best doctors of France and England have seen her, and tried every sort of remedy. She is now 72 years of age.

We ascended the Torre Tavira one bright sunny afternoon; it is the signal tower, and the best to obtain a good view from. From here one sees how very nearly an island Cadiz is; the narrowest sandy strips of land joining it to the continent. The roofs of the houses are mostly flat, and all dazzlingly white. The towers somewhat relieve the monotony of the buildings.

The climate is not always agreeable; the hot damp winds are terribly depressing, and headache-giving. On these steamy days everything is moist, inside the houses as well as out; water trickles down the walls; one's very clothes become damp; and during the time the atmosphere is like this, the sky is dull and the sun does·not shine. It resembles a Turkish bath more than anything else, and is quite as unpleasant and enervating.

CHAPTER XV.

GIBRALTAR.

To leave Cadiz, except by sea, is a very difficult matter, the trains starting at 5 a.m. for any place beyond Jerez, and then they do not go further than Cordova; hence most people are driven to choose the water, and if the weather happens to be as we had it, the sea like a river, a cloudless sky and a hot sun, the trip is most enjoyable. We were bound for Gibraltar, and though we afterwards learnt we might have gone by land, sleeping two nights on the road, and roughing it a little, we were told at the time that it was impossible; the roads were impassable by a carriage, and mules were uncertain; there were no inns, and plenty of robbers. However, there is no doubt the sea journey is the easiest, the quickest, by far the least expensive, and the scenery is magnificent.

We were on board the "Adriano," a clean boat, with an extremely courteous captain, by 7·20 a.m.; she was advertised to sail punctually at 7·30, but we did not get under way till a few minutes past 8. As we rounded the town, it stood out like a mass of frosted silver in the rising sun-light, till, as we steamed along and left it in the distance, it looked like a mass of white ruins rising up from the sea. Soon we lost sight of it, then passing Torre Gorda, Isla de Leon, the Castle of Santi Petri, we saw the town of Medina Sidonia lying back on the side of a mountain, and Chiclana, which we did not see, as it was buried in a valley to the left, the scene of the murder of poor Blanche of Bourbon, the unhappy queen of Pedro the Cruel. Then Barrosa appears, so famous in the war of 1811, quickly to be succeeded by Conil, with its quaint-looking windmills, till at length we round the point and enter those waters so celebrated, and the very name of which must arouse enthusiasm in the breast of the most apathetic Englishman. We are now on the very spot where the battle of Trafalgar was fought, where, on the 21st of October, 1805, Nelson won the great victory that cost him his life. The battle took place on the Cadiz or western side of the bay; at the point of land which juts farthest into the sea, stands a lighthouse, nothing else marks the spot; the sandy coast would hardly permit of any monument, if even the Spaniards would, but it requires none; it is a hallowed spot, and one that is marked indelibly in the heart of every man, woman, and child, that claims to be a British subject.

The great rush of water in the Straits, the calm sea, and the breeze there was, being in our favour, contributed altogether to send us rapidly onwards, and we soon saw Vejer on the hill, and Bolonia on the coast;

then we passed the ruins of Belon, till rounding the point we saw Tarifa in the distance, and the grand panorama of the African coast stretching so far across the Straits, that it seemed from this spot as if no sea lay between the two continents. Apes' Hill, the highest point of this African range, gradually however receded as we approached, and as we neared Tarifa, twelve miles of water separated us from the empire of Morocco.

At Tarifa we landed passengers, and took in some. The large barrack-looking building, which stands out as about the only decent house in the town, is where Guzman *el Bueno* (?) allowed his child to be murdered, this patriot preferring his boy's death to surrendering Tarifa, which every one else had refused to hold, but which he volunteered to do for one year. This Guzman, who is buried at San Isidoro, near Italica, is said to be an ancestor of the Empress Eugénie. The women of Tarifa are eastern enough to wear their faces covered over when in the streets, their eyes, or rather only one, being visible.

From Tarifa to Cabrita, which is the western point of the bay of Gib, the range of hills is covered with aloes and cactus; the former is used for making a material from the fibre which is taken from beneath the outer skin of the leaf, and the latter is grown for the prickly pear, which the people eat; it is grown without the least labour or trouble, so that it thoroughly suits the taste of the Spaniards, who find most things good that are had so easily. Now the grand old Rock rising like a giant from the sea stands before us: its very look seems to forbid progress if the faintest excuse rendered it necessary. It is seen better when the bay is entered, for then you have it from beginning to end, from south to north, wholly before you. The town is principally built at the northern end, though it stretches in straggling houses right across the base. The steamer had to land passengers at Algeciras before we ourselves landed; this occupied fully half an hour, so before we put our foot on land we had been nine hours on board, and we only just got in before gun-fire, which was then at 5·45 p.m., and after that neither love nor money will gain admittance through the closed gates, so that it was with a little anxiety we watched our progress across the bay from Algeciras. Both the embarking at Cadiz and the landing at Gib have to be done in small boats, but it is a matter of no difficulty or even inconvenience, and the distance is short. All along the coast of Spain the same plan is necessary.

It is difficult to describe our impressions on landing here after three months' travelling in Spain: it seemed as if by some magic we had been transported to Dover (always excepting the climate), the British flag flying at all points, the English soldier, the English sailor, the streets well paved, and of an ordinary breadth; the English-built houses, with the English sash-windows; all was such a wonderful change from Spain and its customs and people, it was difficult to realize the fact, that though on British territory we were not in old England.

The Club House Hotel was full, Griffith's was being painted, the Hotel Espagnol was full, so we were compelled to put up at the Hotel de Paris, of which report spoke ill, but which we found no reason to complain of, excepting in the way of dirt, and that surpassed all we had ever met anywhere in our travels over Europe; but we were told the hotels were alike in this respect, the Club House being as bad as any. We had very good rooms, and extremely good living, the roast beef and steaks being better than what we have frequently had in London. Everything in the house, from the poker and tongs to the red-moreen and white (?) muslin curtains that adorned our sitting-room windows, was purely British, the pride of the Gib-ites being that they have not a plate or cup and saucer that does not come from their own mother country. English is spoken in all the shops, though generally with a slight accent. Irish outside-cars and old-fashioned high cabs ply for hire; there is no fixed tariff, but they are not unreasonable, though it is best to inquire what the charge will be. One Hansom cab, drawn by a mule, adorns the Rock. Every English comfort may be had here; it seems surprising that it does not become a winter station for invalids, it is not more difficult of access than Malaga, and has advantages it is impossible to find there, or elsewhere in a really warm climate;

there are English doctors, English chemists, a delicious climate, and one has but to look at the swarms of chubby-faced children to feel assured it cannot be very unhealthy ; and the least healthy season is in the summer, when invalids would not be here. The "Garrison Library" is one of the finest of the kind in existence, every periodical is taken in, and every book is in it that any one can want or require. Plenty of gaiety for those who like it; a pack of hounds, a theatre, concerts, balls, and dinners, always something going on, and a post daily overland, no small advantage to many, and all the while surrounded by English comforts and English friends. Foreigners are not allowed to reside on the Rock even for twenty-four hours, without obtaining a guarantee from some one, but there is not the slightest difficulty in this surety being got if the person is respectable.

To Europa Point is a charming drive; facing you is Ceuta, a large town on the African coast, now belonging to Spain; turning the point of the Rock to the east, the Bay of Granada is before you, and the blue rocky mountains bordering the Spanish coast up to Mijas. The governor has his summer residence here, or Cottage, as it is called, a low spreading house, which, from its being due east, with the perpendicular rock at its back, must be cool enough. From Europa Point to the "Lines" is three miles, and the Rock is only double that in circumference; the highest point is between 1400 and 1500 feet. Looking at it from the bay, the outline at the summit is like a Gulliver lying asleep with his knees drawn up; the silouhette of the face is very perfect. The "Lines" are on the north side of the Rock, and on a level piece of land which looks as if the Rock must have once been an island. The English sentry boxes are placed across from the bay to the Mediterranean, they are painted dark, whilst the Spanish are white, and they are placed much closer together than ours. Between the two is a strip of land called the Neutral Ground, and neither the Spanish nor English soldiers if in uniform cross it; it is "Nobody's." The cemetery is at the base of the rock, close to the Lines, and outside its wall are many flat stones placed any way, and all ways, with Arabic inscriptions; these are the graves of Moors that died at Gib. Here also is the cricket ground and racecourse, and reviews take place, and the men are exercised here. It is, in fact, the only level piece of ground sufficiently extensive for such purposes, though the place called "The Flats," at the opposite end, at Europa Point, is sometimes used for manœuvres.

Up to the Signal Tower is a delightful ride or walk; the Rock is a mass of verdure on this, the western, side; you ascend by a tolerable road with wild flowers growing in thick profusion all around. At the summit the view is magnificent at every point. Though we looked long and patiently, we failed to see even one monkey, there are but very few now remaining, though none are ever killed; they are extremely timid, and have only to see a shadow for them to make a hasty retreat. Returning we stopped midway to visit the Galleries; they are a wonderful sight; blasted out of the solid rock they run round the perpendicular sides, causing them to be alive with cannon, which peep out tier above tier all along. There are two large excavations, called "Cornwallis's Hall," and "St. George's Hall;" in the latter it is said Lord Nelson was entertained; the only drawback to this being a fact is, that the hall was not made till after the great hero's death, and that it was still being blasted at the time of the siege of Gibraltar. On the queen's birthday all these guns are fired, the salute beginning at the signal station (where in the morning and at sunset the gun is fired daily), then it continues gradually downwards, from the upper galleries to Willis's battery, when the troops finish it off. The Moorish tower here, forming a sort of entrance to these galleries, is said to be one of the oldest in Spain; it is kept merely as a relic, no use being made of it.

To Catalan's Bay is a very nice walk if the wind is not too high; you go round by the north front, keeping at the base of the rock till a foot-path leads round to the east side. Here all is barren and the rock almost perpendicular. About a quarter of a mile over a heavy road, a mule track, brought us to Catalan's Bay; a few houses occupied by artillerymen nestle beneath the shelter of the rock; they are built on sand, though some feet above the level of the sea. There is a little

Roman Catholic chapel, but no place of worship for protestants. One woman told us there was no use in going there, as she "could not understand the gentleman, but there was nowhere else for them."

About three miles on the other side of the Lines, driving along the hard sands, bordering the bay, we come to a neat little village as much English as Spanish, called Campamento, and then turning inland to the north, two miles further on we reach San Roque, a clean, nice little town, perched on the top of a hill. The view from the Alameda is splendid. There is a good Plaza de Toros, and three churches, the parish church being extremely full of gaily and sadly dressed virgins. The town was built by the Spaniards when they lost the Rock in 1704, Sir George Rooke having taken it during the War of Succession; then it could not defend itself, now it bristles with cannon. San Roque has infantry barracks, but the infantry is wanting. Many of the officers' families come here during the summer months, when the heat of the Rock is almost unbearable; it is so much easier of access than Tangiers, which takes from three to four hours to reach, nor is it so expensive.

The Cathedral—the protestant church—at Gib, is not striking outside, unless as being plain, but inside it is intended to be pretty: the architecture is in imitation of the Moorish. A monument on the right hand side of the altar is erected to the memory of General Don, to whom Gib owed a great deal. To him are thanks due for the beautiful Alameda, which from a desert he has converted into delightful gardens. Here the "Shade Tree," as they call it on the Rock, grows to an enormous size. It is an African tree, and is rightly called the *bella sombra*. The Virginian aloe is in great perfection and profusion, the rich red flower covering the rock at this season. There is a charming little cottage a little beyond the Alameda, called "The Aloes," from the masses of this plant that grow about it, but in summer the green rock is white, all verdure is parched up. In one part of the Alameda is a bust of Wellington, placed on a column taken from the ruins of Lepida, and erected there by Sir George Don, in 1820; in another part is a bust of General Elliott. Not far from the duke's pillar is a flat stone, covering the earthly remains of a silversmith, (and three of his children,) who, after living here for twenty-three years, died in 1800, at the age of forty-two. Why he is buried here, when consecrated ground lies not many yards beyond, is a mystery. This little cemetery has not been used for many years; it is very small and very full.

There are Roman Catholic churches, and a Roman Catholic bishop, thus the Rock is rich in possessing two; there is also a convent where pupils are taken. The people born on the Rock are called "Rock Scorpions," not a pretty name for them, but they do not seem to mind it; if you ask a man what he is, he will tell you he is "a scorpion." On one of the old gateways leading from the town to the Alameda, are still to be seen the arms of Spain.

The oranges at Gib are delicious, far finer than any we got in Spain, but then they come from Africa, as do many other of the good things that are to be had here.

CHAPTER XVI.

MALAGA.

To get to Gib is much easier than getting away from it. Boats are said to run twice or thrice a week between the Rock and Malaga, but for many a long day may you disport yourself on the Rock if waiting to get off by one of these. They advertise to start on a given day, but you learn on the eve that they are waiting for a vessel to arrive to take and give cargoes, which vessel never does arrive, and so you may go on not only from day to day, but from week to week. This was our case, till finally we were driven to go to the expense of chartering a steamer for ourselves. This may be done for 25*l*. from Mr. Bland's firm, a courteous, obliging company, and their steamer, the "Hercules," a trim, tidy little boat, and rapid, and capable of weathering a fearful sea, as was our misfortune to experience. The deep-blue sky over head, and the awful sea we were pitched and tossed about on for seven hours, formed a strange contrast. A levant wind was blowing, the worst for those bound for Malaga from Gibraltar. The rounding of Europa Point on that morning will never be effaced from our memory, not if we live to be old enough to forget everything else. The sea soaked us through every five minutes, whilst the hot sun kept us steaming. Then, when we did get into harbour—a blessed moment—the officers of health kept us one hour and ten minutes whilst they finished their dinner, before they chose to give us "pratique." However, at last we were let land, the small boats fighting for us as crabs might do under different circumstances; then on putting our foot on shore we were greeted by the custom-house officers. At length we were let go to our hotel, worn and weary. The "Fonda del Alameda," is a very fine house, and we had beautiful rooms ready; but there were certain comforts wanting here that we had left behind at Gib. However, we found it, for Spain, a very good hotel.

The coast scenery from Gib to Malaga is said to be very beautiful, but we admit honestly we did not see a vestige of it; we were far too ill to open our eyes, still less to lift up our head. And supposing we had, should we have thought it beautiful or anything else under the circumstances?

Malaga, the sunniest spot in Spain, a trap to catch every sunbeam, a bright beautiful place, it may well be the favourite resort of invalids. For the tourist or lover of art there is little to interest. It is situated in a lovely plain, yet walks are few, and drives fewer; there is little of art in or near it; but for those who seek health, and prefer to be where there are none of those sights that *must* be seen, it is the place of all others for them; they will find little to disturb the monotony of their life.

The cathedral, begun by Philip II., is a huge pile, heavy and uninteresting, with one tower completed; the other has yet to be finished, but when, no one seems to know or care: so many of the finest of the Spanish cathedrals have but one tower finished. The interior is lofty and grand, but there is little to make us care to visit it more than once. In the chapel of La Virgin de la Rosario is a painting, by Alonso Cano, of the Virgin and Child, and monks and nuns looking up at them. It is said to be the last painting he ever did: it seems unfinished, especially the Virgin's head. In the chapel of the Incarnation the altar is entirely of red marble, whilst figures in pure white marble are placed in niches, which form a great contrast, but it looks heavy. There are two monuments on either side of the chapel. The Virgin *de los Reyes* is thought to be well executed; but it is so dressed up that it is like a doll: the figures of Ferdinand and Isabella, in kneeling posture, are to the right and left of it. The pulpits are handsome: they are of red marble. The *coro* has some good carving, attributed to Pedro de Mena, a pupil of Alonso Cano. There are two organs, both very finely toned. The view from the tower is very grand: the best time for ascending it is towards sunset; the shadows then on the near mountains are beautiful.

The "Sagrario" has a magnificent Gothic gateway, but it is in a terrible state of dilapidation, and entirely bricked up. We found little worth seeing inside: the high altar is like all in Spain, a mass of heavy gilding up to the roof, with niches and figures placed in them. The same side as the old doorway, the wall is inlaid with azulejos. Opposite is the hospital of Santo Tomas: the little bit of Moorish architecture at the entrance, and the window with the horse-shoe arches and azulejos are pretty. The church of Los Santos Martires is a mass of white and gold and gaudily-dressed figures, and as little like a place of worship as Madame Tussaud's rooms. There are Virgins of every kind—young and old—happy and miserable—with the Saviour and without—great and small—black and white—dressed in gauze, spangles, and wreaths—and black, gloomy, and mournful. In every corner there is an image, but among the whole there is not one that has the slightest claim to merit. The church of Santiago, once a Moorish mosque, has nothing now but the exterior to show its antiquity: the steeple and bricked-up original entrance are good. The church of Santa Clara, attached to the convent of the same name, is pretty, and the *altar mayor* light, and in good taste. This convent was built and founded by Ferdinand and Isabella, in 1505.

At the convent of Victoria, a Moorish flag hangs in the chapel over the high altar, and a Spanish one opposite to it: the Moorish flag, which is on the right hand, was taken by Ferdinand during the siege of Malaga, and is the identical one that was hoisted at the tower when the town surrendered. This convent was built in 1487, and was founded by San Francisco de Paula. Ferdinand's head-quarters were here during the siege. It was one of the many convents suppressed in 1835. Now no monks remain; only one sorry, sighing, but fat and courteous priest resides here. The carved and gilded high altar is not without merit, the subjects on it chiefly representing the taking of Malaga. There are several copies of Alonso Cano's painting, but only one original, "San Antonio de Padua," and that is not finished, and terribly injured. There is a very beautiful "Virgin of Sorrows," carved by Menes. The dome at the back of the high altar (beneath which the Virgin is placed), representing the Conception, is very richly ornamented—a great deal too much so; it is a whole mass of plaster decoration.

The Spanish cemetery is near to this convent: there are some very fine monuments in it, and though it is surrounded by high walls in which there are tiers of niches one over the other, for coffins to be shoved in—this being the usual method of disposing of the dead in Spain,—the centre, which is very well laid out, has many graves covered with richly-carved monuments. The view from here is magnificent; it is on rising ground, and commands both sea and mountains. Far away from here, near to the coast, is the Protestant burial-ground, and the only one that is recognised by the Spanish government. It is situated on a height overhanging the sea, and well planted with beautiful flowers and very fine cyprus trees; it is a pretty spot, with well laid out walks, and extremely well kept. Thanks, for this concession by the government, are entirely due to the late Mr. Mark, who was consul here for many years. His son succeeded him, and is the present consul. This grant was made, as a tablet records, on the 11th April, 1830. Mr. Mark is buried here; also Robert Boyd, an unfortunate but enthusiastic Englishman, who suffered the penalty of death, when only twenty-six years of age, with forty-nine other victims, who, under Torrijos, were convicted of conspiracy in 1831. A monument is erected to their memory in the Plaza del Riego: this tribute of admiration was raised in 1842, when the then authorities viewed their conduct in a different light.

Not far from the Protestant cemetery, a sailors' hospital is being built. A Mr. Noble, an Englishman, came to Malaga a year or two ago, and died within a fortnight of his arrival, and suddenly. He is said to have been poisoned by the use of copper saucepans, used in cooking at his hotel. In consequence of this event, inspectors go round at certain periods to enforce the use of vessels which are in a proper state. Mr. Noble, when dying, left 5000*l.* for the erection of this hospital, an institution, he heard, that was greatly needed.

The large square building near the port was a tobacco factory; it is now converted into a custom house. The bishop's palace is close to the cathedral; it has nothing to recommend it. The *patio* is bare and unbeautiful; the staircase common, and a still more commonly-painted domed roof.

The Moorish castle, on the summit of a conically-shaped hill, well repays the labour of climbing to see it, if even the sun be as blazing hot as we found it. The view is most magnificent: mountain, valley, and sea: and clad with such verdure that it seemed impossible that we were only at the end of January; the sea rippling and sparkling beneath the bright sunshine; the sky so darkly blue and so cloudless;—it was by far the finest scenery we had as yet come across; but then we had now only entered on the picturesque part of the country.

The fortress and palace—for it was both—was a famous stronghold of the Moors. It was built towards the end of the thirteenth century. One horse-shoe gateway still remains; all the ornamental portions of the architecture, for which the Moors were so celebrated, have been destroyed. The siege of Malaga was very terrible, second only to that of Granada in its horrors. In the town, near the Alameda, is another very fine marble gateway of the horse-shoe form; it is built up and huddled round by bricks and mortar. There is little value set on these relics by Spaniards, nor can they understand how people can come from any distance to see them.

The Alameda is the fashionable promenade. It is a very broad, dusty walk, with plane trees forming an avenue, and between them statues and busts, and two fountains, one at each end. Every statue and bust has its nose broken off: this was done one night not long since by a tipsy man, who had no nose himself, and as he walked along he began to think it was very hard that he should have none and all these marble figures possessing them, so he began at one end and deliberately went the round and broke off every nose. On Sundays and festivals the band plays; then all the Malagenians are seen in their gayest attire, which, however, is never very gay to northern eyes, for black is so much worn. These Spanish women have no idea of what we understand by home: they have a house to live in, and rooms for people to see; but they pass their existence in a dressing-gown in their bed-rooms, or in the streets in a dress with a couple of yards sweeping the ground; and if they have a silver jug and bason in their own room, and a box at the theatre, they are satisfied. It is as common to see the silver jug and bason in a lady's room in Spain, as it is to see ivory-handled brushes in England; it is as universal a wedding present as a butter-dish is with us. To pass their evenings at the theatre is what they like best; there they see their friends, and are not troubled as they would be if they received them at home. The theatres at Malaga are not good; the best is El Teatro del Principe Alfonso: it is large, clean, comfortable, and well lighted, but having—in common with all others throughout Spain, Seville alone excepted—a horrible smell. The performances are bad, the singing vile, the acting absurd. We saw the "Traviata:" it was dreadful. They cannot afford to pay good singers, as the boxes, let by the year, are at a very low price, and others for the night one can have in the best part of the house for eighty reales, and a stall for sixteen, entrance included. A *baille*—a ball, as they here call a ballet—followed the opera; but Spanish dancing is very ungraceful—they throw everything about but their legs. Their heads, arms, and petticoats are in all directions, whilst their legs remain as if leaded. The women are generally very fat and heavy. Then the noise of the castanettes or the clapping of the hands, the one or the other always being their accompaniment, wearies. The music is very wild, and wonderfully devoid of melody, and the singing of the Andalusian is the most unmusical we ever heard; it is between moaning and howling.

There is at present no bull-ring here; owing to a dispute between the proprietor of the circus and the owner of the land it was pulled down, so for the present they are obliged to have recourse to a circus of small dimensions, in the Plaza de Victoria, which will not admit of anything beyond fights with young bulls, which are never killed. They do not commence till the carnival, then they have them every Sunday.

There are two country houses, situated about three miles out of Malaga, the gardens of which are almost worthy of being called botanical gardens. La Conception, the farthest off, is a modern house, but the garden may date back centuries; one or two of the palm trees are magnificent; the cocoa and coffee plants were growing here; and under glass, but with no artificial heat, were some very fine pines. The ground was carpeted with violets, scenting the whole air. San José, the other, is on a much larger scale; there is a great deal of water about it, and a large greenhouse; but the whole is less well cared for, and the house, a large rambling building, more like a farm-house than a gentleman's residence. The views from both are magnificent, they stand at the foot of a range of low mountains, others towering up behind. There are two drawbacks to them, however: the one is to reach them—the bed of the river forming three-fourths of the road; and the other, that except for a couple or three months they are too hot to live in; being so far from sea, they do not benefit by the breezes. The sugar cane grows about here in great abundance; in the town there is a large sugar manufactory; the sugar is very white and clear. Sweet potatoes, *patatas de Malaga*, is another of the specialities of the place; they are much eaten all over Spain; either plainly boiled or preserved, they taste very much like a not over good chestnut;

in appearance they resemble exaggerated kidney potatoes. They are sold here about the streets ready cooked, just as chestnuts are sold with us. They also eat great quantities of the "cactus fig," or "prickly pear," they are sold about a dozen for a farthing.

There is a fine clay found close to Malaga, out of which figures and groups are made representing the various costumes of the country; some of them are extremely well executed, especially those of Cubero. They are about a foot long, and the single figures vary in price from 100 to 150 reales, according to the care with which they are painted. The shops here are not more tempting than in any other town in Spain. There are more *Escribanos*, letter writers, to be seen here than usual: either the Malagenians must be more ignorant or great lovers of letter writing. These men sit in door ways, and under arches, with little tables before them, having paper, pen, and ink on them, ready to write letters or anything else for any one on the payment of a few cuartos. Some style themselves, by a card which they suspend against the wall, "public and private writers," others only "private." You rarely see them unemployed, the would-be letter writer dictating beside them : these are generally women.

The beggars in Malaga are as bad as in Seville, and the deformities worse and more numerous. One set of them go about as acrobats,—nothing can exceed the horrors exhibited.

The *sereno* keeps his nightly watch in a peaceful

manner here, whistling the hours and half hours as they did at Jerez, only here one single whistle alone gives notice that an hour has struck; perhaps this may be that the cocks crow here through the night, and the man is wise enough to think there is noise enough. Excepting at Mentone, in the south of France, we never heard cocks crow at midnight as they did at Malaga.

To see Malaga at its most interesting time, one ought to be there in late autumn, in order to witness the process of grape-drying and raisin-packing. But was ever anybody anywhere at the right season? Throughout we were always told, "Oh, you should be here in spring;" or "You ought to have been here two months ago," or "two months hence." We, however, visited Mr. Clements's stores: his are the largest and most worth seeing; of course we were told the best were shipped off; still we saw here such raisins as we have never seen in England, some an inch long, and looking, but for their colour, more like French plums. Where are all these splendid raisins to be found? for they come to London direct. Mr. Scholtz, the Danish consul, is the principal wine grower, and has the largest stores. There are four kinds of wine: the sweet mountain, the sweet muscat, the pale dry, and the Malaga sherry; this latter is exported to England in large quantities as sherry; it is made from the same kind of grape, only the land causes that from Jerez to be so very far superior. The process of wine-making varies very little, and though we had heard it all before, we listened patiently to the end, and then tasted the "mother butt," which nourishes so many: it seems a marvel she is not worn out; in these stores this old lady bears the date on her of 1788; this is the rich dark sweet mountain wine, and priceless in itself. After all good has been extracted from the grape, warm water is poured on the crushed dried refuse, and vinegar is made, which is highly prized for household use.

English service is performed twice every Sunday, at Mr. Mark's house, the British consulate. He has had a large long room very prettily fitted up for the purpose.

CHAPTER XVII.

GRANADA.—THE ALHAMBRA.

FROM Malaga to Granada there are two roads, and several ways of accomplishing the journey, but after every inquiry we found the easiest and best was to hire a carriage to take us to Loja, which we could reach by starting at eight a.m., as soon as the diligence, which left at six, if we had sufficient relays of mules. This, therefore, we did, and leaving all our heavy baggage at the Alameda Hotel, at Malaga, we started with sufficient for a fortnight, in a kind of omnibus, with eight mules, changed three times en route, and arrived at Loja at 3·30 p.m. We paid 9*l.* for the carriage. The scenery the whole way is magnificent. The view of the *vega*, or plain of Malaga, as it burst upon us every now and then, winding up the steep ascent of the hills, was beautiful; it was nearly two hours before we quite lost sight of Malaga. From about an hour after leaving Malaga we found the road well guarded by armed gendarmes, two always together. This is a necessary precaution, as this mountainous, wild, untenanted land is one of the few parts of Spain still infested with brigands. Only so lately as on the 28th of January of this year, one of the wealthiest Malaga merchants was taken, and a ransom of 40,000 dollars demanded for him. He was on horseback at the time, and at no very great distance from the town. Strict directions were sent by himself, in his own handwriting, to his personal servant, telling him to go by a certain road to a certain spot, on the 1st of February, and if some people, who were minutely described, were not met at a given place, he was to return on another day specified, and if he failed in any order given him, his master's life would pay the penalty. The celebrated brigand of Spain, the gallant highwayman who does everything like a gentleman, is José Pacheco, of Cordova. He is a personal friend of many a Spanish noble. The anecdotes related of his magnificence, munificence and impudence are legion. He once seized two highwaymen himself, that were not under his orders, and delivered them up to justice at Cordova; of course the statement of the men that Pacheco was their accuser was laughed at; his disguises are so perfect that he is never recognised.

We, however, reached Loja without any more startling adventure than the fall of a couple of mules. We passed two picturesque towns on the road, Colmenar and Alfarnate. Till within an hour of Loja the scenery is extremely wild and grand. Tiers of mountains, looking in the distance as if they had bubbled up in peaks out of one huge mass, the fan leaf palm growing in bushes, the sides of the near hills covered with vines—the "mountain" wine is made from these—and along the edges and close to the road is a profusion of broad-leaved blue flowers.

Loja is a large town, and was once a fortress of great importance, being considered by the Moors as the key to Granada; they lost it in 1488, and Lord Rivers, brother of Henry VII.'s queen, lost his teeth during the siege. Isabella the Catholic recompensed him with a pretty compliment. Loja is like a huge mound, with its fortress, now a mere ruin, on the top. The streets are narrow; but since the opening of the railway from here to Granada new houses are springing up, and the people stirring themselves. Marshal Narvaez, the late prime minister, was building himself a very fine house; now that his death will stop its completion there is a talk of turning it into an hotel; one is much wanted, though there was a new one opened just before we were there. The Genil runs at the foot of the town, and is crossed to reach the Alameda and the railway station. The Alameda is very prettily laid out, and the range of mountains, the "Sierra Nevada," are well seen from here, the pure white uneven mass looking very beautiful against the deep blue sky. For weeks had we now seen this same cloudless sky, and we began to understand what a gentleman, a native of Malaga, said to us, that he sometimes longed for clouds and cold weather. If he lived a year in England he would understand how we pine for a blue sky and sunshine.

Loja to Granada is two hours by railway, the carriages are the most comfortable and the cleanest on this short line that we have yet seen in Spain; then it has not been long open, so they still look new. About a quarter of an hour after starting from Loja, we suddenly came to a stand still, and were all requested to get out, and walk over a bridge that had partially given way, and which must of necessity some day go altogether; so the train went first, and we followed, having to walk some four or five hundred yards; nothing happened, and we got in again. Had it been pouring with rain, this little pedestrian excursion would not have been very pleasant. The latter part of the journey the road passes through the Duke of Wellington's property, the Soto de Roma; it is said to yield from 5000*l.* to 7000*l.* a year. A house is being built on it; in the old house there are some Moorish remains. An estate, called El Molino del Rey, was also conferred on the late duke; they do not join, but they are both near together.

We reached Granada at last; we arrived at six, but before we got away from the station and through the town it was too dark to see anything, anxious as we were to get even a dim glance at the Alhambra. To most English people Seville and Granada are Spain— the former with its riches in art, and the halo of romance with which its very name is surrounded; the latter with the Alhambra and a host of antiquities at every turn. We went to the "Washington Irving Hotel" within the Alhambra grounds; very comfortable, beautifully situated, and so clean, one might imagine the proprietor had been brought up in Holland. On looking out of our windows the next morning, we were delighted with the surrounding gardens. A long avenue cut through the centre of a hill, the slopes on either side wooded by 8000 elms, that were sent as a present by *the* duke in 1811 to the Spanish government, and were planted here; they were planted too thickly, and have shot up thin and poor-looking. The violets on these hills during the spring perfectly scent the atmosphere and colour the ground; bunches of them are thrust under your nose at every step by some urchin looking out for a *cuarto*.

Granada is 3500 feet above the level of the sea, and the hill on which the Alhambra is situated is between one or two hundred more; around this hill are walls, with towers at various points, the whole forming, in the time of the Moors, one of their most powerful strongholds. It was commenced in 1248, and finished in 1314; the walls are of immense thickness, but not very high. The principal entrance is by a grand horse-shoe gate; over it, an open hand is engraved; this is succeeded by a smaller horse-shoe arch, over which is engraved a key; then the entrance continues by a winding way, till you issue out on the other side through another horse-shoe arch: through this entrance no four footed animal is allowed to pass, as a small chapel is now erected here, and thus no risk of an indignity being offered to the Virgin must be run. Immediately to the right is the Torre del Vino; a beautiful double arch, ornamented with lace-like work, and with *azulejos* above, used to be the entrance to it; now you enter it by a common door at the side. This tower belongs to Sir Granville Temple; he bought it about the year 1849, from the queen, to whom the entire Alhambra belongs. He has let the house to a French photographer. To the left are the ruins of the old fortress, and the Torre de la Vela, so called from the great bell which is hung here, and which rings, or rather tolls, out a dismal notice to the people every night, letting them know that the hour for irrigating their lands is at hand. This same bell is supposed to possess a peculiar charm on the 2nd of January, as whatever maiden rings it, is certain to secure herself a good husband during the coming year; the louder she rings the better will he be, thus the noise is deafening during the entire day, and not a maiden within reach but is sure to be up there. The view from this tower is very grand, as indeed it is from any spot on these heights. We watched a sun-set one evening;—the deep glen to the right, with the Darro running through it and coming down from the snowy range of mountains, the Sierra Nevada, which tower up like piles of silver against the blue sky;—straight before us the magnificent *vega*, the luxuriant plain of Granada, rich in gardens and groves, and in the midst of them we could see, tinged with the setting sun, the town of Santa-Fe, which Ferdinand and Isabella built after their camp was destroyed. In this then hamlet Columbus arranged with the queen how his voyage to America was to be effected; he had left in disgust and despair, resolving to do for another country what his own refused to let him do for her, when Isabella, the Catholic, recalled him to her side, and the Western world was her reward. The eye never wearies at gazing at this panorama, but the red hues that still capped the Sierra Nevada were fast leaving them cold and grey, and we turned homewards, not joyously, but silent and thoughtful: there is something in these scenes with which we were surrounded, all ruins of the past, their decayed grandeur, the dilapidations and desolation, that is calculated to depress the spirits rather than elevate them.

By far the most prominent-looking building in the Alhambra is the shell of a palace, occupying the very centre of the hill, which Charles V. began in 1526. In 1633 it reached its present state, and has remained so ever since; the interior gives one the idea that it was built in order to have bull fights in the *patio;* this is very fine, with thirty-two marble columns around it. The façades are all handsome, but it so blocks up and closes out *the* palace, that it is with difficulty the entrance to it is found. Passing round on the right side of Charles V.'s palace we came to a mass of dirty little houses, almost forming a village. The rents all go to the queen, the Alhambra being the private property of the reigning sovereign; so they can let or sell, but in the latter case the purchaser has to pay an annual fine to the crown; in fact, rendering the proprietors tenants that cannot be turned out. A little further on is all that is left of a once celebrated Franciscan convent; it is now portioned out in lodgings; the church is utterly bare, with white-washed walls; where the altar was, there is a recess with a little tracery work round. It was here that the coffins containing the bodies of Ferdinand and Isabella rested, awaiting the completion of their present tomb in the cathedral. Here also the remains of the Great Captain were placed previous to their being taken to San Geronimo. The *patio* has nothing but its columns to recommend it; all is in ruin, with squalid misery around. The convent was built by converted Moors, as most of the great buildings in Granada are that were erected after the conquest, which accounts for Moorish architecture being so prevalent, even after their dynasty was at an end. Their grand mosque was utterly destroyed, and the church of Santa Maria, behind Charles V.'s palace was erected on its site; it was built in 1581.

Amidst a little wilderness stands a small mosque, which, together with the Casa de Moneda (mint), was purchased by an English colonel, for many years a resident of Madrid, who, with praiseworthy exertions, has restored the mosque; and if no one had ever seen Moorish work, they would enter this building and gaze on it with great admiration; the walls and arches are the original, the decorations alone are new. In a room higher up is preserved a marble slab, with Arabic writing on it, giving directions as to how coins are to be struck. This formerly was in the mint, the whole of which Colonel —— sold, even to the building materials; only this slab and two lions were unsaleable, being too heavy to be carried away. The two lions used to stand on either side of a tank in front of the mint; now they are at the entrance of the garden in which is the mosque. The Marquis de Zafra has a very decent-looking house near this. Continuing straight on is the Torre del Pico. It is the only tower that remains quite untouched; it is as it was in the time of the Moors: the window is very perfect and very pretty. Beyond this were the stables of the Moorish kings; they are bricked up to prevent mischievous boys and sight-seers from completely destroying all traces of them. We now passed the Puerta del Hierro: it still retains the original door and bolt, which bolt is closed every night. Farther on is the Torre del Candil, then the Torre de las Captivas, where female Christian prisoners were kept; next to it is La Torre de las Infantas, where the Moorish princesses once resided, but which is rendered more interesting after reading Washington Irving's pretty tale about it. The last existing tower is the Torre de la Agua. Sebastian created such havoc here, that little else but ruins remain. At this point the aqueduct crosses the road which brings the water down from Mula-Hacen to Generalife, and from there to the Alhambra, down into the Darro. Boabdil cut the ravine which borders the Alhambra on this side to divide Generalife from it, as he gave that palace to his son; the earth wall thus created appears much more like a built wall, a crust of salt and magnesia forms on the surface, giving it the appearance of layers of mortar: cattle are brought here to lick it off, which results in their giving not only very fine milk, but a plentiful supply. This huge wall forms, in summer, the residence of the poor, as many as can find accommodation: they take up their abode in the great openings that exist, looking like giant rabbit-holes, and live rent-free and cool. A curious stone found amidst the ruins of Illiberis, said by its inscription to be dedicated by Valerius to his wife Cornelia, —the only name legible to us on it—is placed at the corner of the Torre del Homenage, and imbedded in it. It was so put by the Moors.

The exterior of the Alhambra Palace is so simple and plain that the contrast becomes ten times more striking with its fairy-like interior. The entrance, a mere common doorway, the original one being blocked up by the huge building erected by Charles V., leads one straight into the beautiful palace of the Moors. To give a thorough description of this wondrous mass of exquisite workmanship is impossible; we are utterly incapable of doing it justice, but a slight sketch we will attempt. Its beauty cannot be exaggerated, and with all we had heard of it we not only were not disappointed, but found it surpassing all we had pictured it. We entered first the court of Los Arrayanes, or Myrtle Court: a large piece of water in the centre, surrounded by hedges of myrtle, gives the name to it. This water is now filled with fish, but it was used formerly as a bath. It is surrounded by an exquisitely-worked gallery, and at each corner are recesses which were used as sentry-boxes for the eunuchs who kept watch whilst the ladies were bathing. The fretwork and honeycombed roofs of these recesses are beautiful; they are in a very perfect state, and in some portions of them the original colouring still remains. This court is 150 feet in length and 82 in breadth. Leading out of this, on the right, is the celebrated Court of Lions, so called on account of the twelve lions which support the marble fountain in the centre; the fragile, delicate appearance of this court is beyond description. It is surrounded by galleries, supported by 144 slender-looking marble columns: the lace-work ornamentation of the walls, the stalactical pendants with which the roofs are formed, with here and there the rich colouring still perfect, render the whole more like fairyland than anything we are accustomed to see here. To the right is the Hall of the Abencerrages, so called from the massacre of the thirty-five cavaliers, who, according to tradition, were beheaded here by Boabdil's order, because one of these Abencerrages was supposed to be in love with his queen Zoraya: it not being quite clear which was the guilty man, all were doomed to die. Here our guide, Emmanuel Bensaken, *el Moro*, as he is called, pointed out to us large stains in the white marble, which is said to be the blood of Boabdil's victims. The Hall of Justice occupies one entire side of the Court of Lions; the beautiful Moorish peristyles, are so slight and fragile-looking that one can hardly understand how they support the weight of the arches. There are some queer paintings on leather here, executed by a Christian slave. In a recess stands a splendid vase; one handle is, unfortunately, broken off. This vase Boabdil filled with gold, obtained from one of the neighbouring mines, and intended taking with him when he left his palace; but finding jewels of greater value and more portable, he left this behind, and the Spaniards benefited by its contents. There are several tombstones belonging to the Moorish kings placed against the walls. The arcades of open filagree-work are lovely; it is difficult to understand how all this has withstood time, earthquakes, and wars; perhaps more injury has been done to it by lawless soldiers than even the terrific shocks of earthquakes it has survived.

The Hall of the Two Sisters, so called on account of two enormous twin slabs of marble in the pavement, is opposite the Hall of the Abencerrages: this is a beautiful hall, large and lofty; the lower part of the walls are covered with tiles (*azulejos*) on which are emblazoned the escutcheons of the Moorish kings. The name of Abdallah frequently occurs. The upper portion is ornamented with the most exquisite stuccowork, looking like the richest and finest embroidery. This work is said to have been invented at Damascus; it is all intermingled with texts from the Koran and love inscriptions. The recesses in the wall are for couches and ottomans; at the entrance to all the apartments are small recesses for placing the slippers which used to be taken off before entering. In this hall is the only "dark-eyed window" remaining in the palace. It is so called because the ladies were able from these windows to watch what was going on below without themselves being visible.

Going round Alberca Court, we entered, by a magnificent Moorish archway, the Hall of Ambassadors, a glorious apartment, with windows cut through the thick wall, looking down to the valley below. The ceiling is very fine, of cedar-wood, and the walls a mass of elaborate rich tracery: this hall is beneath the Comares Tower, the highest portion of the whole building. It was here that Boabdil was confined with his mother, Aija-la-Horra, by the orders of his father, Aben Hassan, who, having married a second wife, a Christian slave named Zorayda, and had two sons by her, was instigated by her jealousy of Boabdil to have his eldest son put to death, and as a preliminary step, he was imprisoned with his mother; but she effected his escape, letting him down from the window in a basket. The most perfect portion of the Alhambra Palace is the Chamber of Repose: it is reached now by a long, dark, narrow passage, and beyond it are the large marble baths used by the kings, sultanas, and royal children. This part has been thoroughly restored, and the colouring is exquisitely rich. There are numbers of apartments, each more beautiful than the other; it is a maze of loveliness, fitted only for what it was,—the abode of houris. One could not imagine the *tocador*, the toilet-room of the sultana, to be used by an ordinary mortal. In this pavilion, open on three sides, there is, in a corner, a large flat piece of marble with holes: over this the queen stood, and was perfumed before presenting herself to the king. For such, this palace was a fitting abode: they have passed away from the Western world; yet, in roaming through these fairy-like apartments, we could almost conjure up some dark beauties, and imagine them still the occupants of this Paradise. At moonlight, with the dark shadows cast around, and the white marble pillars, each increasing the effect of the other, one may easily indulge in these dreams; and if the distant sounds of music reach the ear, which, in the present day, with hotels within a stone's throw, they are very apt to do, one may carry on the delusion and imagine love, music, and poetry still to form the sole thought and occupation of the languid, listless beauties of the harem.

The palace is kept in perfect order, and well protected from further injury, either by accident or from mischief. It is being thoroughly restored, but the work goes on but slowly, owing to funds not being very plentiful. An artist named Contreras has been entrusted with its restoration; it is thought that in about twelve years it will be completed. Señor Coutreras has a studio which was well worth visiting; he has blocks of the Moorish work, exact copies, in miniature, of various parts of the Alhambra Palace, both plain and coloured. They vary in size from eight to twenty inches, and in price from ten to forty dollars. We brought one or two of them to England, thinking they would look well inserted in a wall, but the difficulty is to find a fitting site. Coutreras has been commanded by the Emperor of Russia to superintend the erection of a palace at St. Petersburg similar to the Alhambra Palace. He it was who executed the stucco-work sent to England, and erected in the Crystal Palace as a model of some portions of this palace.

There are some people who compare the Moorish palace at Granada with the Alcazar at Seville; yet to our eyes the comparison is no better than it would be to compare a cart-horse with a thorough-bred. The *azulejos* (tiles) are finer at Seville, not those in the Alcazar but in the summer-house; at the Alhambra Palace they have been so terribly destroyed.

The keeper of the keys of the palace is a most obliging, communicative man if you happen to go in without a guide; but he is a bitter enemy to all of them, from Bensaken downwards; indeed, a deadly feud seems to exist between Bensaken and most of the people who have anything in their care to show;—perhaps it is, that when he is there their fee is smaller;—he is the best guide in Granada, though nearly past his work now. He has a son he is trying to palm off on his patrons when he can; but his capabilities are not remarkable. Bensaken's father was a Moor, his mother an Englishwoman, and he was born at Gibraltar.

CHAPTER XVIII.

GRANADA—*continued.*

The Generalife Palace, once belonging to the son of Boabdil, the last Moorish king that reigned at Granada, stands on a hill looking down upon the Alhambra. A large gateway on the high road leads into the grounds. This property now belongs to the Marquis de Campotejar; he resides at Genoa, and is known there as the Count of Palavicini-Grimaldi. He is descended from Cidi Aya, a Moorish prince, who was rewarded by Ferdinand with this palace for having turned Christian. Originally it was a college, and purchased by Boabdil for his son Omar, whose love of the flute was so great, that the noise he constantly made nearly drove his father wild; so he came here, where he could make all the noise he liked without annoying anyone. When Boabdil quitted Granada, never to return again, Omar followed.

The garden without the gate, which leads to the inner garden, has a very fine avenue of cypresses, one or two of great height, around which the thick stems of old vines cling, reaching nearly to the top; some pomegranate-trees grow here, celebrated for their fine fruit. The enclosed garden is a mass of bound-up cypress-trees, forming all sorts of shapes, and tied together at the top, making arches over the tanks of water : excepting violets, which peep out of every little hole and corner, hardly any flowers are to be seen. The garden is in terraces, and in a lower one is a myrtle against a wall, which dates back to the Moors; the root is of an enormous size. Between two tanks is a place domed over by laurel and myrtle-trees, called a *suca*, where they sometimes drank coffee and smoked. One pepper-tree grows here, sent by Count Palavicini from Genoa; it is the only one in Granada. On the third terrace is the famous cypress-tree called the "Lover's Tree," where Zoraya is supposed to have met her Abencerragian lover; it is a magnificent tree, of enormous bulk and height; it was planted in the thirteenth century. At the summit of the hill, which commands the house, are the ruins of a mosque, where Boabdil is said to have invariably retired for peace during any row, till his uncle, El Zagel, with whom he was sometimes on good terms, though at heart hating each other, sent word that all was quiet; hence this spot is now called *La Silla del Moro*. The view from this spot is, if possible, finer than that from the bell-tower in the Alhambra.

The house itself is a disappointment; the little Moorish work that remains in it is so filled in with whitewash that it is difficult to define the lacy pattern, so beautiful of itself. A massive pine-wood door, inlaid, and swung on a pivot, as all Moorish doors are, leads into a hall, where the decorations are rich, and the ceiling inlaid and coloured; this leads into what are termed the picture galleries, two ordinary rooms, but divided by a prettily-ornamented vestibule, which would be worth removing the whitewash from to show the stucco-work beneath; the ceiling here is also inlaid. In the first room are the portraits of Ferdinand and Isabella, and their direct descendants, among them Philip II., the husband of Mary of England. In the second room are likenesses of the ancestors of the present owner of the place, beginning with Cidi Aya; there is also a portrait of Boabdil, *el Rey Chico* (the little king), as he was called; El Zagel, his uncle; and a picture with two ships, those in which Columbus left the Old World to seek the New. A light, arched gallery, running along one side of the garden, leads to a little chapel; there is nothing worth looking at in it.

The owner of the Generalife never comes to Granada, nor does he do anything that shows he takes the remotest interest in it. He keeps an agent or manager in a house which belongs to him in the town, called *La Casa de Tiros*. This is a very curious house; the frontage is very extraordinary looking, with huge figures of soldiers standing in recesses, like saints in alcoves. The large massive doors, which admit into the covered court, have the walls so built behind them, that when they are open they touch them; this is for protection, to prevent any one concealing themselves in what would otherwise be dark recesses. The staircase is wide and handsome. In a large drawing-room, where there are a few good paintings, is a ceiling painted with the portraits of the Christian ancestors of the present owner, also portraits of Ferdinand and Isabella. There is a beautiful Titian, in a closed case; it is the head of the Saviour, and before this picture mass was said in the presence of the troops, before going into battle, during the siege of Granada. There are two paintings by Alonso Cano, a Christ's head, and one of St. Francis. In another room are two old Moorish metal plates, and two muskets; the great treasure preserved in this house, however, is Boabdil's sword, which is said to be very beautiful, and, of course, is very interesting; but we failed to see it; each time we went some excuse was made—the agent was absent, or it was too early or too late, so we gave it up; but it does exist, for people have seen it.

The most interesting house in Granada is the Cuarto Real; it was formerly the residence of Aija la Horra, Boabdil's mother; it now belongs to the family of Pulgar, descendants of the Great Captain. One room alone has been left with Moorish work, and that is the large room facing the entrance, and used as a lumber-room; the grand doors are still there, but in ruins like the rest, the beautiful engraved work filled up with the destructive whitewash so dear to Spaniards;

the arches are very fine, the elaborate work, partly seen and partly imagined; the light, perforated windows above, all so ill-used, with ladders resting against them, and poles stuck about, that if some little change is not made, a few years will cause the disappearance of all traces of the existence of this once beautiful palace. The ceiling is a very fine specimen of the *artesonado*. The *azulejos* are extremely pretty, some of them white and gold, very delicate looking; none of these exist elsewhere. In the garden is a wonderful vault, between forty and fifty feet long, formed of cypress and myrtle-trees, the trunks of the myrtles of great thickness; this arched promenade is about twenty to thirty feet high, and ten to fifteen in width: it is closed at the end by the trees.

The cathedral is erected on the site of the great mosque, which was totally destroyed after the conquest. It was built by Ferdinand and Isabella, and commenced in March, 1529. It is a grand, massive pile, but the interior looks bare, and the eternal whitewash has not been spared. The *tras-coro*, which faces you on entering by the principal door, is of coloured marbles, all found near Granada; it is handsome, but out of keeping with the rest. The dome over the high altar is 220 feet high, and decorated in white and gold; the last arch, opening over the *coro*, has a strange appearance from behind the altar, as it is scooped out, to render the shape of the dome perfect; the arches are magnificent, they are 190 feet high. Around the dome are seven large pictures by Alonso Cano, representing scenes from the life of the Virgin; the smaller paintings below these are by Bocanegra. The coloured windows, seen from the end of the church, are very effective, and give a slight look of warmth to this cold, white building. The high altar, though seemingly of marble, is only painted wood. On the right and left are the effigies of Ferdinand and Isabella, and above them the heads of Adam and Eve, carved by Alonso Cano, but they are so high up it is difficult to judge of their merits. All archbishops are buried beneath a grating, which is before the *tras-coro*. The *coro* has nothing to see in it. Two doorways, one leading to the Sala Capitular, and the other to a large recess, are handsome; over one is a very fine alto relievo by Torrigiano, representing Charity; next to it is a "Crucifixion," painted by Bocanegra. The organs are very much gilt, and showy-looking.

There is a very fine painting of "La Virgen de la Soledad," by Alonso Cano, in the chapel of San Miguel; the marble altar of this chapel is handsome. A little beyond it is the chapel of Santiago; above the saint's figure, which is on horseback, there is a small painting of the "Virgin and Child," said to be by St. Luke. The altar retablo is very massive, as, indeed, all in the church are. Mass is said before this little picture on the 2nd January in every year, the anniversary of the conquest of Granada. It was a gift from Innocent VIII. to Isabella the Catholic. In the chapel of La

Virgen del Rosario are two heads, carved by Cano; one, St. John the Baptist, dead and laid down: the other, of St. Peter, erect and full of life, forming a great contrast to St. John's, which, from being coloured, is very horrible. In the next chapel, that of La Virgen de la Antigua, is the image of the Virgin which was brought with the Christian army, and carried before the troops when they were marching towards Granada. This Virgin and Child Isabella had such veneration for, that she desired it might be placed in this chapel, with her own portrait and that of Ferdinand, life size, and in a kneeling posture, right and left of it; they are painted by Juan de Sevilla. The chapel is extremely gorgeous; the mantle forming a canopy over the Virgin is very graceful and effective. In the chapel of the Holy Trinity, there is a "Holy Family," by Atanacio; and a "Saviour and St. Joseph," by Ribera. In the chapel of San Francisco is a "Magdalen," and "St. Peter," and a head of "St. Sebastian," by Ribera; also, "The Saviour Bearing His Cross," a "St. Francis," and "The Saviour with the Virgin," by Alonso Cano; these pictures form the retablo over the altar. Alonso Cano was a minor canon of this cathedral, and he carved and painted many things for it. He was a native of Granada, yet out of this church few of his works are to be seen. Two very large paintings to the right of the high altar are by Bocanegra. There is a Crucifix in one of the small side chapels, the Saviour has a large mass of bushy hair, tied back from off his face; the whole is more than painful. Against the walls between the chapels a notice is painted, in large black letters, that whoever is seen talking with women in the church, will be fined two dollars and excommunicated. This was put up at the time of the Inquisition, and still remains, unheeded, but as a curiosity. The beggars here are abominable; they are a frightful nuisance all over Granada; they will follow you any distance, and finally will lay hold of you, to force you to give: out in the streets one has a chance, but here in the church one cannot get rid of them; and they will keep so close that one is in fear and trembling that if one does not give, one may get.

The Capilla Real, built by Charles V. as a resting place for the remains of Ferdinand and Isabella, is by far the most interesting portion of the cathedral, which it joins and communicates with, but is otherwise independent of it. The exterior is Gothic, and very rich looking; the initials Y. and F. are in shields all round it; the door leading into it from the cathedral is very fine. The magnificent iron railing is by Bartolomé; it is partially gilt; on the other side of it are the beautiful alabaster tombs of the conquerors of Granada, their daughter, " Crazy Jane," and her husband Philip le Bel. These exquisite monuments were cut at Genoa by Peralta. The details are wonderful: though not quite so elaborate, they are much in the style of the Miraflores monument. The effigies of Ferdinand

and Isabella lie side by side; they are said to be portraits; Juana la Loca, beside her handsome husband, whom she loved so little in life, so much in death; her face is calm and peaceful, a contrast to her troubled life. It was by Isabella's request that she and her husband were buried in Granada. Beneath are the coffins containing their remains; the staircase by which you descend is very awkward if you care for your head; nine chances out of ten you will give it a blow. On common wooden benches stand five time-worn, coarse-looking, roughly-made coffins. Initial letters alone distinguish one from the other. The fifth coffin is that of Prince Michael, elder brother of Charles V., who was killed when seven years of age by a fall from his horse. The coffins are not even paired, but placed on these shelves or benches, Isabella at one end, Ferdinand at another, and the whole is sadly at variance with the beautiful sepulchres above.

The high altar of this chapel royal is extremely curious; the retablo is magnificent, the lower portion of it represents scenes from the conquest of Granada; thus, Boabdil followed by Christian prisoners, dressed as Moors, is delivering the keys of Granada to Cardinal Mendoza, who holds out his gloved hand to receive them; the cardinal is on horseback, as well as the king and queen. There is also a scene representing a whole batch of unhappy Moors being baptized by monks; this retablo was executed in Charles V.'s time. To the right and left are effigies of Ferdinand and Isabella, said to be exact likenesses and correct representations of their dress.

There are many interesting relics in the *sacristia*: amongst them the sword, sceptre, and crown of Ferdinand; the handle of the sword is of gold, the sceptre and crown are silver gilt; and the banner of the Christian army brought to Granada, and the flag which was hoisted on the Bell Tower in the Alhambra, and was the signal of victory given to Isabella who was standing at the time, watching with beating heart and strained eyes, beneath the laurel-tree, are still in existence at La Bebia. In the same repository of treasures is Isabella's missal, exquisitely illuminated; it was the one she always used, and had it on the occasion of the grand thanksgiving mass after the surrender of Granada; this is placed on the high altar on every 2nd of January, the anniversary of the conquest. Beside it stands her jewel-box, from out of which she took the jewels she gave with her own hands to Columbus, to enable him to start on that voyage which led to such magnificent results to his country, but such bitter ingratitude to himself; the box is silver gilt. Cardinal Mendoza's robes, embroidered by the Catholic queen, and presented by her to the cardinal, are also here. In the centre of these things is a beautiful painting, on wood, of " The Adoration of the Kings," by Hemling; the frame is silver gilt. A few pictures adorn the walls of the sacristy; the most interesting are four small paintings, which were formerly in the private chapel of the queen, and a large picture, representing the unfortunate "King Boabdil taking leave of Ferdinand after having delivered him the keys of the town." This scene actually took place at a little spot on the banks of the Genil, where there was a mosque; at this place Ferdinand and Isabella awaited the dethroned Moor, and bade him farewell; this was at three in the afternoon, on the 2nd of January, 1492, the ancestors of Boabdil having ruled the country for 777 years. This little mosque, of which an original arch still remains, was converted into a chapel, and dedicated to St. Sebastian, and on the outer wall is a marble slab, on which is written an account of this farewell scene. From here Boabdil went to Almeria, and as he reached the summit of a low mountain from whence a view of the town and plain is obtained, he turned round to take a last look, and with a heavy heart turned away; this hill has ever since been called "El ultimo Suspiro del Moro," The Moor's last sigh. From Almeria Boabdil went to Fez, and died more gloriously than he had lived.

The *Sagrario*, parish church, joins the cathedral and chapel royal; it is very handsome and showy; there is a fine picture here of "St. Joseph," by Alonso Cano.

The Cartuja convent is an object of great interest; it is situated a little way out of the town. It was built in the early part of the fourteenth century; Sebastiani robbed it of all its works of art and objects of value, and finally it was suppressed by the Spanish government, so there is but a shadow of its former greatness left. The door into the church is of vine-wood, very handsome, by Hermosa. The interior is elaborately decorated with plaster scroll work; there are one or two pictures here by Cotan. The doors leading into the part of the church occupied by the friars are very beautifully inlaid with tortoiseshell, ivory, ebony, and cedar-wood; the framework round them is ebony, inlaid with silver. Here is a picture representing the "Marriage of the Virgin;" a "Saviour's Head," said to be by Murillo; and a "Virgin and Child," by Alonso Cano. The high altar has gilt pillars, inlaid with bits of looking-glass; the plaster decorations around are coloured. Other inlaid doors lead to the sacristy, which is extremely beautiful; the *comodas*, presses where the vestments are kept, are richly inlaid in the same way as the doors, with the addition of mother-of-pearl; these *comodas* are on both sides; above the last two, to the right and left of the altar, are the largest agates that have ever been found in Spain; they are nearly circular, measuring twenty inches by sixteen. The altar is of agate and jasper, with a carved San Bruno, by Mora. On the jasper pillar to the left of the altar is a vein in the marble near the ground, which has the appearance of the Saviour wearing the Crown of Thorns. The marble recesses on either side of the altar, the one for washing the hands, the other for placing the elements for consecration on, are very handsome; the whole is massive and grand, and in keeping. Leading out of this is the sanctuary; it is extremely beautiful; the marbles are magnificent, and all from about Granada. There are four splendid figures, one in each corner, by Alonso Cano: "St. Joseph," "St. John," "St. Bruno," and "The Magdalen;" the latter is the finest—the gentle, sorrowful face, is beautiful; the drapery around them is well arranged. The tabernacle in the centre is entirely of marble, with Corinthian pillars; the *custodia* is of cedar; portions of the marble are inlaid like the Florentine work. The frescos on the cupola are by Palomino. There is a curious confessional chair, used for bishops; it has but one place for the penitent to kneel, and that is in front of the confessor; this all men do in Spain; only women kneel at the side. The ordinary confessionals have three places, one on either side of the priest, with a grating to speak through, these are for women; and one in front, face to face with the priest, this is for men. Two gorgeous frames, with dark, gloomy pictures, and one or two copies of Murillos, hang in the body of the church. Passing out into the refectory, there is at one point a marvellous echo. At the end of this long room is a cross against the wall; it is a fresco, but people have been known to dispute about what wood it was made of! It is a wonderful piece of colouring, by Cotan, and done some 250 years ago.

In the cloisters are some curious paintings, illustrating the life of San Bruno, and others representing various scenes supposed to have taken place in the torturing of the Carthusians by order of Henry VIII.

Some are horrible to look at. One represents the king himself looking out of a window, gloating over the agonies of his victims, who are being hanged; four more, about to be executed, are being dragged along like dead bulls out of a ring. In another, a row of shorn monks are seen, wearing crowns of thorns, and an angel, in the distance, is carrying one straight up to heaven. All the faces are English; in one some Moors are looking on: this is to prove that the English and Moors were, in the eyes of the Spaniards, the only heretics. These pictures are by Cotan. Those of San Bruno are quaint enough also. One, called "His Dream," represents him in bed, with his slippers placed the right way for him to step into them on getting up: almost all these portray some miracle which occurred to this favoured saint himself. It was from this convent Murillo's "Conception"— now in the Louvre—was abstracted by the French, and became, by right of possession, the property of Marshal Soult.

Santo Domingo was also, in its way, a grand old convent: it is now converted into a museum. The collection, with rare exceptions, is made up of ragged, frameless daubs, fitter to burn than preserve. Those worth anything are soon named: one or two by Zurbaran; the finest of them is "The Saviour walking with St. Joseph and Mary after their finding him in the Temple;" an "Ascension," said to be by Alonso Cano, but, though it is not a bad picture, it is not Cano's style; the "Head of Holofernes," by him; a "Kneeling Monk," by Cotan; "The Presentation of the Rosaries to the Friars," also by him,—the last monk in the painting is a portrait of himself. His portraits of Ferdinand and Isabella are thought to be good. His only other work that is worth looking at is a "Last Supper," and that more for the singular fancy of the artist in representing a fight between a cat and dog in the foreground. A "Kneeling Friar," by Risuelo, is not bad; and there are one or two by Juan de Sevilla which, amidst the rubbish around, tell well; but we do not think they would attract much notice in a good collection. The real gem in this *museo* is a small painting, on wood, of "The Virgin's Head:" it is very beautiful, and ought not to be left here. The artist is not known. It hangs near the second window in the last room. Bocanegra has a few monks in the same room. Amongst the hundreds of pictures collected here, these are all that bear even mentioning. There are some finely-carved monks, by Mora and Risueño, forming parts of the seats in the choir; and a frame, containing six very beautiful enamels on copper. This was formerly in the convent of San Geronimo, presented by Gonzalez de Cordova, and removed here on the suppression of that community.

In the centre of the broad staircase leading up to the museum is a hideous statue of an unfortunate lady named Mariana Pineda; this was to have been placed to her memory in the Plaza del Campillo, but the corporation, at whose expense the monument is to be erected, decided this would not do; another, therefore, was executed: for the present it stands in a kind of lumber-room, but as soon as the necessary arrangements are made, it will be raised on the pedestal in the centre of the plaza: it is a fine colossal statue in white marble. This lady was the widow of a Colonel Pineda, and happened to be both young and beautiful; a man named Pedroza is said to have paid his addresses to her, and to have been rejected; he then, in a fit of anger and jealousy, placed, in 1831, a constitutional flag in her house, and then informed against her. Though unconscious of the flag being there, she was arrested, accused of treason, and condemned to death. Her execution took place, by strangulation, in May, 1831, near the Plaza de Toros: a plain white cross marks the spot. Five years later, the corporation of Granada resolved to honour the remains of the innocent woman, and they caused her body to be removed in state, and to erect a monument to her. The pedestal is nearly completed. Besides her own name and account of her death, it bears the names of other victims of liberty; amongst them the names of seven officers who, in 1825, were shot for being freemasons. The Spaniards are never in a hurry, nor can they be made to do things quickly; therefore, thirty-two years is not so out-of-the-way a time for them to make up their minds to raise a monument and carry out their determination. There is little left to finish now—only the ornamental railings round it; but no doubt a year or two more will elapse before Mariana Pineda's statue is actually raised to its destined position.

The façade of the church of San Domingo is very handsome, though in a sad state of decay; it is the work of Diego de Siloe: the initials Y. and F. are above it. Inside, all is very grand; massive, heavy gilding everywhere. The decorations are too gaudy; the few pictures there are, are of little merit. In a chapel on the left hand from the entrance, behind the figure of the Virgin, is a fresco painting of a cross, with white drapery. It is wonderfully done: even when quite close to it, you cannot feel sure whether it is not actually of wood, and the drapery white calico.

San Geronimo is another of those vast institutions which at one time Granada was overrun by; monks and beggars then peopled the town. It is a little better now as far as the monks go: the beggars are as bad as ever. The chapel of San Geronimo is very handsome; to the right and left of the high altar are the effigies of Gonzalez de Cordova and his wife. The Great Captain was the founder, and his sword used to hang above his effigy; but all was destroyed, within and without, by Sebastiani. There were two magnificent organs; only one remains, the other is a mere shell. The *patio* is very fine. The convent is now used as cavalry barracks.

San Juan de Dios is a hospital founded by Juan de Robles, who, because he considered foundling hospitals proper and necessary institutions, was confined in a cage as a lunatic. He died in the sixteenth century, and was canonized a hundred years afterwards. He died on his knees, and in that position he is represented over the entrance : the statue is by Mora. There are two large *patios;* the first is surrounded with pictures representing scenes from his life ; the other has nothing particular in it, but you reach it by passing by a grand staircase, over which is a very fine inlaid ceiling. The hospital is well kept, well managed, and extremely clean.

The Town Hall is a large, plain, uninteresting building, formerly a Carmelite convent. When the queen, Isabel II., visited Granada, in 1860, she stayed here. The façade of the convent, where the Little Sisters of the Poor live, is very handsome.

Granada is full of interest. Every way you turn, and every step you take, brings you to something worth seeing. It would be impossible to describe everything, but the principal objects we will run over.

Leaving the Alhambra hill behind us, we enter the town by a fine Moorish gateway, called La Puerta de las Granadas ; this takes us at once into the Calle de los Gomeles, so called from the house of the great family of that name being in the street; it is the first on the right-hand side. Their ancestor it was who aroused the jealousy of Boabdil, which resulted in the murder of the Abencerrages, the bitter enemies of the Gomeles. At the end of the street is the Plaza Nueva; in the centre is the Chancilleria; it was built by Philip II. in 1584. The façade is handsome, but the *patio* is mean, and the massive stone-work over the staircase in bad taste. It is built entirely of Loja stone, and designed by Herrera. Out of this Plaza, continuing along the Carrera de Darro and passing the church of Santa Ana, nearly opposite is the house of the late Count Montijo, uncle to the Empress of the French. It was from this house that, in 1816, he was taken away in the night by the Inquisition, in a carriage with muffled wheels, and put to such torture, because he was unable to accept all their articles of faith, that he lost his power of speech. At this period his brother, Count de Teba, was living in the Calle de Gracia, No. 12, and in this house the Empress Eugénie was born, and baptized in the chapel of Santa Madalena, opposite. The church is pretty, but nothing more.

A little higher up the Carrera de Darro is the Casa de Bañuelo; this was a public bath in the time of the Moors, and it remains untouched from that period. The marble columns are more perfect than one could expect to find them in such a spot, for poverty and wretchedness reign around. Beyond the large bath is the place where they dressed and reposed. It has since been used by washerwomen, but now it is left as a mere relic of the great past. Nearly opposite are the remains of a Moorish arch, which formed a bridge across the Darro, from the Alhambra to the Mint, but it was destroyed by Sebastiani. The Alameda, at the end of the street, is the promenade for the middle classes. Now in the present day, there is not the same distinction amongst the people there used to be. Formerly they were divided into three distinct sets, which were called Blue Blood, Red Blood, and White Blood: the Blue was royal and the highest of the nobility; the Red was the gentry and middle class; and the White the people. They each had everything apart and distinct, even to their Alameda and café, and never dreamt of intruding where they had no right.

To the left of this walk is the quarter called the Albaicin, because peopled originally by Moors from Albacete, who, on the conquest of that place, fled to Granada for safety; it is inhabited by the poor only. There are two houses in it, joining each other, called Las Casas Chapis; they belonged to merchants, and were seraglios. In the first, the roof of the verandah around the *patio* is carved larch; only two marble pillars remain. There is a fine arched doorway, ornamented with stucco work, and another handsome door; but all destroyed with whitewash. The original well is remaining, and still used, but not for the same purposes. In the second house the *patio* is in a much less tumble-down state; there are five arches, with the decorations tolerably perfect; the stars to the right and left of each arch are very pretty; there is a doorway prettily ornamented, but again the whitewash has done its work.

Ascending the road, we reached the gipsies' quarters, which consist of large excavations made on the side of a hill covered with cactus. They reside here in great numbers. At the entrance of this strangely populated hill, some Spanish families reside, but their caves are far cleaner than the gipsies': all, however, are whitewashed inside. They do not live here rent-free; each has a landlord; one peseta (a franc) a month is paid for dwellings that contain but one room (?), and the same in proportion for larger ones: some have three holes inside, the largest contain five. These excavations are the size of rooms in small cottages; the front one is always the largest. The hole by which these dwellings are entered is the only means of obtaining daylight. The moment the occupants see strangers, they all come out, and request them to walk in, and offer them whatever they have, of course ending by asking for money: they don't tell fortunes; this is a trade unknown to them. They wave their hand downwards and inwards in token of invitation, as if they were scooping in something; but all Spaniards do this. The cactus fruit forms their chief food in summer, and vegetables in winter.

They will go out for six dollars, and dance; we had them up one night at the hotel; ten of them, with their captain, a fine handsome man, who does not burrow in the earth, but lives in a decent house in the town. It is a thing to see, but it is not at all graceful; they dance heavily, dragging their feet after them, hardly raising them from the ground; their arms and heads work instead. Their singing is dreadfully monotonous, not the least melody in it, and the noise they make with clapping their hands, deafening. They are always accompanied by the guitar, which the captain plays; he makes up for the disappointment created by the others, as he plays and sings beautifully; and has a deep rich-toned voice. One pretty light piece of his own composition he played with the guitar behind him. There is a very large good room at the "Washington Irving" hotel, where we had this entertainment. They all shake hands with you, if you let them. There is no beauty amongst either the men or the women; they are so fat and heavy; the children are lovely, every one of them is a picture, but they grow out of it very rapidly.

Near to the gipsies' hill, is San Juan de los Reyes; it was a Moorish mosque, and the first consecrated as a Christian church: the old tower is still very perfect. There is here a picture painted by Rincon, which was presented by Isabella the Catholic to this church. The subject is the dead Saviour, with the Virgin and St. John on the right and left; these are portraits of Ferdinand and Isabella. There is a strange picture on the right as you enter, of the Virgin seated in a chariot, and being drawn along like a goddess, the people around her looking very much as if they were hurrahing.

Returning towards the cathedral, facing the entrance to the Royal Chapel, is an old house with a very richly decorated exterior. This building was a university in the time of the Moors; after the conquest, it was used as the town hall, and now it is a cotton spinning manufactory. Not far from here is the old Moorish silk bazaar, Alcaiseria; it is most curious. Eight years ago it was nearly destroyed by fire, but it has been completely restored. The shops are all open, and closed at night by large doors. The walks are not more than six feet in width; it is like a number of narrow passages, with stalls on both sides: at the end of one is the entrance to the mosque; this was used for the workmen. The Zacatin is the street where all their cotton goods were sold; it is now full of bootmakers and silversmiths, two trades that one would imagine must flourish here, so numerous are their shops; yet it being our misfortune to have a pair of boots stolen from outside the bedroom door (most valuable boots they were, for they withstood the hard wear of the pointed stones in a most wonderful manner), when we sent to replace them, it was with the utmost difficulty we got anything like a boot at all that was wearable. Spaniards will steal if they happen to see on another what they want. We heard Lady H——, of L——, had her purse stolen here in the cathedral; this was doubly wicked, for *she* was not a heretic.

Close to the Zacatin is La Casa del Carbon, once a Moorish palace, now a washerwomen's palace. The gateway, all that remains worth seeing, is very beautiful, but fast going to ruin. The work around the horse-shoe arches, of which there are three—the right and left arches were formerly sentry boxes—is very fine, as are also the windows above. There are different assertions as to what this palace formerly was; some say it was a Moorish noble's harem, others that it was the palace of Boabdil's brother: all, however, agree that it was built in the eleventh century, thus making it two hundred years older than the Alhambra palace. In the centre of the *patio* the original well remains.

There are several of these old gateways studded about the town, with Moorish work about them; the finest is one with three horse-shoe arches, leading out of the Plaza de Vibarambla. Granada being the last place in Spain from whence the Moors were driven, more of their work is to be seen here than elsewhere; at every corner is something, and if not Moorish it is of the time of Ferdinand and Isabella, which is nearly the same thing, as the population was entirely composed of Moors, and the buildings were erected by them. Granada is very much improving, the railway has done an immense deal for it. Houses are springing up in all directions, a large hotel is being built in the town, to be called the "Alameda," though visitors will probably patronise the "Washington Irving," on account of its position. Many of the houses in the old portions of the town have no glass to their windows; matting is hung over them to keep out the sun; yet there is no window tax, but glass is expensive. Dried palm leaves are interlaced in the rails of balconies in almost every decent looking house; they are supposed to protect it from lightning,—not that they are efficacious in themselves, but these have all been blessed, and so are charmed. This is not to be seen in Granada alone, but all over Spain, from the palace at Madrid, and the Escorial, down to the peasant's cabin—if he can get it.

The place called the "Threshing Floor of Christ," is where the Moors put the Christian prisoners to death; it is near the Bull Ring. The Bull Ring is a neat building, but small, not holding more than 6000 people.

There are two theatres. The Teatro de Isabel la Catolica is a fine house, with a good company, good orchestra, and a good *ballet*, the Señoras Olaso and Navarro being the chief dancers: the drop scene is wonderfully painted. The other, El Teatro Principal, is not so large, but better lighted: smells in both much on a par. The dancing here was wonderful, but would have to be modified for English spectators; even one of the present day could hardly sit through such a ballet as was performed here before a crammed house. Mdlle. Mora was the attraction; M. Mamert also drew down applause, but it was faint in comparison with that accorded the lady.

We went one day to see an amusing scene, which occasionally takes place on the exercising ground, a large grassless plain on the other side of the pretty little village of Armilla. It is a sham fire, at which the capabilities of the firemen are tested; it attracts all the Granadinos; of course, like every other sight in this country, it takes place on a Sunday. The whole thing was stupid, and if people's lives depended on the house of straw being extinguished instead of their minds being diverted, there would be little hope for them. A huge building of thin planks of wood and straw is erected, and then set fire to; to put this out, men raised on a platform at the back are handed buckets of water, which are given up a ladder; these little tubs are emptied on the blazing mass, but make no more impression than a teaspoonful would do; the fire, in truth, burns itself out amidst hooting and shouting; when the whole thing is over, the firemen are entertained at a *déjeûner*, which to them is the only really exciting event of the day. This fire, by the way, reminds us of the fire tongs used in this country; they are most absurd looking things, very little larger than pincers used for curling ladies' hair, and very similar in shape.

The way funerals are conducted here amongst the poor is distressing beyond measure to see. The bodies are placed in a hired coffin, dressed in their usual clothes, and then carried to the cemetery, when they are turned out into the ground, and covered over. We saw the funeral procession one day of a little child between three and four years old, and at first could not believe it possible that the body was once that of a living child. It was being carried by four boys, in a pink and white box, without any lid, or any covering thrown over the face, which had the eyes wide open; a wreath around the fair curling hair, and a doll lying over the little hands; they held it by cords, and were swinging it from side to side, and laughingly going on their errand; three or four men followed at a short distance, but no outward sign betrayed their being interested in the poor little thing that was gone. On reaching the cemetery, a priest and a few women were awaiting it; the body was then taken out of the gay-looking box, and placed in the ground. These Spaniards are perfect Pagans about death, as they are in many other points, but they have no shrinking from it, they meet it as indifferently as a suttee.

The only private collection of paintings in Granada is that belonging to Don Gravial Arroya; he has some very good ones. Amongst them may be found one or two Murillos, with the original sketch of his "Conception," now at the Louvre; some by Alonso Cano, and a few by Ribera.

In the Calle de San Geronimo are two houses with Moorish architecture about them; in the one called La Casa del Rey, belonging to Señor Ansotti Colonado, there is a fine picture of the "Council of Nice;" the Holy Trinity is over the councillors, and angels are upholding them.

Granada has a large number of Protestants amongst its population, numbering between three and four thousand. They all wear a small gold star beneath their coats, and, Spaniard-like, daggers and revolvers as well. They are a suspicious race, and very imaginative, two characteristics which frequently go together; this does not apply to the Protestant community more than the Roman Catholic; on the contrary, the latter are the most mistrustful of the two; and Mariolatry is carried to such an excess in all Andalucia (one might say all Spain, only then Andalucia beats Spain), that the Godhead is almost ignored, and at best is very secondary. No wonder Protestantism is making rapid strides, though silently; who *could* be a Roman Catholic if the religion of Spain is Roman Catholicism? We would recommend any who are wavering and doubting, and who are more than half disposed to follow in the footsteps of those who have left the Reformed Church for the Church of Rome, to make a tour in the south of Spain, and then spend a week in Valencia, and if *that* does not open their eyes, nothing will; if that does not cure them, they must have some Pagan tendencies that no human means or power can eradicate.

CHAPTER XIX.

FROM GRANADA TO MURCIA.

AFTER a very pleasant fortnight at Granada, we had to make up our minds to move on, though somewhat reluctantly, for we dreaded the long sea journey from Malaga to Alicante, especially as the recollection of our voyage from Gibraltar to Malaga was very fresh in our memory. But when we came to talk the matter over with Mariano Ramos, the hotel keeper, we found it practicable to do the journey by land; and it was agreed he was to accompany us to Alicante; and we were to send our courier (always useless) back to Malaga, to fetch our luggage, take it by sea, and meet us with it at Alicante. The journey by sea would have taken us three nights; the days are spent on land, as the steamers put in at Almeria and Cartagena, to leave and take up passengers and cargoes. The land journey was to occupy five days; but then we would not be losing time, as the scenery was said to be magnificent; and we also desired to gain an insight into this mode of travelling.

We made all our preparations, that is, Mariano did for us. We had a good strong, but not heavy, carriage, omnibus shape, that held six comfortably inside, the coach-box held two, and a famous seat on the roof for four; five mules, and a first-rate coachman, Salvao by name. We took provisions with us, including butter and tea; our basket also contained knives and forks, plates, tumblers, and a table-cloth. The butter came to an end long before it was intended: and had it not been for a rivulet, where the table-cloth was washed, what would it have been? for we were to have been five days only on the journey, instead of which we were nine;—but this by the way.

We started at nine in the morning, a little late as it proved, on Friday, 14th February; a cheery, joyous party, determined to brave all difficulties, and make the best of all disagreeables. What a lovely morning it was, and how grandly beautiful did Granada appear as we ascended the hill, leaving it behind us in the plain, backed by the glistening, glittering Sierra Nevada.

Our first day's journey was to Guadix; for an hour or two our road was one continued ascent, with a rugged, wild, mountainous country around. At Molinillo, a little *venta* mid-way, we rested, and refreshed ourselves and the mules: water, bread, and wine being all the *ventas* can supply, we found the use of our provision basket. We sat in the open air, but in the shade, for the sun was very hot. A *venta* is a sort of inn, yet in appearance it is more like a large shed. An open archway leads into a covered barn; one side is for man, the other for beast. The former is fitted up as a sort of kitchen: jugs, mugs, plates, saucepans, and other utensils hanging round; more than half of these things are beneath a huge chimney, which covers a space of twelve or fourteen feet, taking up fully a quarter of the barn; in the centre, on the ground, a wood fire burns. Beds are not to be had in these ventas; but the *arrieros*, or carriers, who require nothing but their mule-cloth for their bed, frequently stop all night.

As we were generally ready before the mules, we used to walk slowly onwards, and let the carriage overtake us. Around Molinillo there seems to be a perfect sea of earth mounds, looking in the distance like a colossal encampment; each of these mounds forms a dwelling for the gipsy populations which abound in this part of the country. None have windows, many have no doors; inside, however, is much better than could be imagined from the out; and they multiply and increase as in any other above-ground city.

A couple of hours before reaching Guadix, we broke one of the springs of the carriage; this arose from the dreadful roads that must be gone over when passing through villages; we lost more than half an hour in repairing it; and the night being very dark, and the road near Guadix not over good, we were forced to go at a very slow pace, thus not reaching there till seven o'clock. The night was cold, but, as far as we were individually concerned, we were kept warm with fright; that, however, was the only evil, as no attempt was made either to rob or carry any of us off. All who understood the use of fire-arms were armed with revolvers, and Mariano and Salvao had their knife-daggers with them; and this was no unnecessary precaution, as such things do happen as brigands making a descent on unwary travellers.

There was a little difficulty, on reaching Guadix, to gain entrance to the *posada*, that of Naranjos; the people have a habit of going to bed with daylight in these out-of-the-way spots. And how our hearts sank within us when we did get in! The description of one posada, like one venta, will do for all, as there is so little difference in them—so much so, that it would be impossible to recall any one in particular to one's recollection, without making certain notes in connection with each. The entrance corresponds with the venta's; the ground floor—and it is the ground pure and simple—is occupied by animals on one side, and a kitchen on the other; the space in the centre is covered with sleeping muleteers from sunset to sunrise; the mule cloth is laid on the ground, and forms their bed, and their saddle or sack containing the mule's food, their pillow; they never dream of undressing, but give themselves a shake, and curl themselves up like dogs. A flight of stone stairs, towards the middle of this barn, leads up to the rooms which are set apart for travellers who can pay for this superior kind of accommodation; up this we were conducted by the light of a classically shaped lamp, borne by a decent-looking woman. The rooms were off the gritty paved landing; their furniture consisted of one deal table, about two feet by one, two bass grass chairs, and an iron ring, standing stiff out from the wall, in which was fixed a yellow earthenware basin about the size of an ordinary pudding basin—and not a blessed thing besides. The walls were white-washed, and the floor paved like the passage outside, and covered with gritty dust. The windows were mere square openings in the wall, with wooden doors; not a vestige of glass; but being night, this misery was not felt till the morning, when one was forced to dress with the cold air blowing in upon one—for up in these regions the mornings and evenings were really cold—or else by lamp light; the same with breakfast; and this was the case at all the posadas. Beds were forthcoming, of course, only it is the custom to double them up, and stow them away as we do linen; there were a dozen of them in a store room: a wooden frame with a clean mattress forms the whole affair; but they are very comfortable, and linen plentiful and good.

We picked up, on this our first day's journey, a poor little orphan boy, who was trudging proudly along in rags that were not even sufficient for decency, making the best of his way to Baza; he had gone to Granada, thinking he was old enough and big enough to enlist as his brother had done; but this poor child was but eleven years old, and small for his age, so having of course failed, disappointed and hopeless he was returning to his native town. We let him sit on the step of the carriage when going down hill, but he was to walk going up, and this he most conscientiously did. Now, the poor little fellow tried in every way to be useful; there he stood over a *brasero*, fanning away at it, as if his life depended on keeping the embers a bright red; when the sheets were being aired, he held the corners over the fire, so that no portion should escape being heated; and he remained up the last, so as to be assured he could do nothing more.

Butter, tea, and coffee, are things unknown in a posada. Milk is obtainable, but nót without great difficulty. Had we had our own courier with us, instead of Mariano, we should never have seen milk the whole time; as it was we were never without it: once he went himself and milked somebody's cow without leave or licence, much to their fury and indignation when they found it out; in the meanwhile, however, we had drank the milk. Eggs, ham, *jamon dulce*, as they term those cured by snow, and which are extremely delicate, rice, bread—the same beautiful white bread—and good water are always to be had; but with children these things are not everything; yet by Mariano's good management and forethought we never really wanted for any necessary. There is something awfully dreary in these posadas; the whitewash, and bare, empty, be-shuttered rooms, with paving stones for flooring, are depressing after a long fatiguing hot journey; one requires a very cheery disposition to carry one well through such a tour; however, we never flagged, fortunately, till it was over, and then we were intensely thankful we had done it.

Guadix is a large town, beautifully situated; the Sierra Nevada, towering up behind it, forming a magnificent background. There is a bishop, and a population of 18,000. The Cathedral is large and handsome: the pulpits are the most worthy of admiration; they are of marble, and very fine. The town is famed for the manufacture of a peculiar shaped knife, which the natives are as fond of using as having.

We left Guadix at 8.15 A.M., and left Francisco, our little *protégé*, behind us, as we made arrangements with Mariano to pick him up on his return journey, and take him back with him to Granada, and give him some employment. The poor boy ran after the carriage for a long distance, warmly and comfortably clothed, and a smart *manta* over his shoulders. When he turned at last, and waved his farewell, he could contain himself no longer, and he cried bitterly: the child no doubt thought he was losing the only friends he had ever met with in the world. Poor little Francisco! We often talked of him, and wondered if he would continue to remember us. We heard of his safe arrival in Granada, and of his well-being.*

* And now we have just heard that Mariano so ill-treated the

From Guadix to the Venta de Baul, where we made our mid-day halt, the road is very beautiful, but very wild and desolate: we for hours never saw a human being; then we would see a convoy of muleteers winding along the road: these men are always well armed, as they carry on their mules merchandise, with which they traffic as they go along. This is the way commerce is carried on about these primitive parts. They generally sing as they go along: the Spanish *arrieros* are famous for their songs; but the melodies are peculiar, like nothing we ever heard before; and we had plenty of it at all times, for Salvao, our coachman, was renowned for his voice, as well as for his inexhaustible collection of songs. On from the Venta de Baul, the road lies through a mass of tent-like hills, such as we passed by on the previous day; the "Dientes de la Vieja," or "The Woman's Teeth," rearing up behind them; it is like a sea of brown waves: the effect produced is very curious, and the inhabitants of these mounds swell the population to some twelve or fourteen thousand more than exist in the town. The *vega* around Baza is fine, but does not equal Guadix: cork trees grow well in this soil, and the bass grass covers the plain. The Posada del Sol is the best inn here; it is a duplicate of the one we were at, at Guadix. On the Alameda are some of the old cannons, used during the siege at the conquest of Granada;

poor child that he ran away; however, we have taken steps to have him traced and placed in better care.

they are stuck in the ground, and serve as posts; the rings attached to them forming a sufficiently firm hold for the children of the town to swing themselves round by. The wine at Baza is very good, but, indeed, it is rare in any part of Spain not to find both wine and bread excellent. They have a bull-ring here, which the inhabitants think much of, as at Guadix, a much larger place, they do not possess one.

From Baza, which we left at 8.30 A.M., we went to Cullar de Baza, a short day's journey, but we were compelled to stop here, as at Chirivel, the station beyond, there were no beds to be had. We halted for our mid-day repast at the Venta del Peral, celebrated for the smuggling carried on in tobacco; at this venta the finest Habana cigars can be bought for two-thirds less than they can be had for in the towns. The road during this day's journey was arid and wild, the *esparto* or bass grass growing in great profusion; many articles are made of it, mattings, chair bottoms, baskets, and rope; a great deal is exported to England. From the Venta del Peral to Cullar is not much more than a league; a Spanish league being about four English miles; this we nearly walked; yet the heat was intense, for there was no shade, but having once started there was no use in turning back. As a rule these noonday walks were most enjoyable; we left the high road, and cut across the upland paths, sometimes making short cuts, sometimes long detours. One day Mariano very nearly shot a dog for a wolf; we had seen one in the distance on a mountain ledge, and we imagined the same brute now crossed our path within a few yards of us: he was so like a wolf, that it was not till one or two of us got down from the seat where we were perched up aloft on the carriage, and went close up to him, that all were convinced the beast was only a dog.

The Posada de la Plaza is the best at Cullar: facing it is the mayor's house, and the church forms the third side to the square. Inside the church there is nothing to see; but there is too much to hear outside, the bells never seemed to cease, till at last we were nearly driven distracted. The striped mantas worn here by the natives are extremely picturesque, making the dingy miserable looking town bright and cheerful. Three-fourths of the town consists of holes in the earth, dug out for habitations. The appearance of these dwellings is very singular; and they are rendered more curious by the large mud chimney which rises out of what forms the roof. The hills these excavations are made in, lie in ridges; thus in the distance they have almost the appearance of streets, from their rising tier upon tier.

An old Moorish tower crowns the summit of a hill on the opposite side which overlooks the town; the view from it is very extensive, stretching far over mountain and valley. A portion of this ruin had clearly been turned at some time or another into a Christian chapel, from the traces that still remain of homage that has been paid to the Virgin: her initials are engraved on the walls, and a broken image is stowed away amongst rubbish of all kinds.

The children in these towns form a large moving nuisance; they crowded round the carriage when we arrived, so much so, that it was not always easy to get out of it. They followed every step we took, and they came so close to one, that it became serious; and we were either compelled to appeal to some one to free us from them, or else give up attempting to see the place.

We had a tiny room lent us to dine in at the inn, belonging to a commercial traveller; it had a chimney in it, which formed its only attraction, so we had a fire lighted; and in the evening our hostess and her handsome daughter entertained us by a monotonous tom-tom sort of music on the guitar, and a howling accompaniment with the voice. Spanish singing is dreadfully unmusical; it is guiltless of all harmony, and all appear to sing alike. They burst out in snatches, then tom-tom on the guitar, then they break forth again. How tired we were, and how we longed to get away, but manners induced us to remain a little; doubtless, however, the attention and intention were alike unappreciated. On all these occasions, smoking never ceases; so that the room is filled with it, and though the smell is not strong, the atmosphere is suffocating.

Our next day's journey took us to Velez-Rubio. We got off by 8.15 A.M., and reached Chirivel at 12.30

and Velez-Rubio at 5.45 P.M. The road to Chirivel was good; the last league before reaching it, from Vertientes, is called the "Friar's League;" an awful league it is, at least six miles. At the venta here, in addition to the usual provender they supply, we had a sweet radish, very large and thick, with a rose-coloured skin, more like a carrot in size; the taste was something between a bad apple and a turnip. From Chirivel to Velez-Rubio, the road lies along the bed of a torrent, and we were obliged to hold tight to keep our outside seats; ruts, huge stones, mud, water, and every possible impediment we could, we did encounter. A new road is being made, but when it is to be completed is a question no one would like to answer. Flax is grown about here in great quantities, and gives ample employment to the people if they choose to work; but Spaniards don't care for labour; if they have enough to eat for the day, they take no thought for the morrow. All about these mountain roads we frequently saw rude wooden crosses, formed by two sticks, or two pieces of cane: this marks the spot of some violent death, preceded of course by robbery. These crosses have mounds of stones around them, as it is the custom for all passers-by to cast one at the foot of the cross. Some we saw were very recently erected; the cross new, and the stones few. These victims are generally muleteers, who, instead of joining a convoy, brave the dangers of the road alone; or, perhaps, have started in the hope of overtaking one.

The Posada del Rosario, at Velez-Rubio, is a tremendous house, a perfect barrack, but otherwise resembling the rest, bare and comfortless in the extreme. We always entered these inns with a sinking heart, and left them with indescribable delight, for the days were enjoyable beyond measure. This house was built in 1785, by the then Duke of Alba and Medina Sidonia, eleventh Marquis of Villafranca, as a tablet, in marble, over the entrance informs all wayfarers; it seems impossible, from the utter absence of everything but size, that the building could ever have been intended for a palace. We had a big, white-washed room as a sitting-room; there was a huge chimney in it, by which we succeeded in burning holes in the sheets and pillow cases, for we had a roaring wood fire; the room belonged to some one else, who lent it to us for a few hours, sitting up the while, for otherwise the usual occupant would have been in bed. Outside, on the long, broad landing, more like a gallery in size and length, there were mounds of red pepper, which by morning were stowed away in sacks. This red pepper is the common pepper of the country, made from *pimientas*, a capsicum of great size, grown here in quantities; fortunately it is not strong in smell, any more than it is in taste, so we had no sneezing fits.

From Velez-Rubio we went to Lorca. The road as far as La Puerta de Lumberas, is awful; we re-entered the bed of the torrent, which we left the night before, and bounded over a certain portion, till it became too serious a matter to trust our necks on the outside of the carriage, or the inside either, so we all turned out to walk, which we did for a long league. The carriage, miraculously enough, did not come to pieces, thanks, we believe, to the springs having already been broken and so well bandaged up, that they were better than before; nor did the mules break their legs, though one, Pelegrino, the leader on this occasion, turned right round at a very awkward point, and deliberately pulled in the opposite direction; however, after strong opposition offered in the shape of violent kicks, he was induced to go on the right way. It was no wonder the poor beast tried to turn back, to see what was before him was quite enough even to make a mule hesitate about going on; Salvao, our cheery singing coachman, declared, after we were safe over our difficulties, that once or twice he had nothing but the atmosphere to drive over; this was when he had to drive along the side of a steep hill, without a sign of a road, and that was so awkward looking that we branched off into a mule track, expecting every moment to hear or see the carriage upset. A road in process of being made, loomed temptingly in the far distance, like a thin white thread; the contractors have received three millions of reals for its completion; it will be a great boon for man and beast when it is finished, and so allow the river bed to be left for what nature intended it; to look over portions of this road, it seems as if it were simply impossible for a carriage to pass it —frightful torrents or earthquakes could alone have produced such a jumble.

We stopped at La Puerta del Lumbrera for our noon-day meal; the Posada de Nuestra Señora del Carmen, though calling itself a posada, and not a venta, is less clean than we generally found such places, and is in a village, which to us was not half so enjoyable as were the inns on the road side. The torrent runs through the centre of the village, cutting it in two; the portion on the right is formed entirely of holes dug in the side of the hill, in which the greater part of the population lives. The country about here is very pretty; there is less of the bold mountain scenery, and more hill and dale, with vegetation; the peasants dress in very bright colours, red or yellow petticoats, and coloured bodies, contrasting admirably with their dark complexions. From Lumbrera to Lorca are three long leagues, but we got in by 5, having left Velez-Rubio at 8·20 a.m.

We went to the Posada de San Vicente, but it was very dirty, and altogether objectionable, so we made an appeal to the *amo* to tell us if we could not find better accommodation in the town; he then admitted we might do better if we went to a Casa de Huespedes, or boarding house. Whilst some of the party went to see rooms, the rest remained at the posada; the room we were in was on the ground floor, the window looking into the street; in a few minutes there was a crowd round it, equal to that which surrounds a police court if some noted criminal is expected to appear; there were, fortunately, iron bars all the way up, or they would have come into the room; up these, however, boys climbed, till the grating was a mass of faces; this not being enough, a woman called Caroline came in, and seated herself close to us, and began to talk in French, hoping she did not intrude, but hearing visitors had arrived, she came to pay them some attention; we found out in a moment that she was crazy, and therefore we called to the *amo* to turn her out; she was dressed in dirty silks and finery, and ought to have been kept shut up. It was, therefore, with no little feeling of thankfulness that we heard rooms could be had at the house of Pablo de Pedro, 10, Calle de la Parrica, and with a relief that amounted to pleasure, we found very comfortable, clean, well-furnished rooms. The good old maiden sister told us they had kept the house for twenty-four years, and her first boarder was an Englishman, so she looked especially kindly on all our country people, and treated us accordingly. We had an excellent dinner, excellent beds, and felt as if the house was a paradise, after what we had met with.

Lorca is a large town, with 30,000 inhabitants; there are some good houses, a fine cathedral, several other churches, but nothing remarkable in any; gold and whitewash, images and paintings, rendering them all very much alike. The old castle is worth going up to see, because of the view; the scenery around is very grand, and the *vega* magnificent. The beggars surpass all the beggars in any other part of Spain; they lay hold of you and positively howl at you, and do everything but pick your pocket, which they probably would do if they thought to succeed.

We left Lorca at 7·45 a.m.; we halted at noon, at Alhama; there are three Alhamas in Spain, all celebrated for springs: these are subterraneous. The road from Lorca is arid and uninteresting, it is straight, for miles not a turn, and the cactus and aloe alone relieve the monotony of the brown barren soil. At Totana the oriental scenery begins, which only terminates on the other side of Elche; the flat-roofed houses, the magnificent palms, the blazing sun and deep blue cloudless sky, all tend to give an eastern appearance to this part of the country. Every here and there are hills, topped with the ruins of Moorish towers; all the land about them is arid and wild, whilst hemp and flax grow plentifully in the *vega*, giving a bright rich look to the plain. They cleanse the fibre in a very primitive manner at the corners of the streets.

Our provisions were unfortunately a little the worse for wear; they were nearly eaten away, and we were reduced to-day to a box of sardines, and the frugal produce of the venta, but we did very well on the hope of the future; that night we were to reach Murcia, a considerable town, with a fonda, or hotel; yet the " Live, horse, and I'll give you corn," was unfortunately not fulfilled; we had buoyed up ourselves with the hope of finding a good hotel, and consequent comforts, whereas that of the " Francesca " was very bad; had it been called a posada, we might have spoken of it in terms of admiration, but as a fonda it fell lamentably short of what it should be, and what it might be, for the house is good enough, and large enough, but there is enough dirt in it to frighten away even a pig, and the smells are awful.

CHAPTER XX.

MURCIA.—TO ELCHE AND ALICANTE.

THE approach to Murcia is beautiful; you see it for miles ahead, with the Cathedral tower, giving it in the distance a look of Seville. The palm-tree is studded about here and there, growing to an enormous height, overtopping everything, and laden with the graceful drooping bunches of fruit. The *vega* is very rich; everything grows without man's hand interfering; beans were grown to their full size, peas plentiful; fruits belonging more especially to tropical climates grow about here and in the neighbourhood. But the Murcians think more of silk than anything else; the quantities of mulberry trees show how they trade in it. The silk they manufacture is more celebrated for its durability than its beauty. Mantas, the coarse scarfs worn by the peasants, are all manufactured here, yet Murcia is about the worst place to buy them in, as all the best are sent away. The dress of the Murcian peasant is very like the Greek; they wear very wide white drawers, which, being gathered in at the waist, and falling only to the knee, very full, seem to be a petticoat; their legs, which are much more like walking-sticks than legs, are covered from below the knee with a legging of stocking material, but having neither toes nor heels, only a strap passing under the sole of the foot; their shoes are called alpargata, they are hempen soles, with tape sandals. Round the waist they wear the bright red sash, common all over Spain. It is wound round several times. Their jackets are of velvet, generally ornamented with large silver buttons, their sleeves open, and a white or red handkerchief bound round the head, or a cap shaped like a man's nightcap. Above this they wear the *manta* when cold; the colours of it are very bright. They throw it round the shoulders in the same graceful manner they do the *capa*, or cloak, in other parts of the country. They always carry a peculiar stick, with a tremendous crook at the head of it. The women's dress here also differs from that worn in the western and southern parts of Spain. Nothing is black but the mantilla; all the brightest colours are to be seen; their petticoats sometimes very much embroidered or flounced; the dress fitting tightly to the body, all very becoming to their pretty gipsy faces. They have beautiful hair, and great quantities of it. There is a merry heedlessness in their manner, which alone renders a marked difference between them and the Andalusians.

Murcia is not an interesting town. There is little to see, and less to do that can occupy one's time, which we found hang very heavily the second day, on our hands. The walks are being made, the streets are being made, the houses are being made, and it is the railway does all this; but during the bricks and mortar era, the town is disagreeable. There is a Plaza de Toros, but bull-fights occur during the summer only; a theatre, not a bad one, by any means, for such a town; and the usual other public buildings that are totally devoid of interest to the ordinary traveller, unless they happen to contain some great work of art, or that their architecture is remarkable, which in no instance is the case here. The Cathedral is the principal thing to see. We began by ascending the tower, which, like the Giralda at Seville, we walked up by an inclined plane, that is, as far as the clock tower, where there is a very good whispering gallery; from that point we went up by a corkscrew staircase to the summit. The view around is very fine. The range of mountains which divides Murcia from the sea, the splendid *vega*, the quaint-looking town at our feet, looking so blue and white and yellow, from the strange fancy the Murcians have of painting their houses this colour; the flat roofs, and occasional towers, rendered it different to the generality of panoramas. The finest entrance to this one-towered church is by the Portada de los Apostoles; the door is handsome; the other undomed ought-to-be tower is girdled round by a massive stone chain, in compliment to the Velez family, whose badge it is; inside the church is a chapel belonging to them, which is handsomely decorated with stone carvings; in it is a painting of St. Luke writing his gospel, by Francisco Garcia. In the body of the church is a beautiful Virgin and Child; it might be by Alonso Cano, but nothing is known about it. The pulpits are peculiar; they are more like two jam pots of iron, projecting from the screen of the high altar. There is some good carving in the choir, and also in the sacristy. The great treasure in this church is a relic left to it by Alonso el Sabio, being nothing more nor less than his own inside. This precious gift he bequeathed to Murcia, because it was he who re-took the town from the Moors, who again got possession of it after its first conquest in 1240 by his father, San Fernando. All the valuables formerly here were appropriated by the French.

In the Church of San Nicholas is a large carved image, over the high altar of the saint, by Cano. The expression of the face is beautiful, and at a little side chapel there is a small figure of San Antonio in the dress of a Capuchin friar. It is wonderfully carved, but little value is set upon it. A mile or two out of the town is the immense College of San Geronimo. It is an institution where young men are educated for priests; it is one of the largest in Spain. The walks are pleasant about Murcia. There are two Alamedas; one, across the river Segura, is open all day; the one on the town side is only opened in the afternoon. The former is much the largest and much the prettiest; it abounds with flowers, and along two high borders of cypress trees, cut so as to form hedges, are placed blue-painted iron seats. The effect produced is extremely pretty, for they seem in the distance to be beds of bright blue flowers. There is a monument here, erected to the Comte de Florida Blanca, in 1848. Many of the houses in the town have embossed fronts; they are much admired by the natives, but by no one else. One house facing the side entrance of our hotel still retains two Moorish doors. The stone-work over them is massive and handsome, but the two columns right and left have been cut through the centre, and rubbed down to nothing. The streets are gay enough, and remind one somewhat of Genoa, but the shops are not a bit more tempting than elsewhere. It is very fortunate there is nothing to induce people to fritter away their money, as enough goes with the ordinary expenses that of necessity are incurred.

We left Murcia at 8·25 A.M., and but for an accident we might have reached Elche by 5·30 P.M. The road as far as Villa de Callosa was extremely good; we passed through Orihuela, a large picturesque town, with flat roofs, square towers, and domes. There is a beautiful gateway here belonging to the College. The cathedral, repaired and enlarged fifty years ago, is like any other. The presses for the priests' vestments are curious. At Callosa we made our noon-day halt; it is six leagues from Murcia, and beautifully situated, with palms growing in thick abundance. The church, dedicated to St. Martin, is handsome; the pillars are said to be of marble, but they did not look like it;

the decorations were all gilt, giving a gaudy look over the whole. After leaving Callosa, we branched off the main road to enter an infamous mule track, which, however, admitted of wheels, but certainly not of springs, but then we had none left. This was the nearest way to Elche. From this sorry point there was little scenery but that of the purple—and such a purple!—hills in the distance.

About a league, certainly a friar's, from Elche, we came to a bridge which spanned a ravine; the bridge had no sides to it, and was not more than eight or nine feet wide; we had the mules harnessed three abreast in front, and the outsiders objecting to their position, they nearly squeezed "Coronela," the centre mule, to death by pressing her between them; but at the critical moment of passing, Coronela summoned up courage to push too; the consequence was that Pelegrino, the outside mule on the right, being unable to withstand against two pushing him, was shoved right over; luckily the wheelers held hard, and so saved the whole of us being pitched into the ravine. In a moment we were all out of the carriage, and Salvao, with his dagger-knife, instantly cut the traces and let poor Pelegrino, who never before so resembled Mahomet's coffin, down into the hollow; he so fell that half his body came beneath the bridge, and big heavy stones rolled on the top of him. The difficulty now was to draw the poor brute out. This was first attempted by the tail, which certainly would have been out the first but for the shouts raised by us all to stop that, then all available hands were lent to drag him by the traces. This after a time succeeded, and after a good deal of persuasion he was induced to get up, which we never thought he could do, imagining if his neck was not broken his legs must be; but nothing of the sort, the only harm done was to the harness, but he was very much shaken, and had to walk very slowly into Elche. We now regretted we did not follow the order which is tried to be enforced throughout Murcia, of not driving three animals abreast. The law, however, is not for the sake of safety, but that a heavier tax is claimed when the horses or mules are put lengthways: thus you pay for horses harnessed tandem double what you pay for a pair harnessed abreast. Cox, a little village we drove through before reaching Elche, is nestled in palm groves. It is a quaint-looking little place, so clean and white-looking that one felt disposed to spend a day there, only that is what one cannot do, there being nothing but a venta in the village.

At last we got to Elche—but late, it was quite dark —and we had to thread our way amidst the muleteers, who were already on the ground in the posada fast asleep. Though this town is but three hours from Alicante, and almost every one goes from there to see it, for it has not its second in all Europe, yet there is nothing but a wretched posada to put up at. How thankful we felt at the idea of this being the last we should ever have to stop at—which it wasn't; but this by the way. It is called the Posada Nueva de Tadea, and has a disadvantage which none other we stopped at ever had, that of a horrible smell. Hitherto we found this disagreeable quite confined to the theatres and Murcia; but the posada here shares the distinction.

Elche is a charming spot. It is embedded in a forest of palms, the roads are cut through tracts of land covered with them; thus there are thickly grown avenues branching out in all directions. By ascending the tower of the church of Santa Maria one can understand the extent of these palm plantations: all round, nearly as far as the eye can reach, there is nothing but palms, and they are magnificent; we have never seen any that can come up to these. It does not require any very great stretch of the imagination to fancy oneself in the east: the white-looking town, the flat roofs, so Oriental, even the people themselves do not look like Europeans. The interior of the church is handsome; the Virgin, to whom it is dedicated, is enthroned above the high altar and canopied over with massive gold ornaments. The doors of the church are in the Moorish style, but of a later date than the period when the Moors possessed the Kingdom of Valencia in which Elche is situated.

We took a long rambling walk in the palm woods; they produce so perfect a shade that the air beneath them is quite fresh. An old lady who died some little time back, and who owned several divisions of the palm-planted land, bequeathed them, together with her house property, to the Virgin. These are called *La Huerta* (farm or orchard) *de la Virgen*. Of course the Church of Santa Maria, or rather the priests, claim the revenue derived from these lands. Many of the palms are tied up, making them look like the backbone of a whale, as by this process they become bleached, and are thus rendered fit for the decoration of churches for Palm Sunday, and the balconies of houses, which, as we before remarked, is believed infallible against storms. They are called Las Ramos. The fruit falls short of that which we get in England, which comes from Africa; still they are sweet, and taste fresh and pleasant when gathered from the tree. With even the enormous demand for palm leaves in Spain, Elche can supply it and not miss them.

There are 22,000 inhabitants, a theatre, a hospital, five churches, one convent, and no Plaza de Toros, but they manage bull-fights now and then all the same. They get nothing but rain-water, and every drop is carefully preserved, and not without need, for rain is not plentiful at Elche. The way the peasants drink here, and indeed all along the road we travelled, is unlike any other people. They have bottles made on purpose; they are globe-shaped, with a long neck to hold by, and out of the centre is a curved tube; a cork is in at the top; then they hold it up in the air about a couple of feet from their mouths, throw their heads back, and then pour down their throats a pint at a time without the least distress, and they never choke. This is wine they drink in this manner; for water and coffee, when they get it, they have mugs or jugs of coarse earthenware,—glass is too precious for this class of people to use tumblers,—and by this mode of drinking the mouth does not touch the bottle. In many of their ideas they are nicer than the peasantry in northern countries.

From Elche to Alicante the drive is hot and dusty, and the scenery nothing to speak of. Alicante is seen in the distance like a pale-grey mass at the foot of a pale-grey rock, all barren, bare and dusty. The climate is beautiful in winter. Cold is very rare, the extent of evil in the way of weather is the high wind which, though not cold, is abominably disagreeable, as from the great quantity of fine dust, which is like powder, it blows up at times into such dense clouds that you cannot see a yard before you. We were greeted with one of these dust-storms just as we were driving into the town, and the mules had to be brought to a standstill; we could not see where we were going, or what was before us. When it passed off, we found a large heavy cart close in front of us; fortunately it, too, had pulled up.

There is a capital hotel at Alicante, Fonda Bossio; every comfort short of fire-places, but really they are not wanted here, or were not during our stay; the living excellent, and the landlord most obliging. Could it be by contrast we thought so much of this hotel? It may have been, yet it still stands out well in our recollection.

The day after our arrival we took leave of the mules, carriage, Salvao and Mariano, and not without real regret, for the journey was most enjoyable: all so well-managed, no trouble, no worries, not even a cross or disagreeable word was spoken that could mar the harmony of the whole. Mariano got a return "fare," a Frenchman and his wife. They had no servant with them, could not speak a word of Spanish, had nothing but French money, took no provisions, and would not be advised. We paid 30*l*. for the carriage, besides Mariano. They paid 5*l*., so he vowed he would go back by way of Cordova; therefore they had but Salvao, who could not understand a word of any language but his own. Did they ever get to Granada? If so, in what plight, we wonder? The lady started in a violet silk dress, a yard on the ground. If she only had known what we did, she certainly would have cut it short, as perhaps they did their journey. We did pity them as we saw them start off; yet a kind of satisfaction we enjoyed when we remembered we had done what they had to do, and under such adverse circumstances.

Alicante has very few walks. The Paseo de la Reina in the town is the "promenade," and is crowded on Sundays. The streets are wider than is usual in

Spanish towns, and the shops are tolerably good. There are four churches: San Nicolas, the principal one, was built early in the 17th century. It is a fine handsome church with paintings which, if not bad, can hardly be called good. The others are Santa Maria, San Francisco, and the chapel belonging to the Carmelite convent. The English Consul, Colonel Barrie, is a Roman Catholic, and married to a Roman Catholic, which renders it disagreeable for the English, no service being held at the Consulate; however, prayers are read every Sunday at the house of a Mr. Carey, and those who like may go; the only thing is, no one hears of it unless inquiries are made. Many English merchants used to reside here, but, with the exception of five or six families, all are either dead or gone.

From the old castle on the summit of the grey hill which backs the town, there is a good extensive view stretching over land and sea. There is a bull circus and a theatre; we were told it was a very good one and a good company, but we did not go ourselves. There used to be a good collection of pictures, but they have disappeared like the English; perhaps they went together. There is a tobacco factory; but it is a dirty place to visit, and not worth it; in fact, none are but that at Seville. We were sent to see the garden of the Conde de Pino Hermoso; in itself a proof of how little there is to see at Alicante, as this was not worth walking down a street to see, still less the expense of driving a league and a half along the dusty high road, with a blazing sun scorching one up. It might be mistaken for a cemetery at first, the railings enclosing it being painted black and white, and arranged in the shape of a bundle of arrows spread open across shields, which resemble arrows in a heart, a symbol the Romanists are very fond of. The principal attraction, and what gives rise to the gardener's pride and admiration, is the fantastically cut cypresses; the garden is full of them, and bad coarse statuary studded about, the price of each figure being duly told.

Not far from here, immediately on the coast, is a plot of land, or rather sand, consisting of several acres, which has been purchased by the Earl of A., who for the last four years has lived in Bossio's hotel. Here he has built a mass of walls, some high, some low, some so narrow they look like chimneys; against one of them there are three recesses that look as if they were intended for furnaces. Large open spaces are closed up by immense iron gratings; what his object is no one knows, and perhaps no one cares, but on this jumble of useless erections he spends his time and money; the workmen are sometimes occupied by doing nothing more than carrying one load of stones from one spot to another, with no view beyond their removal. The life the poor man leads is terrible; he has two rooms in the hotel, and he lives in them entirely, never allowing them to be touched; they are a heap of dirt and rubbish; baskets, sheep skins, tin pots, earthenware pans, and every conceivably useless article. He has no servant, and only allows one waiter in, who brings him his dinner; this, however, he is very particular in having good and properly sent up. His whims are all given in to, and he is watched as closely and carefully as he can be, but by no one except the hotel keeper. It seems strange none belonging to him, not even a friend, can be found who would look after him, with some more tender feelings than mere duty prompts. In the summer he will leave for perhaps a month or six weeks, but not longer; he returns again to the hotel and his miserable life. And yet this man had once a great intellect, and in years past had a turn for mechanism, which has not yet died out; only his inventions now are utterly incomprehensible, being articles of the queerest, quaintest form. Fortunately he is, so far as it goes, in good hands. Bossio is a kind-hearted man, and is sure to see that he is treated with respect and care by the servants. A simple act he performed not long ago will show the man he is, and he deserves it should be recorded of him. A lad in rags, and starving, applied to him one day for charity; Bossio asked him what he had been doing, where he came from, and so forth; and finding the boy had tried to earn an honest living by watching and taking care of goats, and that he was an orphan, he took him into his hotel and gave him employment. He worked steadily and industriously, but in all his leisure moments he might be seen with a pencil and any scrap of paper, drawing. Bossio watched him, and found he showed a very great talent; and in the goodness of his heart he resolved to give the lad a chance, permitting him to study a certain amount of time daily, and now his drawings are wonderful; he is shortly going to Madrid. His name is Vicente Tortosa, and Bossio is going to place him where he will have proper instruction, and there is no doubt in time his name will be better known than it can be by its simple mention here.

CHAPTER XXI.

VALENCIA.

THE direct line of railway from Alicante to Valencia being now open, we were able to make the journey in eight hours, including three-quarters of an hour at La Encima, where we changed carriage, and where dinner may be had. We left Alicante at 3.15 P.M., and reached Valencia at 11.10 in a storm of wind, hail, and rain. The scenery was beautiful all the way as far as we had daylight to see; at Sax, a station some two hours from Alicante, there is a wonderful ruin of a Moorish castle perched on a sugar-loaf rock. Almost on the summit of every peaked mountain some ruin is to be seen; it reminded one of the scenery on the Rhine.

Valencia is a very fine town, without being a pleasing one, of upwards of 100,000 inhabitants; it is especially rich in churches and relics; there is a cathedral and fourteen parish churches, all of them containing something of interest. Valencia is celebrated as being the first town in Spain where a book was printed, the subject of it being the Virgin and her miraculous powers; here also the Serenos, or watchmen were first organised in 1777, and it was here Queen Christina abdicated.

The cathedral, as a church, is not very interesting, after having seen those of Burgos, Toledo, and Seville. There is nothing decided in its architecture, it looks patched up, and very dark at the circular end behind the high altar. The principal entrance, the Porta Cœli, is the least handsome; the doors are copper-gilt, and a medley embossed on them of palm trees and roses; the other two gates, the Puerta de los Apostoles and the Puerta del Arzobispo, are gothic. The church stands where formerly stood the Roman Temple to Diana; it was commenced in 1262 and enlarged in 1482, the loftier portion of the edifice being the part added. There are three aisles, the centre filled by the *coro;* the *trascoro* is of alabaster, and contains twelve alto-relievos of sacred subjects, each divided by marble pillars. The choir seats are Corinthian; the gates are bronze, and very handsome; the organs are well carved. Over the high altar are two painted doors, said to be executed by Leonardo da Vinci; there are three subjects on each door; when these are opened the panels inside are disclosed, also painted in the same way; all the scenes relate to the life of the Saviour and Virgin; the interior is occupied by a finely wrought bronze gilt *retablo* in the Gothic style, with a Virgin and Child in the centre niche; passing round at the back of this is the Saviour, with a chalice and wafer by Joanes; the chalice is the same as the Santo Calix. To the left of the high altar, suspended against a painted shield, are the spurs, curb, chain, and bit which belonged to Jaime I. There are forty-two chapels round the church and choir, all with paintings more or less good. Over the altar in the Capilla de San Pedro (the second on the right, if you enter by the Porta Cœli) is a "Saviour with the Wafer," by Joanes,—a very favourite subject of his; it is an exquisite painting; in none of his works is the colouring softer or more brilliant; the hands are especially beautiful. Portions of the alabaster screen, which formerly was a part of the Altar Mayor is preserved here. This beautiful work of art was destroyed by fire on Easter Sunday, 1460; a dove with lighted tow, intended to represent the Holy Ghost, set fire to it. The frescoes on the walls are by Polomino, that on the ceiling is by another artist, and possesses no great merit. In the Capilla de San Miguel is an exquisite Virgin's head by Sassoferrato, and above it, a picture of the Saviour, standing with a globe between his feet; this picture is said to be very ancient. Facing San Miguel's Chapel, in one of the small chapels which surround the coro, behind the retablo, which draws down, is a most exquisite Ecce Homo by Ribalta; it is glazed over and in good preservation. We had to get on to the altar to see it properly, and also to have candles, and by these means it may be seen very well. Over the font is a painting, attributed to Joanes, but not at all in his usual style, of the Saviour being baptized by St. John. In a chapel behind the high altar is a Virgin and Child beautifully painted; the mother's expression is so tender and loving, the child is very natural; it is glazed over, but not thought much of, because it is not known by whom it is.

There are three *sacristias*, one leading out from the other. Over the entrance, in the church, is a large painting of "Christ bearing His Cross," by Ribalta; it is terribly dirty, but a very fine picture. The first sacristy was once a mosque: a portion still remains of a Moorish door, which is now raised up, forming an arch over the entrance, with large iron spikes projecting; beneath the matting of the floor we saw where the well was. In this sacristy, fixed up in a small case against the wall, is a tooth of San Cristobal, the giant saint, who adorns most cathedrals in this country. He is said to have been a Saracen ferryman, and is always painted standing, with the Infant Saviour in his arms. There is a very good copy here of Murillo's "Dead Christ and the Three Marys;" also a small painting of the "Virgin," which belonged to King Jaime I., and was carried before his army at the conquest of Valencia. In the second room is the ivory crucifix, which belonged to San Francisco de Sales; it is very beautifully carved; an exquisitely painted "Ecce Homo," a copy of Joanes; the "Saviour and the Lamb," by Joanes, but hardly worthy of him; and a few other paintings by unknown artists. In the third room is a "San Francisco," by Ribalta; "Conversion of St. Paul," very fine; a "Holy Family," a

"Last Supper," and portraits of the "Blessed Ribera," and "St. Thomas of Villanueva;" all by Joanes. There is one painting by Espinola, "Abraham and Isaac," but the colouring is not good.

Off this last room there is a chapel, a domed, almost circular room; here are kept the relics, about the largest and most valuable collection in Spain. They are placed in three cupboards. In that on the left, is to be seen the right hand and arm of St. Luke; it is like a piece of black wood, and very small for a man; next it is a drawing of the Virgin's head, executed by St. Luke, and set in a silver frame; standing as a pendant to St. Luke's arm, is a leg of St. George, but this is not so interesting (it has not a foot to stand on). Besides these there are at least forty bones and bits of rags arranged uniformly and in handsome casings. In the right-hand press, in a glass-case, is the mummy of a little child, one of those sacrificed by King Herod at the Massacre of the Innocents; it is dreadful to look at, even though it is perfectly black. A book and mantle belonging to St. Vincent Ferrer, Valencia's great saint; the mantle is black; the book is a Bible, written in ink by his own hand; it is beautifully done. A statuette of the Virgin, with a portion of the Infant Saviour's belt placed in the centre of the figure, with a piece of glass over it; the belt is red (it could not be any other colour for Spaniards); St. Augustin's mitre, a very small one; a shoulder ornament belonging to Archbishop Ribera, the "Blessed Ribera," as he is generally called; a bit of the banner of St. George, which he held when destroying the dragon. The other relics in this case are of minor interest, excepting the jaw of St. Bartholomew, which we must not forget to mention—the lower jaw; it is under glass like everything else. And now we come to the centre cupboard, in which the most precious relic of all is kept: this is the Santo Calix, said to be the actual cup used by our Saviour at the

Last Supper; it is of agate; the foot is also original but is divided from the cup by a stem forming a portion of the setting, which, of course, is not of the same period, but is very beautiful and simple, yet very costly; it is of the purest gold, studded at the portion round the foot with magnificent whole pearls and emeralds; the two handles are also of chased gold; the whole is very beautiful; it is kept in a silver-gilt casket, with subjects relating to our Lord's life, in relievo on the sides. Only a priest can show this relic, and when it is taken out all are obliged to kneel, when the priest allows it to be kissed, a privilege, in truth, if our Blessed Lord's lips ever touched it.* In this division of the cupboard, which is within an extra lock and key, is kept a piece of the sponge which was presented to the Saviour with vinegar in it, when on the cross; also two pieces of the cross, and a crystal case containing some six or seven thorns from the crown of thorns; and one alone, larger than the rest, with some of His blood on it, which was given to the church by St. Louis of France. On the shelves above, is the *Baculo* or Staff of St. Augustin; a small gold toothcomb with precious stones, which belonged to the Virgin; some of the myrrh presented by the wise men of the East to our Saviour in His cradle at Bethlehem; a seamless garment worked by the Virgin's own hands for her Blessed Son; and a portion of a tunic worn by the Saviour. Surely these are relics enough for a whole country; yet there are other churches in Valencia where they actually show what is more wonderful, more precious, than all these put together; but of that presently.

* This cup used to be exposed on the high altar every Holy Thursday; but owing to an accident which once happened when it was being moved, this has been discontinued.

The Sala Capitular of the cathedral is a magnificent structure, with a richly carved alabaster altar, and in good keeping; it is the finest thing in the church, and at a little cost this chapel might be restored sufficiently to render it worth a pilgrimage to see. It was built in 1358 by Peter Compte; it was here, being bomb-proof, that the Bourbon family sought and obtained refuge during the War of Independence. Over the altar is a Crucifixion by Alonso Cano, almost life-size; but the brow is narrow and receding, and the features small and pointed, and unlike the usual works of this great master. Hanging around the wall is a chain, said to have been taken from the gates of Marseilles, and brought here as a trophy; but another account is that the French came with a fleet to try and gain possession of the "Holy Chalice," and that this chain in some miraculous manner caused the destruction of the ships; and so they had to return without the sacred relic. There is a third story, and a very long one, printed on a sheet of paper and framed, and hanging beneath the chain; but it is too long and too uninteresting to relate here.

In a room leading out of this are kept the altar ornaments and massive silver statues of saints. Amongst the former there are two *Frontales*, which belonged to St. Paul's Cathedral, and were sold after the Reformation; they are richly embroidered in gold and silver. The subject of the one is the Crucifixion of the Saviour, and the other the Resurrection; in this latter is represented a building with turrets, supposed to be the Tower of London; they are twelve feet long and four wide. Two others are massively handsome, with relievos in solid silver decorating them; one of these, with the vestments to match, cost 22,000 dollars. The subject on the altar ornament is Peter being released from prison by an angel. The *custodia* is very magnificent, with the stand for the Host studded with precious stones; the ancient one, which the French melted down and carried off, was, we were told, far superior even to this. There is quite a regiment of silver busts and statues. The statue of St. Vincent de Ferrer stands on a silver pedestal; in the centre of his body is a hole in which his mantle, already mentioned, is placed when he is carried in procession; this effigy is about four feet high. The next is that of St. Vincent the Martyr, but no connection of, or with, the other St. Vincent; it is so massive and heavy, and all silver, that it takes eight men to carry it when it is taken out for processions; part of his body, but which part it is impossible to ascertain, is placed behind the piece of glass inserted in the chest. The silver tabernacle for the silver statuette of the Virgin is very pretty; around the stand the silver ornaments hang so that they ring when it is moved. Louis XI., the saint king, is here in silver as far as his waist, and as large as life; it is on a massive silver stand. Inside the body, in the centre, is Louis' skull; glass is over it, so it is easily seen, but the sight is very unpleasant, the teeth giving it a ghastly appearance. Does France admit that their saint king's skull is here? Next to it, and the same size, is St. Thomas, and his skull is here too, only the teeth are gone; no doubt each one forms a precious relic in some other church. There is another silver St. Louis, but he is a local saint, full length and solid silver, with the exception of the face, which, as well as that of the King of France, is of painted wood; there are several others, but of saints, and perhaps sinners too, that we never heard of. The vestments are very gorgeous and rich and numerous; but looking at these never gave us the remotest pleasure, any more than it would to go through a lady's wardrobe, and they are somewhat similar, with their cambric and lace, and satins, and velvets.

Close to the cathedral, and with a communication by a bridge thrown across the narrow street, is the chapel of Nuestra Señora de los Desamparados, Our Lady of the Unprotected. Outside it has no pretensions to a church, and appears to be modern; yet it was built in 1667, but was so thoroughly repaired some forty years ago, that all traces of antiquity are lost. It is oval in form and surrounded by marble pillars, with gilt capitals. The dome is painted by Palombini, and represents the Coronation of the Virgin by the Holy Trinity. The image of the Virgin, which is placed over the high altar in grand array, is covered over by a painting representing the Mother of the Saviour; on feast days and festivals this is wound up like the curtain before a stage, and the gaudy bejewelled effigy of the lowly handmaid of the Lord is exposed to the faithful for worship. It is said by some that this image was miraculously carved by three angels, but others state it to have been executed by mortal hands in 1410, by order of Benedict XIII. This Virgin during the Peninsular War was created Captain-General of Valencia, and carried in state about the town. The rival Virgin in Valencia is La Purisima, in the Compania, the church of the Jesuits; it is a painting of the Virgin by Juan Joanes, and is a lovely picture; the story connected with it is this: Father Martin Alberro, a Jesuit, was in the year 1602, or very near that period, seated under an orange-tree in the cloister garden adjoining the church of La Compania, when the Virgin appeared to him, and desired him to have her painted as she would describe. She then said she wished to be represented in a white tunic and a blue mantle, with the moon at her feet, the Father and Son crowning her, and the Holy Ghost appearing above the crown. Upon this, Father Alberro sought the great Valencian painter, Joanes, and entreated him to undertake the task, which he did, and finished most exquisitely. The soft, meek expression of the Virgin is very beautiful. Right and left of the picture in the same lateral chapel where this great work hangs, are two paintings, the one representing Charles III., on his visiting Valencia, coming to this chapel, and a tablet beneath records his instituting this Virgin the patroness of Spain on 29th September, 1771, in token of thanksgiving for the birth of his grandson, afterwards Charles IV., who in the other picture is being presented to the "Purisima" by his mother. In the adjoining chapel is the representation of the whole apparition, carved from the wood of the identical orange-tree under which it happened; this work, a beautiful alto-relievo, was executed at the expense of a devout lady whose name is unknown, and is said to have cost something enormous.

The Colegio de Corpus is one of the most interesting churches in the town. It was founded in 1586 by Archbishop Juan Ribera, afterwards canonised; he enacted many strange laws which were to be strictly maintained under severe penalties; one was, that any priest who was out of the college after a certain hour, was only to gain admittance by being ignominiously hoisted up in a kind of bread-basket and taken in at the window; this leniency, however, was only shown on the first offence, the second time the penalty was dismissal from the society. Another, prohibited women from being admitted to certain portions of the edifice, the great *patio* being one of the places they would defile if their feet touched. They were also forbidden to enter the church unless wearing a mantilla, and the kind is even denoted; they must not be of lace, but of some opaque material, and of course black.

The church is in the Corinthian style, and contains some very good paintings. A magnificent " Last

Supper," by Ribalta, is over the high altar; the portrait of the man who represents Judas is, they say, that of a boot-maker against whom Ribalta owed a grudge; the apostles are kneeling round the table, our Lord is sitting. Above this is a beautiful "Holy Family," by the same master. The dome which canopies the upper half of the church is painted by Matarana; the miracles of San Vicente Ferrer are portrayed on it. In the chapel of Las Animas, the first on the right of the high altar, is a painting by Zuccaro, on lowering which the embalmed body of the founder, the "Blessed Ribera," is discovered; he died in 1611. It is in a very handsome glass case, richly ornamented, with the archiepiscopal robes and the crozier between the legs. The chapel is too dark, and the sarcophagus too high up, for the exhibition to be very disagreeable. In a chapel opposite there is a beautiful painting, by Ribalta, of St. Vincent being visited when ill, by the Saviour and angels; but the light is so bad that without candles it is impossible to see it.

The *Reliquario* leads out of the *Sacritias*; there are two. The relics are arranged in a large press, with handsome folding-doors. Curtains hang before them; when these are drawn, the whole remain disclosed. A priest and a couple of brothers accompanied us; the priest held a stick, and pointed them out one after the other. Amongst legs and arms, and other bones, enough to make up a good many perfect skeletons, there were three pieces from the cross, five thorns from the Saviour's crown; the leg-bone, from knee to ankle, of St. Vincent Ferrer; a book of church ceremonies belonging to him; a piece of the shawl worn by the Virgin over her head (this is placed in the centre of a small image of herself); the skull of one of the innocents massacred by Herod; the skull-cap of the holy founder, El Beato Ribera; an excellent bit of carving, excessively minute, of scenes from our Lord's life; the retablo of a small altar, containing three pictures by Joanes (the subjects are "The Crucifixion," "The Descent from the Cross," and "The Resurrection;" this belonged to the founder, as also a crucifix in ivory and bronze). In a pair of crystal cases similar in every way, are the two most precious relics of not alone this church, but we should say, as far as one of them is concerned, of all the world. It is hair said to be cut from our Saviour's head; the other is of the Virgin's, fair, almost golden coloured. That called our Lord's is dark. We were not required to kneel in presence of *this*, which, if genuine, would indeed claim our adoration; but the cup is another affair altogether; but these are verily *Cosas de España*, and that is all one can, or indeed need, say about them.

Over an altar in the Chamber of Relics is a picture representing a dead bishop, with an angel on one side and a devil on the other, with the Saviour above. This picture was greatly valued by the Blessed Ribera, and always hung in his own room. In the Rector's rooms are some fine paintings by Ribalta, but mantillas are not admitted within this sacred dwelling.

The ceremonies of the Church of Rome are here carried out to their fullest extent; high mass on all occasions is on the same scale of grandeur as it would be in other churches on great festivals only; something is always going on, the priests are kept well employed, and the church destroyed with the flame and smoke of candles and incense. Every Friday, soon after ten o'clock, when high mass is over, the "Miserere" is sung; the church, always dark from the very few windows there are, is now rendered darker still by the curtain being drawn over the only one, at the end facing the high altar, where a gleam of sunlight ever manages to enter, thus rendering the gloomy appearance necessary for the theatrical performance that follows. The priests now enter in procession, wearing violet vestments, the altar being covered with cloth of the same colour; numberless candles are alight, and everyone kneels down in silence. After a minute or two, the "Miserere" begins, beautifully sung, and Ribalta's picture of "The Last Supper," which, as we before said, hangs immediately over the altar, is lowered by unseen, but not entirely noiseless machinery. This grating disturbs one a little. A dark violet curtain is seen in its place; this is slowly drawn to the right, when another with stripes becomes visible, which is presently drawn to the left; then another is seen of a paler hue. This, like the other, is withdrawn to the right, another to the left, and then one paler still, almost grey, like a thin cloud, remains. This, after a few seconds, is parted in the middle, and drawn on either side, when the effigy of Our Saviour, crucified and dying, is disclosed. The effect is wonderful, yet the whole thing is too theatrical to be very painful; though the face of Our Lord is terrible, the agony is so faithfully represented, that for a moment a shudder passes through one. Right and left, as if suspended in the air, are two candles, which cast a lurid light over the head and shoulders. This vision, for such it seems to be, remains till the conclusion of the "Miserere," which goes on uninterruptedly the while; then the curtains fall again one after the other, as when raised, but more rapidly; the picture is drawn up, and all seems as if one awoke from a dream. In silence the priests withdraw, and the people retire.

San Nicolas was once a Moorish mosque; it now looks like a huge twelfth-cake turned outside in; it is a mass of coloured plasterings, but otherwise a fine building. To the right and left of the high altar are large frames, each containing several charming pictures by Joanes; his colouring, for which he is so celebrated, is seen in these to perfection. The heads of Our Saviour and the Virgin, painted on wood, in the sacristy, are by him; they are very fine. The high altar had just been regilt when we saw it, therefore it looked very gorgeous and rich.

In San Martin there is a "Crucifixion" by Ribalta,

but in a very bad condition. There used to be a "Dead Christ with the Three Marys" by him, but that has been removed, which means in this country sold, for though they do not tell you so plainly, there is hardly a picture in any church that cannot be bought if a sufficient sum is offered. A copy then replaces the original, and nothing is said about it. Over the principal entrance is a statue of St. Martin on horseback, of course, dividing his cloak. It is renowned for its enormous weight; the statue is small and ugly. Beneath the portico of one of the side entrances is a large stone placed against the wall in honour of St. Vincent de Ferrer, and in memory of the fourth century of his canonization, erected by the churchwardens in 1855 over another stone on which the saint had stood and preached. There are some fine azulejos in this church, as there are in a great many in this town. Tiles were first manufactured in Valencia, and they are still made in very large quantities.

Santa Catalina has a lovely tower, built in 1688. The view is very fine from here, but the cathedral tower is the best to ascend for seeing the country round. The church is Gothic, and once contained some fine Ribaltas, but the French destroyed them. The decorations are white and gold, and images in all directions. The only painting worth looking at, is "The Saviour with the Wafer," probably not an original, but a very good copy of Joanes. This is on the door of the custodia on the high altar. It was in this church we first learnt that it is forbidden to enter churches in Spain with the *capa* or cloak thrown over the shoulder; all are obliged to pull it down, and let it hang before going in, just as much as it is necessary to enter with the head uncovered.

The retablo over the high altar in the Church de los Santos Juanes is by Muñoz; the cupola is painted by Palomino; the whole church is in such a state of dingy dirtiness, that whatever paintings there may be in it worth seeing are so coated over with dust that the subjects are hardly visible. In the sacristy is a small carved crucifix, very beautiful.

In the Church of San Andres, in the Chapel of St. Joseph, is a "Holy Family," by Joanes, a perfect gem; it is well preserved under glass. Another very fine picture, also by him, is in a chapel facing; the subject is "The Saviour after the Crucifixion," being tended by two angels, and the Father looking down upon him.

The Escuela Pia is a charitable institution, founded in the beginning of last century. They can receive about 150 in-door pupils, which they entirely support. When we went over it there were 120 boarders, and 1070 day-boys. The church belonging to it is a grand rotunda, surrounded by small chapels. To the right of the high altar is a carved image of Sta. Marcia, who was martyred: her throat was cut, and this is shown in her effigy. She is dressed very gorgeously, with diamonds in her hair, and rings on her fingers; she looks more like a sleeping eastern princess, but for the ghastly gash in her throat. In the centre of the wall behind the case she lies in, all her bones are placed, and a tumbler full of her blood; the former are arranged as they ought to be, as far as the size of the box they are in admits. Every chapel has a group of carved images hidden by paintings really not bad, and at any rate worth a dozen of the rubbish behind; yet on festivals the pictures are all rolled down, and the images exposed. The high altar has two handsome green marble pillars right and left, and a well-carved crucifix in the centre; beneath is a sweet head of the Virgin, a little picture about ten inches square, protected by glass. In the gallery that runs round the entire church, where a woman's foot never treads, is a picture by Ribalta of San Antonio holding the infant Saviour, and angels looking on them. In the patio close to the church door is an azulejos representation of "The Virgin at the Pillar, with the Child Jesus." A notice beneath informs the faithful that according to the archives of the church, whoever shall repeat one Ave Maria before "Our Lady of the Pillar," or any of her images, will gain an indulgence of 9570 days.

In the church of San Salvador is the miraculous crucifix called "El Cristo de Beyrut," which we were informed came all the way from Syria by itself, and floated up the Guadalaviar against the current to Valencia. The miracles said to be performed by this image are both wonderful and numerous. It is a huge, ungainly, ill-shapen figure, thirteen feet high, of a dark reddish-brown wood, and the hair hangs down like dusty black wool; this hair is considered as the greatest marvel of the whole, it being the same that was on the head when, seven hundred years ago, it landed at Valencia. The Sacristan said many believed it to be the work of Nicodemus, executed the year following Our Lord's Crucifixion. A gold crown has been made for it, weighing ninety-three ounces; this is put on for great occasions. The image is exposed every Friday and on special days. Two pictures in the church to the right and left of the high altar, represent events connected with the reception of this wonderful effigy at Valencia.

The only gallery of paintings in Valencia is what is called the Muséo. The building was formerly a convent of Carmelites. There are 1125 pictures in it; the few good are almost lost amidst the quantity of rubbish. The cloister walls are completely covered with old tattered and worthless paintings; the good ones are in two rooms leading one out of the other; the best are— A Crucifixion, 411, by Alonso Cano; San Francisco embracing a Crucifix, 569, St. John the Baptist, 582, A Crucifixion, 676, San Bruno, 759, Portrait of Pope Calixto III., 815, all by Ribalta; the Virgin, St. John, and Mary Magdalen, 579, by Cristobal Zariñena; St. Sebastian, 581, and St. Theresa, 711, by Ribera; Ecce Homo, 661, The Assumption of the Virgin, 683, The Last Supper, 700, and The Saviour, 701, by

Joanes; The Virgin and Child, 671, by Leonardo da Vinci, but the child is not pleasing; The Communion of Mary Magdalene, 672, and a passage in the life of San Luis Beltran, 719, by Espinosa; the Birth of St. John, 758, by P. Borrás; a Holy Family, on copper, 767, school of Corregio; the Portrait of a Lady, 793, by Goya; 857 is the portrait of King Jaime, and as such is a curiosity—the painting is not good. There is a sketch, 392, by Alonso Cano of the Infant Jesus. The Saviour at the Pillar, and Sta. Theresa, 396, by Gaspar de la Huerta, is not devoid of merit. There is one very beautiful mosaic, 757; the subject is a centaur hurling a stone at a tiger; the country in the background is wonderfully well done.

The convent must have been very large and very fine; the *patio* has four splendid palm trees in it, but the garden is completely overgrown with weeds. In a room at the end of one of the long galleries are a number of interesting old relics gathered from various parts of Valencia; amongst them is the altar of the first Christian chapel erected in the town, which was in this very convent; Jaime I. laid the first stone; it has paintings that deserve a better position; and a curious alabaster representation of St. Vincent the Martyr, with his inside hanging out as if gored by a bull; the alabaster is beautiful, the subject treated differs.

Near the cathedral is the Casa Consistorial, a very fine building; to the right, on entering, is a room in which the archives of the kingdom of Valencia are all kept. The ceiling is very rich; it is carved in panels and then gilt, here and there touched up with colours, red and blue, sufficient to throw up the gilding. Above is a splendid room; here in days of yore was the "Salon de Cortes;" the ceiling is the same as below, but not gilt, and the room is loftier. Around it, immediately below the ceiling, is a cornice, then pillars, and beneath them a gallery all richly carved; the division panels are all carved with different subjects. Around are frescoes representing the various members of the Cortes, civil, military, and ecclesiastical. Among the latter is St. Vincent Ferrer; they are painted by Cristobal Zariñena in 1592; the retablo of the altar at the end of the room is also his work; here mass is said on feasts and festivals. The Virgin and Child are prettily grouped; the Virgin's face might be a portrait of our Queen, it is so very like her. The *frontale* is beautifully embroidered in silver and gold.

There are three small rooms or courts adjoining; in the second is a wonderful "Crucifixion," by Ribalta; the Saviour is dying on the Cross, the Virgin and St. John are standing at the foot; the agony and despair depicted in the poor mother's face, with her clasped hands and head thrown back are too life-like not to be painful; the Saviour is looking up to heaven, his body quivering with pain, but the expression of resignation is perfect. St. John seems as if his grief was beyond control, and that he hardly knew whether to turn to the poor bereaved woman who had been committed to his care by his Lord, or to sink beneath the weight of his own misery. It is a wonderful painting, the most beautiful of Ribalta's we have yet seen. In an ante-room, leading to the Hall of Justice, are portraits of all the kings of Spain from Jaime I. down to Ferdinand VII. The sword of Jaime I., and the keys of the town, which were presented to him when he entered Valencia as its conqueror, used to be kept here, but they have been removed to the "Ayuntamiento" or Town Hall.

There used to be a good collection of pictures at the Conde de Parsent's house in the Calle de Carniceros, but the best have been removed to his house in Madrid, though one or two still remain:—"Christ breaking bread at Emmaus," by Ribalta, is fine; there are two of the same subject, but there is no difficulty in discovering Ribalta's—the other is very bad; also by him the "Martyrdom of St. Catherine;" the "Saviour with the Wafer and Chalice;" "Sacrifice of Abraham;" "Melchisedec" and a peasant, two life-sized portraits by Orrente, the two last are very good; the Saviour kneeling on the Cross, and the Holy Father looking down upon him, by Senent Vila, the subject though peculiar is well treated; the Saviour's upturned face is full of resignation, though his up-lifted arms seem to be pleading for mercy.

The house itself is a very wilderness in size, the rooms are handsome, but all empty; yet they are being repapered and decorated with fresco paintings on the ceilings. The count, like all Valencians, seems to prefer the capital to reside in, and rarely comes here.

The house of the Marquis de dos Aguas, which has the appearance outside of an embossed Valentine, or a coarse wedding-cake, with a tremendous marble doorway, *not* however used as an entrance, is inside most beautifully fitted up and decorated. It is entirely modern, and only very recently finished: the ceilings are perfect works of art; the walls are hung with damask satin, according in pattern with the furniture of the room. There is a profusion of gilding and looking-glasses. Like all Spanish-built houses, the rooms lead one out of another around a *patio*. The ball-room is inlaid with coloured marbles, and the arms and initials of the Marquis; the place for the musicians is so constructed that they cannot be seen, and they enter from behind into the small room, which in front has the appearance of a panel in the wall only. Leading out of this is a lovely boudoir, and beyond it a room entirely fitted up with Dresden china furniture; that is, the frame-work of the chairs is wood, rendered invisible by china laid over it; the cabinets are panelled with it, and the frames of the looking-glasses all china; the table is inlaid with it. Whether the room is comfortable for occupation we cannot tell, but it is very lovely to look at. The walls are hung with blue and white satin, which agrees wonderfully well with the rest. The room beyond is a toilet room, hung with white satin and a little sprig of flower over it; the dressing-table has a drapery of crape festooned, and wreaths of flowers entwined in it. Another room is entirely Chinese. The whole is more like a fairy palace than an ordinary mortal's residence; there is not a thing about it to denote occupation: not a book, not a writing-table; the only life about it is below, where, beneath the upper *patio* which is glazed in, and leads off to the dining-room, are the stables, and there some sleek fat horses turned lazily round at our approach. All was in excellent order, stables, carriages, and harness-room, but they were kept too hot. The Marquis employed only Spanish architects and Spanish artists in the construction and fitting up of his house, and it certainly does them great credit.

The Valencians rejoice in a very fine "Plaza de Toros." It is the largest and best built in Spain, and can hold 18,000 people; though the arena is not so large in circumference as that of Madrid, the building far exceeds it, and is much cleaner and in better repair. We went to see it under far more pleasing circumstances than witnessing a bull-fight, as it was a masque ball, which took place on the last day of the carnival, that we "assisted" at as spectators; and though it was during the afternoon, and all the dresses and decorations had to stand the trying glare of daylight, it was very pretty. A flooring was placed in the ring and decorated with orange and white flags, the Spanish colours, with festooned drapery of pink and white; a green hedge was placed round the inner circle of the building, giving the whole a remarkably gay appearance; a good band played, the masked danced as if they were there for that and nothing else, and evidently enjoyed themselves. The building was tolerably well filled with spectators.

There are two good theatres here, clean, nice houses, well-lighted, and comfortable seats. At the "Teatro de la Princesa" they occasionally have Italian operas. At the "Teatro Principal" there is a good company, but no singing.

The market is large and well supplied, and is best seen in the early morning, when the fresh vegetables and fruits look delicious. Here is the grand old Gothic built "Lonja de Seda," or Silk Hall; it has three aisles divided by six spirally-fluted pillars. The three gateways to the left are very beautiful; the centre one leads into the garden, which has nothing to recommend it in itself, but the windows and battlements are very fine. The "Lonja" was built in 1482. In the hall, from 9 A.M. till 1 P.M., trade is carried on in raw silk, sold in huge hanks, which are suspended round wooden stalls.

The walks and drives around Valencia are not numerous. About two miles along a dusty avenue is the "Grao," the actual port of Valencia, for the town stands far away from the sea. A magnificent sea wall, jutting out a mile, forms a splendid harbour and a fine walk, only to get there is the nuisance. The "tartana," the only hackney carriage in the place, is a most extraordinary conveyance; it looks like a carrier's cart, and on two wheels. Five out of six do not own springs at all, and those that pretend to them might as well, except for the name of the thing, be without them. The driver sits outside on a little seat fixed against the right side by the shaft; within they are roomy and clean, and comfortable when they are standing still, but once on the move it rattles one's bones together, and one feels after a drive as if one had been bruised and beaten all over. They charge six reals the first hour, and four for the succeeding ones; and it is enough, considering that they only go at a foot's pace.

Just outside the "Tapia," or city walls, which were built by Pedro IV. in 1356, and are very fine, and still in a tolerably perfect state, passing through the Puerta del Cuarte, are the Botanical Gardens, but with little to see in them. A square plain, ploughed in some places, trees in others, some magnolias, but not anything like the size of those at Seville, two glass houses filled with untidy-looking plants, and some ugly but fine specimens of the cactus, comprise the wonders to be seen. The only really good things are the violets, and they are exquisite; the flowerless beds are bordered with them, the air is laden with their perfume, and they almost repay one for the disappointment in all else.

The gardens belonging to Baron Rothschild, of Madrid, are better worth visiting, but they are badly kept. Four times a week hampers with fruit and flowers are sent to Madrid; what remains over is sold. He only comes once a year for a week or ten days' visit, and just before he is expected a little weeding takes place. There are greenhouses and hothouses, and therefore some interesting tropical plants. Close to it, in the same road, is "La Huerta de Soler" strawberry gardens, but nothing is flourishing this spring in Valencia; even the strawberries, generally plentiful at this time—the beginning of March—are not yet ripe; the severe winter has told on all vegetation. The oranges we had here were the worst we met with in Spain, celebrated though they are. It may be that it is a bad year for them, or perhaps, as with sherry at Jerez, the good are all sent away. The rice is very good, and it is grown and eaten here like potatoes in Ireland; no dinner is a dinner without it. It is stewed in grease and generally handed round the first dish after soup.

The prettiest walk is the "Paseo de la Glorieta." Elio, the royalist, made this garden, and was murdered in it in 1820 by the Constitutionalists. In 1823 he, like poor Mariana Pineda, of Granada, had justice done his memory, and honour paid to his remains some time afterwards. Adjoining this "promenade" is the Plaza de Tetuan; the gardens are pleasant. The Captain-General's house is here: it was formerly a convent founded by Jaime the Conqueror. Close by is the tobacco factory, a large square Herrera-ic building, as dirty inside as they all are.

On the site where formerly stood the gate known as "La Puerta del Cid," that idol of Spain having made his entry as conqueror through it, is a marble slab against the walls of the Temple Church, stating this to have been the spot where the Tower and Gate of Bab el Schadchar stood, afterwards called the Temple, where King Jaime's royal standard first flew on the 9th October, 1238, and which spot was afterwards conceded by him to the Templars, then preserved by the military order of Montesa, but demolished for the extension of the city in 1865.

The post-office officials at Valencia are worse than any in any other part of Spain. We had been for some time without letters, and between doubt and anxiety we requested the head man at the office to be so good as to let us see the letters he had for foreigners bearing the English post-mark; but he would not till we had given him the numbers which were attached to such names as we thought might be for us. So we picked out on chance "R., Esq.," "Post-office," and one other which we now forget, as it was not for us. But the other two were both distinctly addressed, and no excuse for their intense stupidity; but no one should ever put "Esq." on letters intended for the continent. During the last week of our stay at Valencia no papers reached us; all were stopped on the frontier because of a riot at Toulouse. What that had to do with English newspapers is neither here nor there; it was sufficient excuse for the Spanish government to be annoying.

CHAPTER XXII.

TARRAGONA.

BARCELONA may be made in a day from Valencia, leaving at five in the morning; but for people who are not in a hurry, the best thing is to sleep at Castellon the first night. By taking the mid-day train Castellon is reached in three hours and a half. This line has the best carriages on it, and the cleanest in all Spain. We went to the "Fonda del Ferro-Carril," formerly the "Parador del Leon," and a "parador" it simply is, with all its miseries and discomforts; however we were not likely to meet with many more of them, so we made the best of it.

The chief point of interest between Valencia and Castellon is Murviedro; the ruins of the old castle crown the whole summit of the hill; the walls appear to be very perfect. The little town at the foot of the hill was formerly on the sea, but the waters have receded nearly two miles. Its history dates back to 1000 years B.C. It was originally built by the Greeks and rebuilt by the Romans; then came the Goths, who were succeeded by the Moors, and they were driven out by the Spaniards. The great attraction to the tourist is the theatre; it is placed on the slope of the hill, and so built as to have enabled the spectators to enjoy the magnificent view afforded by the grand range of hills and at the same time protected from the sun, the castle hill sheltering it from the south and west.

Castellon "de la Plana" is six leagues further on, a dreary little town with a tremendous long avenue leading down to the sea: we took a moonlight walk here, and mistook a railway-station lamp for a star! Jaime I. built this town and it is celebrated as being the birthplace of Ribalta the painter, who was born in 1551. It is full of churches and convents, notwithstanding many having been suppressed—they must have formed the entire town before. The churches are all so pitch dark, literally speaking, that it is impossible to see anything. The Parroquia, or parish church, was being repaired whilst we were there, and as the roof was partially taken off we were able to see the bricks, mortar, and dust accumulated within; the churches certainly shun the light of heaven in this country.

The Church of the "Sepulcro" has an altar which tradition states to be the work of angels—it may be anybody's, and one story is good till another is told, especially when all is in the dark. There is not one window in this church and the doors of course are kept closed; the reason for this can be but to frighten people. We heard a deep moan in a far-off corner, and with beating heart we groped our way to the door.

The people have little to do here, nature does everything; but they are an indolent set—groups of men standing about, with their striped mantas and coloured handkerchiefs over the head, with seemingly nothing to do but smoke; they remind one of the labourers waiting in the market-place to be hired, but if they thought there was a chance of their being hired they would not be there, in fact they would take care to be nowhere.

From Castellon to Tarragona is a long fatiguing day. We left the "Fonda," or, to call things by their right names, the "Posada," at 7·30 A.M., the train leaving a few minutes after 8, and we only reached Tarragona at 5 P.M. Tortosa is not a bad place to stop at, where a break in the railway occurs, the bridge over the Ebro not yet being completed. About a mile before entering Tortosa we were turned out of the train into an omnibus. A hurricane was blowing, and it was all we could do to keep our feet; the violence of the wind as it came across the plain was frightful, carrying everything that was not very heavy before it. However, we jolted along without any disaster over the rickety wooden bridge into the town. An hour is allowed for dinner, which we had at the station, and was good enough. The old town is worth seeing. It is well situated, the magnificent river Ebro skirting its base. It looks well from the opposite bank, and is much more imposing in appearance than reality.

The Cathedral was built in the fourteenth century, on the site where stood the Mosque. Amongst the relics preserved here is one of great reputation, known as the *Cinta*. The wonders this miraculous girdle is able to perform is best known to those who have tested its efficacy, which is said to consist in saving women in child-birth, and removing any difficulties with which such cases are frequently attended. The towers of the churches here are mostly octagon, and continue to be so all the way till Barcelona is reached.

Cabrera's mother was executed here by the order of General Nogueras, in February, 1836. The poor old lady died for the sins of her son, whose deeds of blood and cruelty are familiar to all.

Three hours took us from Tortosa to Tarragona. The road skirts the coast all the way, and the scenery is very grand, the vegetation rich and fertile, and the purple hills to the left forming a beautiful back-ground. On nearing Tarragona, however, the country is less green-looking, the chalky nature of the soil in the immediate neighbourhood giving it a grey, dried-up appearance. Tarragona is well situated on an eminence, some few hundred feet above the sea level. The glare and dust are excessive, the climate is good and very healthy. The town at first gives one the idea of being a grand pile of ruins; all appeared still and deserted. Even the railway seems to shun a too near approach, as if afraid of disturbing the terrible silence that pervades the whole place. Tarragona has hardly yet risen out of the depths of misery and desolation into which it was cast by Suchet in 1813, when the streets flowed with the blood of the women and children who, by his orders, were butchered wholesale. The Oliva fort, where he entered the town, is even now pointed out by the inhabitants with an irrepressible shudder. It stands a little out of the town to the south-west. To the east and nearly facing it is the Archbishop's Palace, with its fine old square tower. The scenery is very grand. The carob-tree, vines, and aloes cover the land. The pod of the carob here forms food for man as well as beast. The vines produce the Benicarlô wine, a rich full-flavoured red wine.

Past Monte Oliva, leaving it to the right, the high road winds round, and about a mile further on, in a deep valley, is all that remains of the magnificent Roman aqueduct now called "El Puente del Diablo." A double row of arches span across the valley of 700 feet; at the deepest part of the gorge the arches are double, the lower tier containing eleven, the upper twenty-five. The width of the aqueduct, which is formed of huge blocks of stone, is five feet and a half. The highest centre arches are ninety-six feet, diminishing on either side as the ground rises. The view from this point is beautiful. Far away to the west is the little village of Costanti. It is said that formerly Tarragona reached to here. There is a very fine church in this place, well worth driving to see. It contains some fine marbles and some good carving. Not very far from Costanti is a building which was a tribunal in the time of the Moors, but nothing Moorish is about it, or anywhere else in Tarragona. The whole is so essentially Roman, that one could fancy oneself in some old Italian city, rather than in Spain.

Sweet-smelling herbs grow in profusion about this desolate place, perfuming the air; also the low growing fan-leaf palm, which, when dried, the people convert into brooms. The ruin of this great aqueduct was the work of the Moors, and when in recent times it was repaired, Suchet again destroyed it, as he did everything he came across.

Precisely in the opposite direction is what is called the Tomb of the Scipios. Here the two brothers are supposed to have been buried. The monument is in the form of a square stone tower of a reddish hue. The upper portion has partly fallen. On the front side, that facing the sea, are two figures; the upper portions are perfect, but the legs are gone. The remains of an inscription are traceable. It is placed within a few feet of the high road, amongst pines and sweet-scented herbs. The calm blue sea, studded with picturesque fishing-boats with white sails, is within a hundred feet of it. The spot is worth visiting, if only for the sake of the glorious view, and the beauty of its own position. It lies about four miles to the north of Tarragona.

The Museum is rich in Roman remains, broken stones, broken statues, broken tombs—all broken; even the coins, like all else in Tarragona; even to the recently built portion of the town everything is in ruins, tumbling down, dusty, and desolate. The Cathedral, with a handsome entrance—but all the figures which adorn it are broken—is of Norman architecture; the choir, as usual, blocks up the centre nave. At the back of it is the tomb of Jaime I.; it is of white marble, and bears the date of 1276. Santa Tecla, the patron saint of Tarragona, lies buried in the chapel dedicated to her, which is built entirely of marble, from the lofty dome to the pavement; the red marble pillars are very fine; the white marble *relievos* are by Salas, a sculptor of little talent, if these are his best productions. The *retablo* of the high altar is exquisitely sculptured. The subjects of the lower tier of *basso relievos* are the various tortures to which Santa Tecla was put, on account of her refusing to marry a man named Thamiro, to whom she had plighted her troth. Her excuse was having vowed herself to a virgin's life, but this availed her nothing, and she was condemned to every description of torment. The Gothic pinnacles are exquisitely carved, and are all marble; those above, which fringe *relievos* of subjects from the life of our Lord, are of wood. In the former there is a spider and a fly carved, not larger than life, but the details are perfect; this was all sculptured by Juan and Guillen de Mota, early in the fifteenth century. A Gothic gallery runs round the inner part where the high altar is placed; to the right is the tomb of the son of Jaime II. He was Archbishop of Toledo and Tarragona. To the left is the chapel dedicated to the "Virgen de los Sastres"—of tailors. They are looked on as a peculiarly fortunate class in Tarragona to be under such powerful protection. The windows are very beautiful; there are two rose windows, one over the "Capilla del Sacramento," the other faces it. They are both very lovely, but especially the latter. The dome inside this chapel is singular from the way it dips on either side, so as not to destroy the symmetry of the vaulted roof. This chapel was built in 1560 by Archbishop Antonio Augustin; he died in 1586, aged 69. His tomb is here, and is a grand work by Pedro Blay; many of the monuments in this church are by him, and some are very fine. The pictures are all daubs, and fortunately not a great many of them. The upper portions of the seats in the *coro* are beautifully carved; the archbishop has two seats, one at the end in the centre, the other at the corner near the high altar; the work of both is rich; the organ also is very well carved. All was done by Francisco Gomez in 1480. The marble fonts for the holy water are supported against two columns, by well shaped marble hands apparently growing out of pillars. Cardinal Cardona's tomb, which forms a division between two chapels, is very handsome; the scroll work is fine.

The Sacristy contains little worth seeing, and all is so dirty and untidy; even the relics are not cared for, they stand huddled together with dust and rubbish. Amongst the things is a pretty little gold cross, studded with precious stones and some fine pearls, a thorn from the Saviour's crown, a Gothic silver-gilt stand, containing twenty-four relics of so many saints, and two huge teeth belonging to some antediluvian animal, which, we were informed, were not kept as relics. In a room up a tower are kept the vestments and *frontales*; both are extremely rich in texture and ornament.

The cloisters and cloister garden are by far the most interesting portion of the cathedral; they are full of fine delicate carvings. There are 316 marble columns supporting Gothic arches, and every arch varies; so do the capitals; not two are alike. On one of these are three faces, all perfect, yet only two eyes amongst them. There are both Moorish and Roman remains here, many of the stones embedded in the wall bearing dates which correspond with their eras. There are five fountains in the garden, which is a mass of flowers, brilliant in colour and perfuming the air, but all are growing any way; no order, no care taken of anything; weeds spring up with flowers and are left to bloom out their time in peace. Even the walks are grass grown; yet perhaps this is more suited to the old cloisters than a neat well-trimmed garden.

Just behind the cathedral is a little church, which tradition asserts to have been built by St. Paul, who is also said to have preached in the cathedral; but tradition relates stranger tales in Spain than anywhere else. However, the church is very old and very interesting. The beautiful cross of St. Anthony, erected in 1604, is on the Plaza San Antonio, overlooking the sea. The slender column, carved with a diamond-shaped pattern all over it, is very pretty; the capital is formed by the Twelve Apostles.

Pilate's house, so called because Pontius Pilate, tradition again says, was a citizen of Tarragona and lived here, is now the prison; from the tower, a splendid view is obtained. The only vestige of antiquity about it is a column embedded in a crumbling wall. The interior of the prison is clean, and there were not many prisoners. One man was being released as we were let in; his crime was being without a pass-paper, necessary for every Spaniard desiring to enter or leave a town. There were but two female prisoners, and each had a child; here they do not part mother and child. The walls are upwards of twenty feet thick on the outer side of the tower, which was used as a telegraph station formerly.

There are constantly being dug up remains of statues or tombs; and coins, rings, and vases occasionally; altogether, there are sufficient antiquities here to supply any demand for a very long period. The people are a dull, heavy set: they want rousing out of their torpid state. There was a waiter at the hotel we were at,—the "Europa," the best in the place,—who said he would be so glad to get away from Tarragona, but if he did, where could he go? So he stayed on, moving about as if a world of care oppressed him; he was but a type of the rest. They feel depressed and weary of their sluggish unchanging life, yet they cannot rouse themselves sufficiently to try and do better. *Quien sabe*, if they did, what might befall them; might they not find themselves worse off? This is their argument, and so they go on, till they become as stupid, heavy, and useless as the old stones amongst which they are buried.

CHAPTER XXIII.

BARCELONA.

VERY different is Barcelona, different not alone to Tarragona, but to all Spain. A thickly populated, busy, industrious, thriving town, Barcelona is more like a young Paris. It far surpasses Madrid; the streets are finer and the shops very superior. Almost anything may be procured here that is to be had in Paris or London; French and English are more generally understood, and one can hardly believe oneself to be in a Spanish town, so little does it resemble one.

Barcelona is reached from Tarragona by railway in three hours and a-half; mountains on one side and sea on the other form the surroundings all the way. The country is well populated, and a look of life pervades the whole. Villages are numerous, and every league one advances one notices an increase of activity and civilization.

The Rambla, a boulevard, half a mile long, runs completely through the town; it is a broad avenue between two carriage roads, where the people assemble in crowds on Sundays, rendering the atmosphere foggy with dust. Here are the two theatres and the two best hotels. We were at the "Four Nations;" extremely expensive: good rooms and bad food. We heard that the "Oriente," just opposite, was better. In continuation of the Rambla is the Champs Elysées of Barcelona; here the *beau monde* drive. On Sundays it is a very gay scene. Handsome new houses are being built on either side, and more springing up daily. Leading off from this drive are *cafés* and gardens, the "Pré Catelan, &c., all in imitation of Paris. Gracia, which a few years since was a suburb, now forms a portion of the town. The drives and walks are innumerable, and occupation for all tastes can be found. Here ladies go into *cafés*—another innovation on Spanish customs; but there is no sitting outside of them yet. Bonnets predominate, especially on Sundays. The lower class, of course, wear the mantilla, which on grand occasions is white; this, seen in church, has a very singular appearance. The shops are extremely good; the best are in the Plaza Real and the Calle de Fernando VII. Capital gloves may be bought here at fifteen-pence a pair; the best shops for them are in the Plaza Real.

The day after our arrival, we drove up to the castle, as from there we could obtain a view of the whole town and environs, which appear more like straggling limbs of the city than villages, so nearly united are they. The castle is historically interesting to us, as on the 14th of September, 1705, it was taken by Lord

Peterborough: this was during the War of Succession. It has been taken again more than once since that. It is called De Monjuich. The hill it stands on rises 735 feet above the sea. It is garrisoned by 600 men. No Spanish soldier—or officer under the rank of captain—is permitted to marry, so they have to wash and mend their own clothes, and do a hundred and one little matters that in England we are accustomed to see the soldiers' wives attending to. They are allowed two meals a day, both of the same description—a sort of stew, in which potatoes and sausages form large items, and of this they do not get too much; their rations would hardly satisfy an Englishman. For drink they are allowed an unlimited supply of water, and their pay is a few *cuartos* a day. But the Spanish soldier can rise from the ranks if he has sufficient of the right stuff in him and the opportunity, which certainly is not wanting in this hot-bed of revolutionary spirits. As a rule, they are a slovenly and untidy set; but picked men are sent here, the Catalonians being always ready to fight, no matter in what cause, provided it be against the existing government. So in Barcelona and Tarragona there is a little more neatness and order among them, the bands play in tune and the men march straight; whereas, in the other provinces, they go any way and play any how. In the south of Spain, you rarely see a soldier with boots or stockings; their feet are bare, and they have on the straw soles with sandals.

The cathedral stands in the old part of the town amidst ancient houses and arches. The principal entrance is still unfinished; it is called "La Puerta de la Inquisicion," as it faces what remains of that building. The interior is gloomy and grand; its great height gives a narrow look to the beautiful centre nave, which, as usual, is unfortunately blocked up by the choir. The upper end behind the high altar is semi-circular. The lofty grey stone pillars seem like giant ghosts in the dim shadowy light, but the whole is very solemn looking, very impressive, far more so than the gaudily decorated cathedrals of Valencia, Cadiz, &c. Here the side chapels are unseen till you are close by them; they stand back, hidden by the columns and darkness, almost in recesses; the light elegant gallery running round the upper part of the building is seen from being immediately under the little light cast down through the stained glass windows. The *coro* is Gothic, and the carving of the pinnacle tops to the seats exquisite. Under these, but above each seat, are the arms of all the knights who in 1518 were decorated with the Order of the Golden Fleece, at the installation held here by Charles V. in that year; amongst them are those of Henry VIII. of England. All is in oak, but not of Spanish growth; the Bishop's seat and the pulpit are very delicately carved. The *tras-coro* has relievos in marble, representing incidents in the martyrdom of Sta. Eulalia; in front of it is a statue of St. Oldegar. The organ is handsome, and is decorated beneath by a huge Moor's head, which hangs suspended from it; the beard is long, thick, and excessively dusty.

The high altar is placed over a crypt where lies the body of Sta. Eulalia, the patron saint of Barcelona. She was martyred in 304 by Dacian, and was seen ascending to heaven in the form of a dove. In 878 her body, which had been missing, was discovered through the sweet odours emanating from it, and brought here and buried with immense pomp and display. Kings and queens and princes, besides the great dignitaries of the church, all attended on the occasion. The chapel itself is very simple. The Gothic retablo of the high altar is copper gilt, with red marble columns on either side. In the "Capilla del Sacramento," or of "San Olegario," lies the uncorrupted, incorruptible and flexible body of that miraculous old man, who was Bishop of Barcelona and Archbishop of Tarragona. He is—not buried, he does not require it—placed, in a glass case at the back of the altar (over which is a good picture by Viladomat); he is dressed in his robes and has on his mitre; his hands, horribly small, black and withered, are adorned with rings; only his nose is wanting, it probably was unable to bear with himself. This ghastly spectacle is exposed to the faithful on the anniversary and octave of his death, which took place on the 6th March, 1136. Two years ago his grace had new clothes put on him. Then his body was still flexible, he was sat upright and dressed; some lady had bequeathed him a new wardrobe.

Outside the Sacristy door are the coffins of Ramon Berenguer and his wife Almudis; they are covered with red velvet, and stand on shelves projecting from the wall.

The Sacristy is dirty and untidy, it contains little beyond the *custodia* and a few relics. The vestments and altar *frontales* are poor; one only amongst the latter is ancient and well embroidered; the subject is the Resurrection, the faces are good. The *custodia* is magnificent, the finest and most valuable in Spain. It is Gothic in design, and of pure gold enriched with precious stones; the pearls are enormous, and there is a black diamond the size and shape of a small bean. When Philip IV. came to see it he took the diamond and ruby ornament he wore in his hat and hung it on; it is there still, as also the Order of the Golden Fleece, which Charles V. wore at the Installation in the cathedral in 1518. A solid piece of gold, in the form of a wreath around the upper part, weighs alone 24 lbs.; a huge crystal, greatly valued as possessing some charm, is set in the lower part. Some ridiculous story is told of its being taken out of a serpent's head. The *custodia* is placed on the silver gilt chair or throne, on which Juan II. of Navarre and Arragon made his triumphal entry into Barcelona, after his victory over the French at Perpignan, on the 28th October, 1473. It takes eight men to carry this immense tabernacle, which is only used on Corpus Christi day; a belt, embroidered in coral and seed pearls, reaches completely round it; there is also a very handsome diamond pendant, which was presented by a lady, and hangs in the centre. The relics are neither rich nor rare :—a handkerchief worked by the Virgin, the material is spun silk, the colour dark dust; wood from the cross, and two thorns, are the principal ones; there is the nail with which San Severo, Bishop of Barcelona, was martyred, and some odd bones of saints.

The cloisters of the cathedral are too heavy and massive, still they are very fine, and would be far better were they not disfigured by the chapels which fill up the vacancies between every arch. There are some old tombstones let into the walls, bearing dates varying from 1300 to 1500. The garden is pretty, with a fountain and a tank, where two holy geese reign supreme. Pepper, orange, and lemon trees grow in it. The entrance into the cathedral from here is magnificent.

The church of Santa Maria del Mar ranks next in importance; the exterior is extremely beautiful, purely Gothic, and very light and elegant in design. It was commenced on the 25th March, 1329, and finished on the 3rd November, 1383. The first mass offered up in the church was on the 15th August, 1384. The interior very much resembles the cathedral, though much smaller, it being only 372 feet in length, yet the choir being placed behind the altar gives an appearance of far greater size. The church, as is usual, is surrounded by chapels, in each and all are one or more virgins; one chapel was formerly Mozarabic. The pictures are so dirty they might be anything, and beneath many are bundles of wax legs and arms, and other portions of the human body. Facing the organ is the royal pew, a heavy gilt projection midway up the wall, which is reached by an invisible spiral staircase. Some of the windows are very beautifully painted, especially the large rose window. The christening font was the sarcophagus which contained the body of Sta. Eulalia, Barcelona's saint. When her body was discovered it was in this stone coffin, close to the spot where "Santa Maria del Mar" now stands. It was preserved as a precious relic, and converted into a font. Sta. Maria Carvellon was baptized in it on the 8th December, 1230. There are some of Viladomat's paintings here, which rank among his best, but one cannot see them for the dirt.

"Santa Maria del Pino" has a single nave; it is a large and light looking church. In a crypt beneath the high altar, called "La Santa Espina," or "del Sepulcro," are two thorns; the crypt is sustained by five arches. The choir is behind the high altar, the rose window at the end of the church over the organ is very fine. The churches in Barcelona are rich in painted windows. They seem to take the place of pictures, of which there is a great dearth; several around the nave of this church are very good. In the chapel of San Miguel is the tomb of the only painter Barcelona ever gave birth to, Antonio Viladomat; he died in 1755. A simple stone let into the wall records his talent as an artist, and marks the place of his burial. The pavement of the church is covered with old tombstones. The exterior is handsome, but some portions still remain unfinished.

San Balem, the church of the Jesuits, on the Rambla, is rich in marbles; there are various kinds, and from various countries; there are a few paintings by Viladomat; and in the rector's apartments is kept the sword which Ignatius Loyola placed at the Virgin's feet at Montserrat.

San Jaime was built at the end of the fourteenth century; it is a handsome church. Right and left of the high altar—which is tawdry and rendered like a child's theatre by a stupid, highly-coloured painting, with sliding scenery, representing purgatory—are two fine door-ways. In a chapel to the right is a richly-coloured rose window.

The church of San Miguel is one of the most ancient in Barcelona; it is some twenty feet below the level of the street, a small, quaint, quiet, little chapel, but extremely dark; the eye must become accustomed to the light before one can even see the way. A rich piece of mosaic pavement is here; it is supposed to have belonged to a temple dedicated to Neptune, having maritime subjects on it; near the altar is some Roman mosaic pavement: the colours are bright and varied. In one of the chapels is a monumental tomb belonging to Francesco Coll, Vice-Chancellor to Ferdinand the Catholic, and afterwards to Charles V. There are two paintings by Viladomat; one the "Divine Shepherd," the other "Angels." The façade of the principal entrance, with its pretty Gothic towers on either side, is a sight for any lover of architecture to feast his eyes on.

San Justo is a handsome church with a single nave; the colouring of the church is warm, the arched roof is lofty and painted with a deep blue. The chapels around it are Gothic; the choir is behind the high altar; it is very ancient and but poorly carved. The organ has a huge Moor's head suspended from it. The church was built in 1345.

Sta. Ana, formerly a college, was founded in 1141 by King Alfonso II. of Arragon and William I., Patriarch of Jerusalem, in imitation of the church of the Holy Sepulchre. There is nothing now to see in the church; the cloisters are the attraction, they are very pretty, and are of an earlier date than the church; the double range of arches are supported by slender pillars, formed of four grouped together, altogether not more than a few inches round. The entrance from the cloisters into the church is very pretty, with windows on either side, having small marble columns in the centre. The *patio* is well filled with trees, and has a large well. All is so still and quiet here, that one might stroll up and down the galleries indulging in dreams called forth by the spot, but for the desecration of the place which is permitted, and which calls forth anything but an odour of sanctity.

There are also some very pretty cloisters at San Pablo del Campo, but they are ruined with whitewash, which fills up all the delicate carvings in the stone-work. There are eight double engrailed arches, similar in form to the Moorish arch, with double pillars in the centre; they now belong to the barracks adjoining. The old door leading into the church has a hand sculptured over it, with two fingers extended, the others being doubled in. This hand has given rise to various stories; one being that it represents the hand of a wealthy nobleman who murdered a cardinal, and in consequence his fortune was confiscated, and devoted to the building of this church, which, however, according to a stone let into the wall, was built by Wilfred II. in 913; beneath the hand a Maltese cross is cut in the stone. The church is cruciform, with a dome in the centre.

Many of the public buildings are extremely interesting. The *patio* of the "Lonja," or Exchange, in the Plaza del Palacio, has four entrances; it is a large square, with statues at each corner, representing Europe and Asia, Commerce and Industry, and a fountain, with Neptune lazily presiding. The marble staircase is handsome. Here are some rooms set apart for the "Bellas Artes;" the art may exist, but most assuredly the beauty does not. Two of the rooms contain only modern pictures, one little better than the other; then in the Sala de Sesiones are some more. Passing through the students' rooms we then entered two or three dingy rooms, dignified by the name of Museum. There are twenty-two pictures in them by Viladomat. The Catalonians are immensely proud of this painter, and yet his productions are not worth very much, except in their estimation. All his works are to be found in his own province; no one has, as yet, thought them worth removing. With the exception of two, the twenty-two paintings are scenes from the life of San Francisco, and were formerly in the cloisters of the Franciscan convent, which no longer exists. Saint Francis, though the founder of the great Order named after him, never thought himself pure enough to offer up mass, in consequence of his having had a vision, in which an angel appeared to him with a glass of water, and told him a priest must be as pure as the water he held in his hand; this St. Francis could not believe himself to be, and, therefore, never dared say it. This vision forms the subject of the best of Viladomat's paintings. A modern Catalonian artist, named Clavé, still living, has one or two good pictures here; his "Ecce Homo," 23 in the catalogue, and "Various Apostles," 24, are extremely well done; the latter is a copy from Rafael's well-known picture.

Facing the Lonja is the Palace, it looks like a cardboard imitation of a Venetian house; adjoining is the house of the captain-general, a handsome building dating four centuries back, but it has been sufficiently "improved" to destroy all marks of antiquity.

The Casa de la Ciudad, or Casa Consistorial, in the Plaza de la Constitucion, with a statue of Jaime I. on one side of its modern entrance (which is very like the Prince of Wales), and Juan Fivaller on the other, has some fine old remains of Gothic architecture about it. The arms of the city, cut in stone, face the entrance; the ceiling is very handsome. The Cortes of Catalonia held their meetings in the large saloon on the left; the door inside, of carved stone, is very curious; the arms of all the towns of Catalonia are painted on the panels of the walls. The throne-room, a lofty half-circle, is modern, as are also the session rooms. The old entrance, on the left side, now nailed up, with its beautiful Doric decorations, is partially hid by the trees in front; there are three windows and one built-up entrance, all beautiful in decoration and carving; over the portal is the figure of an angel, the two wings extended, and over it a richly-worked Gothic pinnacle.

The "Audiencia" is on the opposite side of the plaza; this also has its original entrance at the side, which is still open, and by it we entered. The whole is extremely fine, and deserves careful inspection. Over this entrance is St. George and the Dragon: the entire façade is elaborately decorated with quaint subjects; around the low arches in the court are carvings of monks and monkeys' heads. A fine stone staircase, beautifully carved, led us to a glazed-in gallery where the attorneys sit in little boxes like ticket-takers at an out-of-door show; they are ready for any one who may require them. This Gothic gallery is surrounded by slender pillars, all marble. Occupying one corner is a beautiful entrance leading into the chapel of St. George; on the left hand a door leads to an upper *patio* called the Court of Oranges; the old walls with their finely decorated windows, the rich mouldings, the quaintly carved figures and heads, are extremely fine.. In the large hall to the right are kept the archives of Arragon, which date back to 874; to the left are the Courts of Justice. When we entered, three grave-looking old men were sitting listening to the statement of a case about to be argued before them. Before a case is argued here, a statement is drawn up and read, by an impartial person, and when the judges are thus acquainted with the subjects, the barristers plead their cause. The courts are open to the public, but the public does not seem to take advantage of the permission. No one but those concerned in the question were present when we were there, and we were told it was rare to see any one else. The ceilings are very rich. In the Sala de Gobierno are the portraits of the kings or rulers of this portion of the country, from the Goths to the present Queen. Much of the less ancient architecture here is the work of Pedro Blay. The St. George's Hall is his, and it is a very fine room. St. George was the protector of Catalonia and Arragon against the Saracens, and so constantly appeared at the critical moment that the victories, in consequence, were always on the side of his *protegés*. The *frontale* of the altar for the chapel, used on St. George's Day, embroidered in silver and gold, represents the saint fighting the dragon, and rescuing a young lady attacked by it. This *frontale* is very ancient. Amongst the relics kept here are a rib of St. George, which is in a gold case, and a *redomita*, or small phial, with some of the saint's blood in it: this is enshrined in silver.

The house of the Counts of Barcelona, in the same plaza as the Cathedral, forms a portion of what is now the Convent of St. Clare. The entrance and *patio* are handsome, the staircase of stone is roofed over by an elaborately carved wooden ceiling, hollowed out, and a gallery running round it; it is oval in shape. This was formerly the palace of the Counts of Barcelona, and Kings of Arragon; and the chapel, now in ruins,—but very beautiful they are,—was the Hall of Ambassadors, where the royal assent was given to laws, and any important business was attended to. In this chapel the Virgin is said to have appeared to Don Jaime I. on the 2nd of August, 1218; a chapel was built on the spot and dedicated to her; beneath the *retablo* of the High Altar are the relics of St. Benedict, which were brought from Rome to be placed here. In 1713 this convent suffered great injury from the lawless soldiery of Philip V.'s army. An old Gothic fountain adorns the plaza fronting the church.

On the opposite side of the Cathedral is the house where the Inquisition resided, the terror of Spain, as of every other country where its fearful power was felt. All round this neighbourhood are remains of antiquity: stones let into walls, columns buried in walls, bits of arches built up, and so on. One house has the remains of what is supposed to be the aqueduct which came from Collcerola; but as houses are pulled down and streets widened, these treasures disappear. In the Calle de Moncada are two houses, 20 and 22, which both have *patios* with staircases and columns worth seeing. In the Calle Ancha, 82, is a huge head that had been dug up, placed on the façade of the house, which is very ancient. The ruins of the Chapel of the University are fine; the richly-worked doorways and lateral chapels are built up in a cruel manner, dwelling-houses of a low, poor stamp, peering above them.

There are one or two private collections of pictures, but consisting mostly of copies; the best is that of Don Anton Pascual in the Calle Xuclá, 19, who has nearly 300 pictures, and those contained in the Palacio Vireina, Rambla de San José, 21, where engravings and coins are collected as well. Some of the paintings are really very good, and they are chiefly from the best masters.

At the end of the Paseo de San Juan is a garden, that of "Del General," which is greatly admired by the Barcelonians. It was laid out in 1816, and is now a very untidy mass of flower-beds bordered by box, pepper-trees, and Nefliers de Japan, with fountains and a duck-pond, one pair of swans lording it over all. The soldiers' exercise-ground is just outside of it.

The theatres are very good, and plenty of them. The two principal ones, the "Liceo" and "Principal," are both on the Rambla. The former is a magnificent house, and the finest in Spain. It was built in 1847 on the site of a convent; burnt in 1861, it was rebuilt in the following year. The height of the *Sala* is enormous; there are five tiers of boxes above the pit tier, and owing to the divisions being only on a height with the frontage, they appear all to communicate. The decorations are white and gold, with a little delicate colouring introduced on prominent points; the roof is painted in bright frescoes, and around are medallion portraits of the great composers. It is lighted by 364 jets of gas, ranged, each beneath ground glass globes, in groups around the house. The stalls are covered with crimson velvet and gilt borders; there are close on 900, and the house holds 4000 spectators. Operas are given here on alternate nights; on the intervening nights there are dramas and dancing. The orchestra is pretty good, but the house deserves a better. The *foyer* is very fine.

At the "Teatro Principal," there is acting only; occasionally they have a French company. The house is handsome, but cannot be compared with the "Liceo;" the decorations are crimson, white, and gold. There are 450 stalls; and in front of the first tier of boxes are the "Balcony Stalls." The scenery is old and dirty, the orchestra tolerable. The prices at both theatres are extremely moderate, and about half what London theatres charge.

The Plaza de Toros is close to the port; it can hold 12,300 people In 1827 Ferdinand VII. gave permission to the Casa de Caridad to give eight bull-fights in the year. In consequence of this, in May, 1834, the directors of the charity ceded to a company a plot of ground belonging to them to build an arena; this was done and opened on the 24th July of the same year, on the arrangement of their paying an annual sum to the Charity.

It was in Barcelona that in April, 1493, Columbus was received by Ferdinand and Isabella on his return from America, and here he placed the New World as a gift at their feet.

Barcelona nuts are sold in great quantities, but they cook them before eating them: toasted they term it, though baked would be more correct. The nuts are extremely nice in this way, though not equal to the toasted almonds of Madrid, which are really delicious.

There are two excursions imperative on every one to make who visits Barcelona: the one is to the Monastery of Monserrat, the other to the Salt Mines of Cardona. There are two ways of going to the monastery; the one is to take tickets to Martorell, on the Tarragona railway, and then proceed onwards by carriages to Collbato, from whence you are forwarded by one means or another to the monastery; but the best and most direct is to go by rail to Monistrol, on the Zaragoza line, and there omnibuses are in readiness to convey people straight to Monserrat. The journey takes from four to five hours. It is difficult to see the monastery in the day, and impossible if the environs are to be visited; but sleeping another night at a *posada* we shrank from, as most others would do who had had as much of them as we had; and the *posada* at Collbato could hardly be called even decent, though it is clean.

The one great point of interest to pilgrims (for it is a real pilgrimage) is the miraculous image of the Virgin here enthroned. The story of it, as told at the monastery, is, that St. Luke carved it, and St. Peter brought it to Barcelona in A.D. 50. In 715, when the Moors invaded the country, the Goths hid it in a cave. It was afterwards found by some shepherds in 880, through the appearance of unearthly lights and sweet music. They took the image, and having carried it a certain distance, it would not allow itself to be moved any further; so where it remained a chapel was built to place it in. About the year 970, a Benedictine convent was founded by a Count of Barcelona, the Virgin having done his daughter a good turn. Here the image was enshrined till another new chapel was built, and then Philip II. himself removed it on the 11th July, 1599. Again in 1835 it was disturbed, on the convent being suppressed, and it was placed in the chapel, where it may still be seen. In the sacristy are all that remain of the Virgin's jewels and wardrobe; the rest were thought too beautiful by the French to be thus buried in a napkin, so they carefully removed them. The Virgin is coarsely carved, and does not represent the sweet, soft, and gentle Virgin we like to think she was; the wood is dark; the infant Saviour is on her lap.

There are numerous hermitages studded about this huge, strange, isolated mountain, the highest points of which rise nearly 4000 feet above the sea; most of them are in ruins; the one nearest the summit is that of San Gerónimo. The monks who, in days of yore, inhabited these desolate houses, never left them after once entering till death released them from their self-imposed prison. The views from the various points are magnificent. The miracles worked by this Virgin of Monserrat are, according to Spanish historians, legion. Books are published relating them, all too wonderful for heretic Englishmen to accept.

The *retablo* of the high altar in the church is by Esteban Jordan. An inscription on the wall records that, in 1522, Ignatius Loyola prayed before the sacred image of the Virgin previous to his founding the famous Order of Jesuits. Here he dedicated himself to her, and laid his sword (the one at Belem Church, in Barcelona) on her altar, for he began his career as a soldier; but being seriously wounded at the battle of

Pampeluna in 1521, against the French, he imagined St. Peter came down to him and cured him. From that time the soldier turned saint. The cave he buried himself in at Manresa, about sixteen miles from the monastery of Monserrat, still exists; here he did penance, then paid his celebrated visit to the Virgin, and leaving his sword with her, started for Rome, and gained permission to found his order, which soon became as famous as since it has become unscrupulous, and a by-word for every description of cunning and deceit.

Goethe has drawn the scenery of this marvellous-looking mountain in the fifth act of the second part of his "Faust."

To visit the wonderful salt mines of Cardona, it is best to go direct from Barcelona to Manresa. Coaches then take people through Suria to Cardona for ten reals each. The only thing is, if one had but the courage to sleep at Cardona, one might visit the huge mountain of salt at sunrise, which we were told was the right thing to do, when the rainbow colours on it are very beautiful; but we did not see it. It is astonishing in travelling how frequently one is told that any other time or season would be better to see a place in than the present. This mountain of salt is nearly 500 feet high, and three miles in circumference. One cave is nearly a mile in length; it is called the " Furad Mico." The hill is full of caves and grottos, more like a place excavated for show than the result of mere necessary labour. There are two bazaars—they call them here museums—in the town, where articles made from the salt are sold. They keep very well in this climate, but in our northern damp home they would soon melt out of their pretty shapes.

The night before we left Barcelona we went to see what was termed a "decapitated head." It was on the same principle, no doubt, as Colonel Stodare's "Sphinx," but it was very superior. The head was on a round table, in a small room, hung with dark cloth, and lighted by gas; the spectators—only a certain number were admitted at a time—were within three or four feet of it. The head answered all our questions and requests, from giving us his history to looking at us, and putting his tongue out. He said he had been beheaded for conspiracy in 1534, and that his body was still where it was buried at the time of his death, at a village not far from Barcelona. We have seen many exhibitions of this sort, but none that in any way came up to this one.

CHAPTER XXIV.

FROM BARCELONA TO PERPIGNAN.

THERE are three routes by which one may quit Spain from Barcelona. One is by taking the rail to Zaragoza, and then on to Miranda, which is the junction of north and south; from here, still by railway, to Bayonne. The next is by an unbeaten track over the Pyrenees by Urgel and Hospitalet to Ax and Tarascon; there is only a mule track over the barrier mountains at this part. The journey this way may be done in two days, and the scenery is said to be very beautiful. The third is the beaten path *viâ* Gerona, and this we chose.

We left Barcelona at 1 p.m., and reached Gerona at 4·30 p.m. This line is the first that was opened in Spain; in the beginning it only went a portion of the way. The entire road is populated; villages lie thick together, cottages intervening. The country shows the people to be industrious; it is highly cultivated; not a metre is wasted or neglected. On nearing Gerona the land is more arid, and labour has less bountiful results.

Gerona is not the best town for the traveller to

enter and receive his first impressions of Spain from; the other side, at San Sebastian, is far better. Gerona has nothing but its cathedral, a church or two, and ruins; it looks in a very tumble-down state. Many of the streets are arched over by the houses projecting from the first floor, and supported by large massive pillars; the streets being narrow, this gives them a very dark stuffy look.

The "Fonda Italianos" is the best inn; it is clean and tolerable; the entrance, as usual, through the stables, is the greatest drawback. They cook the dinners (which are by no means bad), the roasting part at least, by the labour of an unfortunate little dog, not even born a turn-spit.

The Cathedral is very fine; it is approached by a magnificent flight of eighty-five steps, divided by three terraces; the view from the top is grand. The principal façade to the church is not good; there is a tawdry look about it, and only one tower to the right, whilst the "Door of the Apostles" is beautiful. The interior, which would be superb, is ruined by the *coro*, and rendered ten times worse again by a huge, ungainly looking organ at the back of it, thus most thoroughly destroying the vista, which, from the church having but one nave with a semi-circular termination behind the high altar, and a double tier of gorgeously painted windows above it, would otherwise have let it rank amongst the finest cathedrals in Spain; but, as it is, it is completely spoiled. The choir is lightly carved; the bishop's seat is the most elaborate, and the two pulpits are fine. The two large rose windows, St. George and the Dragon, and a glory overshadowing the Saviour, one at either extremity of the church, are not so fine as the long ones that surround the high altar, nor so rich as the smaller rose windows. The confessionals are all placed together out of sight in the dark behind the altar. A small light gallery runs completely round the church. Passing by the Sala Capitular out by a little door to the right, are the ruined cloisters, and in such ruins! It is like entering a place where a house had recently been pulled down—heaps of stones and rubbish. Every step we took was on tomb-stones; the floors are literally paved with them, and the walls project in all directions with the stone sepulchres placed against them. The garden is like all else, a ruin; there is a huge well in the centre, overgrown with weeds. It was with relief that we quitted this desolate gloomy place; a door at the side opposite to where we entered led into a sort of lane, steep and stony, which took us down again into the town, which seemed bright and cheery in comparison with what we left behind us. An octagon tower on our right hand standing out clear and distinct against the blue sky, the undulating hills in the background, and the town at our feet, formed a very pretty picture; and it was such a lovely evening.

On reaching the bottom of the hill and turning to the right we came to the College of San Felin. The exterior has some claim, but not very much, to architectural beauty. The principal interest attached to the church is that it contains the remains of Mariano Alvarez, governor of Gerona in 1809, when the town was besieged by the French. For seven long months he managed to hold out; then he was struck down by illness, and his successor capitulated. Alvarez died soon after: how is not known, but he was found in his prison, dead. He was a gallant soldier, and an honest, upright man. Here in this church is he buried; and a visit to his last resting place is more worth paying than one to the visible relics of San Felin, whose head is here, and San Narciso, whose whole body may be seen; but they are thought a million times more precious that the ashes of the man who died for his country.

We had agreed at Barcelona with the Diligence Company on the Rambla, close to the Calle Fernando VII. —(for reasons which will be obvious very soon, we are thus particular in stating where this office was situated)—to hire a carriage to take our party from Gerona to Perpignan; the carriage was to have a *banquette,* or outside seat, to hold three at least; a rough drawing was made of the kind of carriage required, so as to avoid all mistakes. Owing to a slight illness of one of our party, our departure was delayed on the very day we had proposed leaving for Gerona. We instantly sent a telegram to say we could not leave for three days, and made an agreement with the director to pay an additional twenty francs for the delay; at the same time we paid seventy-five francs, the half of the money agreed on for the journey. The coachman, finding the "family" did not arrive at Gerona as he expected—(the carriage was sent over from Perpignan to Gerona, and it had started before the telegram explaining the delay had reached)—came over to Barcelona to enquire the reason. One of us asked if the carriage had a *banquette*; he said it was an omnibus for six passengers, and no place outside, except one by the side of himself. We at once stated it would be impossible for us to travel in an omnibus; that our party was too large, and moreover a *banquette* was indispensable. He shrugged his shoulders, and said the omnibus was roomy and would hold eight, and that the road was so terrific in some parts no lady could possibly sit outside and witness it. This utter nonsense we could not argue against, as we knew nothing about it, beyond stating that our nerves were all strong enough, we were quite sure, for the occasion. However, it ended in (for the moment) our consenting to forfeit the money already paid, rather than make so long a journey in such a carriage; and we engaged another, this time having a written agreement that we should have a *banquette*.

On our leaving Gerona at 8 A.M., with our newly-engaged carriage, which was, in fact, a diligence and six horses; the other, a small omnibus and three horses, started also, the coachman having remained the three days at Gerona, to suit himself or revenge himself. The sequel—a proof of how justice is disspensed by legislators in the south of France—we will give presently.

Gerona gains by distance—in fact, it looks a very picturesque town, as one sees it from the long narrow bridge which crosses the Fluvia. The scenery, with the magnificent range of Pyrenees before us, every minute becoming nearer and nearer and more beautiful, made the time seem nothing till we reached Figueras, amidst pines and olives, with its grand citadel and square towers. The "Hotel du Commerce" is the place to breakfast at; and wise people will so carve out their journey, if they sleep *en route*, which those who go by diligence do not, or rather cannot, as to make this place the one to stop at, instead of Gerona, as the hotel here is far away the best. From here the sandaled shoes and scarlet caps give place to the ordinary leather boots and black caps; the mantilla also is changed to a white flannel head-gear, looking more like the dress of a Carmelite nun.

The last Spanish town is La Junquera; above it, towering over all, and commanding the country around, is the fine fortress of Bellegarde, which Louis XIV. erected in 1679, to show the new extent of his recently gained possessions. The road is very winding and narrow at this part. One seems surrounded and shut in by mountains. Presently a straight, but still narrow road, leads to a small bridge, erected during the early part of the present queen's reign. This is the spot where Spain ends and France begins. On the Spanish side are the officers and custom-house of Spain; on the other, are two marble pillars, bearing the arms of Spain on the south side, and those of France on the north; and there also stand French sentinels. And now we are in France.

It was with no regret we left Spain. On the contrary, there was a sensation of relief at feeling we could not possibly encounter any more *posadas;* and that henceforth a higher degree of civilization would be met with, even at little by-towns, and, in short, that "roughing it" was over. The custom-house officers were extremely civil, and only opened the courier's portmanteau, perhaps for form sake, perhaps thinking that there, if anywhere, tobacco might be smuggled.

The road still winds in and out of the cork and pine clad hills;—the cork-trees grow here to a very large size;—till the base of the Pyrenees is reached, and the mountain barrier between France and Spain is fairly crossed. Now the plains of Rousillon—the wine produced is abominable, especially after the rich full-flavoured wines of Spain—lay before us. Acres and acres of the low, brown, unbeautiful, leafless vines, not pretty even when laden with their fruit in this stunted form, was all the eye had to feast on, unless we looked back. Then, indeed, we were fully repaid for twisting our necks. The purple hills, the snow-capped mountains, with the golden sky and the setting sun tipping the clouds with small thin lines of crimson, was a glorious sight. A sunset in the Pyrenees is magnificent even in spring. The remaining road to Perpignan was uninteresting; nothing but a straight line between an avenue of young plane trees for several miles. On arriving, we went to the "Hôtel de l'Europa," certainly the best, and good, though it does not look promising outside. There was a shadowy resemblance to those comfortless-looking stable-and-coach-house entrances in second-rate Spanish hotels, that for a moment made our hearts sink, and wonder whether Perpignan was far enough out of Spain not to be Spanish. All our doubts, however, were dispelled when once in the rooms. Carpets and comforts met us in every one of them, and fire-places as well; but the charges were high, far exceeding what they should be. But it is not our intention to do more now than give a slight sketch of the journey home. The Pyrenees are beaten tracks; they need little description.

In all towns there are certain "sights;" so here, at Perpignan, there is a citadel and churches, and a great horse establishment belonging to the government, and an avenue of plane-trees, the pride of the inhabitants, and must be seen by everyone. It is handsome; there are three avenues; the centre one for carriages is very wide, and the trees are so trained as to form Gothic arches of an enormous height over each, and when in full leaf must be very magnificent. Perpignan is rich in avenues and trees, but this plane-tree avenue is the king of them.

On the night after our arrival, just as we were going to dinner, a decent looking man came in and delivered himself of a suspiciously legal-looking paper, and of a verbal order that M—— was to present himself at the Juge de Paix's private residence, Rue de la Real, 2, at once. We went off at once, guessing what it was about, therefore we did not waste time in reading the officially stamped document; instinct at once suggested the diligence affair—what else could it be?

On entering a dirty, dingy little room, there stood our enemy, the owner of the rejected carriage, before us, or rather sat, and around him his supporters. The case was stated by his *avocat*, who trumped up a story quite well enough to make one boil with British indignation to think a lie could be so plausibly told. We told ours; we were asked for proofs. Of course we had none, nor had they; we had not even our receipt for the money already paid; we had a witness, but he, being our courier, was silenced at once; and the end was, that this justice of the peace decreed that we must pay 125 frs. as compensation for the loss of time sustained by the diligence proprietor, and 8 frs. 25 cents. costs. We were preparing to pay when another man started up and said, "I warn you if you do not pay here on the spot——" He was cut short, we could not stand *that*. The money being paid, we wished the dispenser of justice a good night. No doubt he had one, as we heard afterwards that the matter had been settled and arranged before we arrived, and the profits were shared. The recollection of this affair is still too fresh not to make us feel excessively indignant.

CHAPTER XXV.

FROM PERPIGNAN TO PAU.

WE left Perpignan for Narbonne by an afternoon train; it only takes two hours and a quarter to get there. There is nothing interesting in the flat marshy land, intersected by lagoons of salt water, which for miles one passes through, nor in the arid looking rocky country nearer Narbonne, where the aromatic herbs grow, on which the bees feed, which produce the highly-scented Narbonne honey. The Hôtel Daurade is the best and nearest the station, but there are odours in the house which form a great distinction to the sweet-scented honey, the finest of which is sold in the hotel; yet here Queen Christina passed two nights on her way into Spain. It is a busy-looking town and possesses a fine Gothic cathedral, which, however, from not being finished in length, seems altogether out of proportion as its height is enormous, reaching to 131 feet. There are three aisles, some of the windows are well painted, and there is some fine old tapestry hung about. The picture by Sebastian Piombo of the "Raising of Lazarus," now in England, was painted for this church.

The Hôtel de Ville was formerly the Archbishop's palace. The old garden is converted into a museum of antiquities; there are some Christian tombs of the third and fourth centuries. The most interesting relic is an altar which was erected to Augustus, 11 years B.C., by the people of Narbonne.

From Narbonne to Toulouse is three hours by the express train. All along this road honour is paid in the shape of columns and monuments to the memory of the celebrated Paul Riquet, who made the canal known as the "Canal du Midi," which joins the Atlantic to the Mediterranean; the work was commenced in 1666 and finished in 1681; now that railroads intersect the country this grand achievement is of little use.

Toulouse is a handsome large town, with long wide streets and plenty of squares and gardens. The hotels are not first rate. We were at the Hôtel de l'Europe; it was only good by comparison with Spanish hotels. We believe the Hôtel de l'Empereur is better; the former has the questionable advantage of being nearer the railway station. The museum is worth seeing, not on account of its extremely bad picture galleries, the largest of which was formerly the chapel of the old Augustine monastery, but for the cloisters. They are very beautiful, and larger than one generally sees. The Gothic arches are supported by double marble pillars, and the light stone work is exceedingly pretty. These cloisters are full of antiquities, which destroy the quiet and solitude that ought to form a part of them. Here, in fact, is the real museum.

The church of St. Servin, built in 1090, is a very fine building, and once had wonderful relics—whole apostles. The tower is octagonal, like those in Catalonia. The cathedral is a singular old edifice, being all one-sided. It was begun by Raymond VI., Count of Toulouse, an excommunicated heretic; that is to say, a convert to the Reformed Faith. The churches all about here are very rich in marbles, which come chiefly from the quarries of Caunes, a place about ten miles from Carcassonne. Toulouse has the sorry renown of being the only town in France where the Inquisition gained a footing. It was first established here in 1221, and the tales of horror connected with it will bear comparison with those of Spain.

From Toulouse to Pau is eight good hours. From Montrejeau, where we stopped half an hour, and had a good scrambling breakfast, the scenery is magnificent. We skirted the range of the snowy-capped Pyrenees, from there on to Pau. No wonder the temperature is so different here; the wind blowing from these frozen regions is enough to icify one—indeed, from Perpignan on, we were shivering with cold. From the station at Lourdes, or just beyond it, we saw very plainly the celebrated grotto where the little girl (now a big one) saw the Virgin, young and beautiful, as she was thirty years before she died. This girl is now in a convent.

A magnificent church is being built beside the spot. The grotto had half a dozen candles burning inside it, flaring up before an image of the Virgin, placed on a small altar. Miracles can still take place in the villages buried in the Pyrenean mountains, but they will soon cease. It is astonishing how railroads and civilisation, to say nothing of what is more important still—education—put a stop to them.

The approach to Pau is very fine; but of Pau, the birthplace of Henry IV., and where, in the castle, his tortoise-shell cradle is so carefully preserved, there is little necessity of saying a word. Every one knows which *they* think the best hotels; every one admits that the winters are very cold, but very gay; and every one agrees (if they have any conscience) that it is unfit for invalids, who are such in truth, and not merely in fancy. We heard it said by a gentleman who had been sent there for health, that but for the name and the honour of the thing he would have been better off in his own native county, Cork, where skating was not one of the winter pastimes, which he found it was here.

Take it in spring and autumn, and Pau must be delightful, excursions are so numerous, and the scenery so beautiful. But there is no use in talking or writing—Pau is the fashion, and as long as it remains so, the sick will go there with the healthy. The sick will die, and the healthy will comfort themselves that " all that climate could do was done." It seems to us that it would be better far to leave the sick at home, and let them die with home comforts around them, than drag them to this beautiful spot to die from the effects of cold unmitigated by English measures against it.

At Pau we bid adieu to our readers, for our next stage is Bordeaux, which we passed through together at the commencement of " A Winter Tour in Spain."

THE END.

BRADBURY, EVANS, AND CO., PRINTERS, WHITEFRIARS.

www.ingramcontent.com/pod-product-compliance
Lightning Source LLC
Chambersburg PA
CBHW031421230426
43668CB00007B/390